FAMILY BUSINESS

FAMILY BUSINESS

AN INTIMATE HISTORY OF JOHN LEWIS AND THE PARTNERSHIP

VICTORIA GLENDINNING

WILLIAM
COLLINS

William Collins
An imprint of HarperCollins*Publishers*
1 London Bridge Street
London SE1 9GF

WilliamCollinsBooks.com

HarperCollins*Publishers*
1st Floor, Watermarque Building, Ringsend Road
Dublin 4, Ireland

First published in Great Britain in 2021 by William Collins

1

Copyright © Victoria Glendinning 2021

Victoria Glendinning asserts the moral right to be identified
as the author of this work in accordance with the
Copyright, Designs and Patents Act 1988

A catalogue record for this book is
available from the British Library

ISBN 978-0-00-827375-0

Printed and bound in Great Britain by
CPI Group (UK) Ltd, Croydon

MIX
Paper from
responsible sources
FSC™ C007454

This book is produced from independently certified FSC™ paper
to ensure responsible forest management.

For more information visit: www.harpercollins.co.uk/green

FOR PETER LEWIS

CONTENTS

PROLOGUE

This is not a business book nor a corporate history, even though it would never have been written at all if a tempestuous family saga had not been inseparable from the story of the business which dominated their lives.

One day, wandering along London's Oxford Street, I looked up, and read the familiar name JOHN LEWIS in the familiar lettering. I wondered, who was John Lewis anyway? After some preliminary investigating, I was hooked. John Lewis was an orphan, born into poverty in a small Somerset town not far from where I was living. He made a pot of money and just banked the lot. His obsession with the family fortune distorted his own life and the lives of his wife and children.

I had no idea at the beginning what an extraordinary family I would be taking on. It is a tale of ferocious conflicts, and rows of epic proportions, between John Lewis and his sons, Spedan and Oswald. In Spedan's case, these involved shouting, face-slapping, emotional blackmail, a kidnapping – and much litigation, between father and both sons and between the brothers, and a spell in prison for Father.

Yet the family never broke up. These were obstinate people of preternaturally high nervous energy. There is glee in Spedan's letter to Oswald recounting a physical fight with Father, hurling the office waste-paper basket at his head. Much in this book is borderline comedic; but there is bleak tragedy too.

That particular row was about Father's treatment of Mother. The story is loud with the voices of women – not only Mother but the brothers' attachments, wives and families, plus a slew of feisty 'shop girls', all contributing to the clamour from private letters and diaries, the public record, and the memories of survivors.

If the family story were all, it would be riveting enough. But the personal is embedded in the equally riveting story of the family firm. In 1864 the young John Lewis opened a little drapery business on Oxford Street, in a narrow-fronted shop which had been a tobacconist's. Fuelled by prosperity and the rise of an aspirational middle class, thousands of dim little shops were swallowed up or transformed into sumptuous shopping palaces, 'universal providers', 'department stores', with glittering plate-glass windows and dazzling floor displays. The new department stores became destinations. Visiting a department store was a sensual experience and an adventure. John Lewis rose on the wave of an unprecedented retail revolution.

His elder son Spedan reacted violently against his father's self-serving business values. Nevertheless he was a chip off the old block, steeped in the romance of retail. When very young, he elaborated a vision of 'Partnership' – of the business as a close community, putting purpose before maximising profits, with every employee having a stake in the enterprise.

Oswald was their mother's darling, destined by her for great things beyond shopkeeping. It was agreed that Spedan was perilously unstable and unpredictable. So he was. He was also single-minded and inspirational. A pragmatist, he saw Partnership as a model for workplace happiness and, as a result, for commercial success. Partnership was to provide an ethical corrective to the inequalities and industrial unrest inherent in unreconstructed capitalism.

The family business did not die with Spedan and Oswald. On the contrary, it thrived. Today, however, the sector is in the throes of another retail revolution. Apparently unassailable department stores, including the iconic John Lewis & Partners, are in limbo. Spedan's ideas of Partnership are being put into practice in some form or other by countless grassroots and community enterprises, and may be part of the way forward for the struggling high streets. Sound ideas don't die – they survive to meet the good moment.

1

SHEPTON MALLET

John Spedan Lewis retired from the chairmanship of the John Lewis Partnership in 1955, at the age of seventy. In the spring of 1959, clearing the attics of Longstock House, his Hampshire home, he decided to take a look at his father's diaries.

'I should have done it long ago,' he told his younger brother, Oswald. He had expected just 'a record of litigation and other matters of business'. But the diaries were personal and Spedan himself figured in them, not always in ways he would have supposed. Quarrels and crises which were cataclysmic for Spedan seemed to have affected his father not at all.

Spedan had read up to the year 1922 – his father died in 1928 – when he dictated an emotional six-page single-spaced letter to Oswald. He had no one at home to confide in. His wife Beatrice was dead. He dictated all his letters, even the most private, to his long-time secretary Muriel, who lived in the house. 'I have no secrets from Muriel.'

Spedan's response to the shock of reading the diaries was to burn them. 'Nearly all of the many volumes that I have found so far are now ashes, and the remainder will be very soon.' They would have been 'a rich picking for muck-rakers' and, for 'an outsider of a much better type, it would have been an extremely tempting combination of the beautiful, the admirable, with the contrary'.

In his book *Partnership for All* (1948), Spedan had written of his father that 'the conditions of his early life had so overdeveloped in him a passion for accumulating money and a dread of losing it that, where money was concerned, he was like a man driven by a demon'. His father's desire for an heir was not 'for the sake of the business as a thing in itself but for the sake of the fortune'.

Father never retired from the family business. He clung on until he died, in his nineties. In his letter to Oswald, Spedan ascribed their father's 'really insane greed of money and power' to early hardship: 'The naturalist, that I was born to be' interprets their father's personality ecologically. He had great qualities of character, and also the nervous energy that Spedan considered essential to success. (He had it himself.) If Father had been reared 'in a fully civilized home', if he had been to a good school and to a good college, 'the world would have seen another Mr John Lewis of Oxford Street'. Some influences in Father's development he would not wish changed, though. He had been 'the delicate boy with several good sisters', and 'wisdom and backbone are factors independent of culture'.

This degree of insight never alleviated Spedan's resentment against his father. Reading the diaries just brought back all the old rows, bullyings, misunderstandings and injustices. 'What a mess life is!'

So who and what was this father – the John Lewis who in 1864 opened a little drapery shop in the narrow premises of a former tobacconist on London's Oxford Street?

★

He was born in Shepton Mallet in Somerset – known familiarly as Shepton, the 'Mallet' deriving from the name of its Norman overlord.

If you drive to Shepton Mallet today, on your way perhaps to Wells, Bath or Bristol, you pass across the top of the High Street – No Entry – and never see the town at all. You are whisked past Tesco and ring-roaded away before you know it.

In the old stone-built town the High Street slopes from south to north, opening out into the Market Square, and continues on downhill. Beyond the square, the thoroughfare narrows, becoming Town Street. On either side of these 'backbone' streets rises a hidden network of lanes, alleyways and courts, following the steep contours of the valley. The network was, in John Lewis's childhood, even more extensive. Old buildings, domestic and industrial, grouped around once-important mills, were bulldozed for re-development. Kilver Street, now just a section of the busy A37, used to be an integral part of Shepton.

The steep and curling alleys and pathways were commonly referred to as 'streets', and indeed some would accommodate a horse and cart, though most are just wide enough for two people to walk abreast. In 1790 the Reverend John Collinson described the town as lying in 'a low, reclusive valley, interrupted with winding, rocky shelves and dingles' comprising around 'twenty streets and lanes which are in general narrow, acclivitous, and dirty' – and that was in a period of optimum prosperity. Some open out into level spaces lined by the fine homes of eighteenth-century mill owners – known locally as 'manors' – and by mullion-windowed cottages. Sheptonians rich and poor lived side by side.

The lanes and alleyways run between the high stone walls of old houses, old factories, mills and warehouses, some built at odd angles to the path or presenting their blank stone backs. Shepton has been in decline for a long time, especially since it lost its rail links in the 1960s; it once had not just one railway station, but two. The core of Shepton is as it ever was, give or take the insertion of a few 1970s architectural statements, gifted to the town by the Showering family of Babycham fame.

Old Shepton has simply remained. Walking the lanes and alleys now it is easy to imagine little John Lewis, in the hungry 1840s, scuttling along in leaky boots on his way to see one of his aunts.

★

When 'old' John Lewis, father of our John, was born in 1798, Shepton Mallet was thriving. The prosperity of this part of south-west England was built on sheep. Wool was the only material for clothing, apart from linen and luxurious silk, and imported Indian muslins. Woollen cloth, in different weaves and weights and dyes and finishes, was spun and woven on handlooms in manufactories or in the upper rooms of Shepton's cottages, and sold throughout the kingdom and beyond. The industry supported the town for hundreds of years, peaking in the late eighteenth century when, out of a population of something over 5,000, 80 per cent were employed in the textile trade, and their employers became gentry.

A little gazetteer, *The Beauties of England*, published in the 1750s, describes Shepton Mallet as 'the Residence of many Considerable Clothiers', before the inevitable description of the unique 'streets' – 'narrow, steep, very irregular and uneven; but well watered with Rivulets, convenient for the Clothworkers'. The actual river which flows through Shepton was more than a rivulet but scarcely more than a wide, fast-running stream, which powered many mills. In the past, it was just 'the river'. Only in the nineteenth century, which did not tolerate vagueness, did it become regularly called 'The Sheppey'.

The writer of the little gazetteer missed the parish church, which lies back from Market Square. The glory of it is its wagon-roof, made up of 350 little wooden panels linked by carved bosses, each little panel painted with a lattice pattern, with carved angels around the sides. Simon Jenkins, in his *England's Thousand Best Churches*, called the roof 'superb', like 'an oaken quilt'. When our John Lewis was a baby, the footprint of the church was enlarged by widening the side aisles.

Not that the Lewis family went to church, as such. Shepton had a community of Quakers, and a Roman Catholic chapel and convent, but the Lewises were Nonconformists, or Dissenters. Very broadly speaking, the gentry and upwardly mobile went to church, and tradesmen and artisans did not. Dissent was widespread in the West Country, and there were four different dissenting chapels in Shepton. (Dissenters dissented even among themselves.) The Lewises attended the handsome 'Independent' Hephzibah chapel, built in 1801 and later extended to house a congregation of 700. John would have received his elementary teaching in the school attached to the chapel.

Opposite the church, downhill across the laneway is the old grammar school, set back in its garden. The great prison, dating from around 1610, squats between the lanes on the other side of the church behind intimidatingly high blind walls. On the west side of town was the old workhouse. These three institutions loomed over John Lewis's childhood.

'Lewis' is a surname frequently adopted by Jewish immigrants to Britain, as an anglicisation of Levi, Levy or Elias. 'Lewis' is also thoroughly Welsh, and the sixth most common surname in Wales.

(To answer your question – the most common is Jones.) Spedan Lewis thought of both Jews and Welshmen as peculiarly suited to the retail trade, and of his father as 'a typical Welshman'. There is no evidence of any Jewish antecedents. The Welsh filtered into the English West Country from the earliest days by ferry across the Severn estuary, part of the continuous commercial traffic between Cardiff and Bristol and beyond. There had been Lewises in Shepton for four generations, and many more Lewises – shop-keepers, tradesmen and artisans – in the towns and villages around. Not all were related, but there was a large, diffuse cousinage.

John Lewis was born on 24 February 1836. His family lived in Town Street, composed of small, terraced shops and workshops with living quarters above. His father, John, was one of many bakers in the town. He married Elizabeth Speed, who was brought up in nearby Cowl Street. Hers was the fourth recorded genera-tion of Speeds in Shepton, and there are memorials to eighteenth-century Speeds in the parish church. Elizabeth was twenty-seven when she married, a year older than her husband. They had five daughters and just the one son, John, the second youngest.

These children were born into a bad time. Prosperity ebbed from Shepton within just three decades. There were some improvements, which provided employment: in 1826 the Turnpike Trust caused the Waterloo Bridge to be built over the river, carrying a road out from the end of Town Street towards Bath and Bristol. In 1848, the workhouse was rebuilt.

A history of Somerset by the Reverend W. Phelps, published in 1839, when our John Lewis was three, describes the cloth trade in Shepton Mallet as 'nearly lost'. It survived the loss of valuable contracts for cloth for uniforms when the wars with France ended. It was the introduction of steam-driven machinery into the textile industry which was its undoing. Sheptonians would have no truck with the new technology, and the manufacturers, from a mistaken opinion that manual labour would be able to compete with machinery, soon found that 'they were superseded in the market', according to Phelps. Another interpretation is that manufacturers were so fed up with the resistance to modernisation that they simply closed their Shepton mills and set up elsewhere. There was, at the time Phelps was writing, just one manufactory of crepe and velvet, 'and some silk throwing', and 'the town is reduced to much distress'.

This was the dismal economic climate when John Lewis's mother Elizabeth died of tuberculosis in the spring of 1841. She must have been the one who held everything together, including the bakery. Her husband died two years later, on 12 April 1843 – not at home in Town Street, but in the old, decrepit Shepton Mallet Union workhouse.

The death certificate is discreet. The word 'workhouse' does not figure, but the informant of the death was James Cogle, master of the Shepton workhouse. Mr Lewis at the time of his death had been an inmate for eighty-nine days – nearly three months, so admitted during the winter. Applications to the workhouse always increased during the winter months. But in order to have reached this depth of hopelessness, Mr Lewis can hardly have been an effective parent even before his wife died.

The failed baker had six siblings who might have helped him, including a successful younger brother, William Lewis, a grocer, tea dealer and tallow chandler on Market Square, married to Eleanor Byrt, from a numerous and enterprising local family. But neither William Lewis nor anyone else in the family saved their brother from the workhouse, perhaps because he had other and intractable problems. His cause of death was given as 'Epilepsy' – a condition still evoking fear and shame and vestigial connotations of demonic possession. There was no treatment. No anticonvulsant is recorded before the late 1850s. The nurses in workhouse infirmaries were female inmates, likely to be illiterate. Medical officers were third-rate because the posts were put out to tender and the cheapest appointed.

Spedan and Oswald Lewis knew that their father came from Shepton Mallet, and that he was orphaned, and had a deprived childhood. He made sure they clocked that. But Spedan and Oswald – prosperous, prominent, confident – never knew of their grandfather's death in the workhouse.

If Spedan had known, he would hardly, in the 1930s, have engaged the College of Arms to investigate the family pedigree, in the hope of acquiring a coat of arms for himself by right of descent. Oswald was warned off the family's past when he was a parliamentary candidate for North Dorset just before World War I. His constituency agent wanted details of his West Country credentials for publicity purposes, and he turned to his mother for information. She herself was from the nearby town of Bridgwater. She replied that it would be 'easier to say that both Dad and I come from Somersetshire, simply, without mentioning the names of the two towns'. This was because 'the fortunes of both my family and of Dad's were at a very low ebb before the younger generation migrated elsewhere and made positions for themselves, and as it is a frequent custom with unscrupulous opponents in parliamentary elections to rake up long forgotten matters with a view to discrediting a candidate – unless fathers, grandfathers, in short *ancestors* – are distinctly a help to a man, it is best not to give any precise information.'

Who looked after the children? The six of them ranged in age between sixteen and three years old when their mother died. John was five. With both parents gone, the girls kept the shop going for a while with cakes and sweets – a trade directory of 1844 listed John Lewis in Town Street, but as 'Confectioner'. The local economy was still tanking. Stocking-knitting had been an important Shepton cottage industry, but there were only five knitters left. And four silk-throwers.

Their mother's family, the Speeds, came to the rescue. She had five sisters, of which she was the second. Her elder sister Christian was already in her late forties when she married James Clark in 1842, in between the deaths of the children's parents. Decades later, Oswald Lewis wrote out in his diary 'Notes About My Father', compiled after questioning the old man about the past. Oswald recorded that his father's aunt, 'Mrs Clark (whose husband was a schoolmaster), brought up Father and his sisters in Shepton Mallet'.

Schoolmaster? No. James Clark was the principal turnkey, or chief warder, at the prison. He rose to be deputy governor. There were executions within the prison walls. Official reports record insanitary conditions, overcrowding and smallpox epidemics. Prisoners developed hernias from toiling on a forty-man tread-wheel which powered a grain mill outside the walls. Uncle James Clark's cheerless profession was something else that John Lewis did not want his sons to know about.

The Clarks lived in Garston Street, over the little river from the prison, and Aunt Christian opened her home to her nieces and nephew. Another Speed aunt, Ann, was the widow of a William King. With a son of her own, she was living in Castle Cary, ten miles from Shepton. John spent some time with Aunt Ann Speed in Castle Cary.

'It is profoundly pitiful,' wrote Spedan, in his 1959 letter to Oswald, 'to read in several years of the diaries' his father mentioning that 'on a particular day in May he started at the grammar school and two mentions that for all his first year he was very unhappy'. That is unsurprising as, parentless and uprooted, John was probably unhappy already, and sudden immersion in a grammar school curriculum could be pretty traumatic. Oswald recorded in his 'Notes' that 'Father was delicate as a child', and that 'about this time a doctor in Castle Cary said, "If you press this boy unduly with mental work he will become an idiot"'. Aunt Ann's doctor may not have said exactly that. But he spotted some disorder in young John, and it was remembered.

The person that John loved best was his eldest sister, Elizabeth. He wrote in his diary, according to Spedan's long letter to Oswald, that 'his passionate love for his eldest sister was largely gratitude for her having secured him even that amount of schooling'. This beloved eldest sister, named after their mother, was twenty-two years old when, aged eleven, John entered the grammar school in May 1847. His intelligence must have been evident to Elizabeth, and her confidence and powers of persuasion considerable. She was at that time a domestic servant in the house of a Somerset clergyman, who may have lent his support to the application. A boy was only admitted to the grammar school for free if he were nominated by the trustees.

Another benign influence was Aunt Julia, their mother's youngest sister, who married Robert Collett when she was twenty. Aunt Julia's father-in-law, also Robert Collett, lived on the High Street and was the registrar who signed off Mr Lewis's death certificate in the workhouse. No secrets there, then.

Aunt Julia and her husband lived in Longbridge House, 78 Cowl Street, where the Duke of Monmouth stayed in July 1685 before the battle of Sedgemoor. John Lewis never lived with them at Longbridge House, because Robert Collett died when his only son, yet another John – John Kyte Collett – was two years old. The cousins were the same age, and John Lewis, when he was two, was still with both his parents and sisters, in Town Street.

After her husband died, Aunt Julia Collett moved to Garston Street, near her elder sister, Christian Clark, and supported herself,

her son John and her daughter Ann Mary, with a little grocery
business. John Lewis spent time at Aunt Julia's house, and John
Kyte Collett too went to the grammar school. They were
companions out of school hours as well, fishing in the river and,
with their gang of friends, trespassing on private property to play.
A favourite place was land belonging to Mr Garton, who made a
lot of money importing maize from the United States. This piece
of land was attached to Langhorne House, his residence on Paul
Street, and the boys were continually being chased out. They
considered these fields to be common property, and indeed there
was a public footpath across them.

John Kyte Collett, outraged by this injustice, did not forget.
Half a century later and in the next generation, Major James
Garton, co-founder of the Anglo-Bavarian Brewery in Shepton,
removed himself to the greater splendour of Clarendon Park near
Salisbury in Wiltshire. Langhorne House and park, and the adjacent fields, were auctioned off at the George Hotel in Shepton.
John Collett, now a rich man, moved in for the kill. (He did not
want the house, which became a Roman Catholic convent
school.) There were other bits and pieces of land available nearby,
and John Collett scooped them up too. Then he had it all planted
and landscaped, and gifted to the town no less than thirteen acres
of parkland and recreation space, with woodland, playing fields, a
lake, and a bandstand.

Collett Park was opened on a fine day in June 1906. Shepton
was festooned with wreaths, floral arches, flags and banners, and
the whole town came out on to the streets. There were parades of
schoolchildren, bands played, speeches were made, and a 'Public
Dinner' given for Mr and Mrs Collett. No other modest Somerset
town has anything remotely like Collett Park within its purlieus;
and John Lewis never did anything remotely similar for his birthplace when he too became rich.

Although John Lewis was, like many overbearing men, something of a sentimentalist, there are only one or two known mentions of his returning to Shepton Mallet in adult life. In 1893, on 7 November, he went to Shepton to visit John Allen, a widowed cheese and corn factor who lived at Highfield Farm on Park Road, and wrote in his diary: 'Seeing JA was unequal to the cold and winds, I walked about the old scenes alone all day. Dined at 1pm with John Allen, then walked to Cannards Grave, back to Charlton round by the stream where I used to catch minnows, through Kilver Street, Garston Street, Lower Lane, Bowlish, up over Ham down to Ham Lane and Croscombe, back through Darshill, Bowlish, back to JA by 5pm.'

We know about this entry because of Kenneth Hudson who, preparing to write a biography of Spedan, was the only person who had a sight of the diaries before Spedan threw them on his bonfire. Just eighteen A4 pages of Hudson's almost illegible handwritten notes survive. There may have been other visits to Shepton, and other reminiscences of 'the old scenes'. It is worth noting that on this particular walk of around seven miles John chose not to remain within the town but spent much time in the outlying communities and countryside.

It is not much to go on. Yet to understand what John Lewis became, one has to follow him in the freedom of the woods and fields, which relieved the orphan boy's insecurity and deprivation; along with the sisters and aunts who sustained him so long as they lived. Shepton and its rural environs, until he was a teenager, was the whole world. Awareness of a world elsewhere extended no more than twenty miles in any direction, and fuzzily. This is not only how people lived, it is how people were. To live among strangers in a strange place was, for the many, quite inconceivable. But John Lewis, and most of his aunts and all sisters, were among those who would have no trouble about moving away and moving on.

The grammar school at Shepton was already antiquated in John Lewis's time, 'a picturesque and curious structure', as described by John E. Farbrother in 1859. It was founded in the seventeenth century by the Strode family – responsible for funding the alms-houses behind the church, the Bread Hall for dispensing bread to the poor, and for most of the charitable institutions in Shepton Mallet, over generations. There was the schoolhouse, and a resi-dence for the master, a chapel, and accommodation at one end for five poor widows. The schoolboys, with the widows, had to attend prayers, morning and evening 'according to the liturgy and usage of the Church of England'. The history of the school, however, was one of gross mismanagement and scandals.

In the 1760s the son of a deceased master usurped the master-ship, claiming a right of heredity, until the trustees had him arrested. He had, meanwhile, hidden or destroyed the 'Ledger Books' and all legal documents relating to the school's constitution and endowments. The school was closed for more than thirty years before being successfully re-established, with 'most of the gentry around, as well as the respectable inhabitants of the Town' sending their sons there. But soon afterwards it was closed down yet again and its bungled affairs placed in chancery.

New trustees managed to reopen it only four years before John Lewis and John Collett started there – and for the last few years 'it has been in a very improving and flourishing condition', accord-ing to Mr Farbrother. He would say that, since he took over as master in 1851. By that time the two Johns had just left.

★

The romance of retail, which informed John Lewis's whole life and that of his elder son, germinated in the small drapery shops of Shepton Mallet, a model which in spite of his later wealth John never really transcended, to the despair of both his sons.

The textile industry may have collapsed, but cloth was in Sheptonians' bloodstream, and drapers' shops remained essential to everyday life. A draper sold woollens and linens by the yard or by the piece, and sometimes silks, in which case the draper styled himself, additionally, as 'silk mercer'. There were no ready-made clothes in John Lewis's childhood. There were dressmakers and tailors in the town, but artisan families had their clothes made at home, stitched by hand. Treadle sewing machines had not yet reached Shepton Mallet.

All John Lewis's five sisters, none of whom married, spent some or all of their working lives standing behind shop counters, as did their aunts. Drapery was the default position, but not all could succeed. Another aunt, Mary Speed, married John Godfrey who had a linen drapery in Town Street. John Lewis told Oswald, for his 'Notes', that Mr Godfrey 'ultimately went mad'.

Both John Lewis and John Collett became apprenticed to drapers as soon as they left the grammar school, but not in Shepton, which was not cut off from its immediate neighbours. Carriers trundled back and forth between the towns nearby at regular hours. Stage coaches, en route between larger towns, stopped at Shepton once or twice a week. Apprenticeships lasted for six or seven years, not necessarily with the same master. John Collett began his twenty miles away, in Bristol; while John Lewis joined his sisters Maria and Ann, who worked in Peter Marquand's drapery in Glastonbury.

Marquand died within a month of John's arrival. Uncle William Lewis now came up to scratch. According to what John told Oswald for his 'Notes': 'On July 6 1851 being then fifteen years of age, his Uncle William took him to Wells, and apprenticed him to a draper called Tusker.'

In August 1955, when Spedan was just beginning to sort out the family papers, he wrote to Oswald:

I remember clearly Father saying he had been apprenticed to a little draper in 'the little cathedral town of Wells', whose wife was kind to him. From Wells he went as an improver to Nicholls at Bridgwater, a business owned and managed by two brothers. ... I have heard Father say that he could remember seeing our grandmother come into the shop with a child, who must have been his future wife ... from Bridgwater he went to Liverpool where his life seemed so dreary and his prospects so poor that he thought of committing suicide. He borrowed a screwdriver from a friend ... and went for a day's outing to London, in the hope of getting there a post, as he did.

We can unpack this, apart from – yet – the bit about his future wife. Joseph Tusker's drapery was on the High Street in Wells, the small cathedral city only a few miles west of Shepton. Sadness hit the Lewis family again the following year, when Ann – the younger of the Glastonbury sisters – died aged twenty. Maria moved from Glastonbury to establish herself at King's, a big draper's shop in Bath.

The writer H.G. Wells started out in life as a draper's apprentice, and left in his novel *Kipps* (1905) a fictionalised account of the experience. He had hated it, and got out as soon as he could. Wells was thirty years younger than John Lewis, so apprenticeship for him, in the 1880s, was certainly no harder, but maybe less intimate and familial. Wells recorded the unrelenting physical strain on adolescent arms and legs of the dead weight of bales of cloth, 'things heavy and difficult to handle in bulk, that one folded up, unfolded, and cut into lengths'. Linen tablecloths were 'collectively, as heavy as lead'. Apprentices did not serve customers, and if not occupied stood by, 'plunged into an abyss of boredom', waiting to fetch and carry goods as the sales assistants required. Bread and margarine, and potatoes, were the staples of the fictional

Kipps's diet. At night 'he dreamed of piles of woollen blankets as he lay exhausted and footsore beneath his overcoat, his spare undershirt, and three newspapers'.

The daily routine of a draper's apprentice as described by Wells was standard, and John Lewis's own apprentices, in his early years as an employer, would have endured the same. Up at 6.30 a.m. in old clothes and a scarf, to dust cardboard boxes, take down the dust wrappers from the goods, and clean the shop windows. Much fetching and carrying for the window-dresser, and packing of parcels. 'Certain sorts of goods that came in folded had to be rolled on rollers, and for the most part refused absolutely to be rolled ... and certain other sorts of goods that came from the wholesalers rolled had to be measured and folded, which folding makes young apprentices wish they were dead.' Then at 7.30 p.m., 'a fever of activity', the 'straightening up' – closing the shutters, hanging wrappers over the stock, scattering wet sawdust on the wooden floors and sweeping up. The front door was locked at 10.30 p.m. and the gas lights extinguished at 11 p.m.

Yet John Lewis seems to have enjoyed his time with Mr Tusker, who was only twenty-eight. The fictional Kipps felt that 'the whole business was unjust and idiotic'. John Lewis never felt that. His energy, ambition and desire were focused on what H.G. Wells, with an irony that John Lewis would never have shared, called 'the whole art and mystery of the trade'.

★

John Lewis's first paid employment, from the age of eighteen, was with Nicholls & Co. in Bridgwater. He was now a shop assistant in a high collar and a tail coat, leaning forward, hands spread, palms down on the counter in the approved manner, to listen to the customer's requirements, always showing her not one but two bales of material, in the hope that she would choose the more expensive. There were few goods on display except in the windows, and no browsing and fingering.

Bridgwater, twenty miles from Shepton, was a larger and busier place than John had yet known, an inland port on the River Parrett near the mouth of the Bristol Channel and thence to the open sea; the main trade was in coal from Wales, and timber bound for the Baltic and North America. Henry Nicholls's shop, one of fourteen drapers and mercers in Bridgwater, had a prime site on Cornhill in the heart of town. According to Oswald's 'Notes': 'He [Father] always said that the good food he had at Nicholls was the making of him. He was still delicate, and was then growing fast.' The inference must be that he was hitherto undersized and skinny. So he grew, but he was always a lean, small man, and always had health worries.

John left Nicholls & Co. and took off for Liverpool, that booming port city on the Lancashire coast with a population, in 1851, of 376,000 people. It had grown by nearly 100,000 in the past decade, and would add nearly another 100,000 in the next. Liverpool was an import–export hub, and its prosperity was based on cotton. By 1850, more than a million bales a year were coming in from the West Indies and the Americas. There was employment for dockers, warehousemen, porters, carters and clerks. Fortunes were made by ship owners, shipbrokers and entrepreneurs. Liverpool was cosmopolitan, with brokers from all over Europe and as far away as Russia opening up offices. The white fluff of samples blew across the flagstones. The opportunity of the Liverpool cotton trade might have suggested a career option. But John Lewis was wedded to retail, and he loved silks.

Just one of Father's diaries, by chance or choice, escaped Spedan's conflagration. It is for the year 1856. It starts in Liverpool. The diarist is twenty years old, already established, and 'living in', at Carmichael's drapery in Church Street. Aunt Mary and Uncle John Godfrey from Shepton – the latter presumably not yet 'mad' – were now in Liverpool, and Oswald's 'Notes' report that: 'While he was there he saw the Godfreys a good deal', and racketed around in his spare time with their son, his cousin Percy.

He wrote the Liverpool diary in very bad French. The first entry, for 7 January: '*J'allais a Argy et je dansais tres beaucoup.*' ('I went to the Argy and I danced a great deal.') On 11 January: '*Je parais la fenêtre avec de fleurs brocatelles pour la fois premier.*' ('I dressed the window with brocade flowers for the first time.') 18 January: '*J'allais a Argy mais je ne dansais pas beaucoup. Je envoyè une lettre a Tante Clark.*' ('I went to the Argy but I didn't dance much. I sent a letter to Aunt Clark.')

Those entries can stand for all. The 'Argy' is the Argyle, a music hall and place of entertainment, with girls. The aspiration always is to 'go home' with one of them, though it's not clear whether John achieves this or not. He writes regularly to Aunt Clark, to his sister Elizabeth, and to his youngest sister Eliza. Aunt and Uncle Godfrey move to London; a fellow employee, whom he calls 'Italy', goes to Manchester to study the fashions. John stays in the shop till half past ten two nights in a row, rolling and 'cataloguing' the ribbons. He likes this work. He goes to chapel on Sundays, sometimes twice. He sends £10 to Aunt Clark 'to pay part of my debt to them' – so the Clarks had given him a float. He gets his hair cut regularly, his boots mended, buys hair oil and stamps and cigars, and keeps meticulous accounts.

There is no indication in the diary to suggest that, as he apparently told Spedan, his life was so dreary and his prospects so poor that he actually thought of suicide. Perhaps it was just a figure of speech. Certainly John is impatient for advancement, applying for a raise in salary and asking his boss, Mr Allard, to let him work in 'Silks'. Before the raise comes through he gets into a fight with a fellow assistant called Creighton who interferes with his window display of ribbons, and Creighton ends up with a bloody mouth. This is the first and by no means the last recorded instance of John Lewis's violent temper. Mr Allard dismisses them both. Next morning John goes to see Mr Allard to apologise and ask to be kept on. He is told to come back in the evening. But Mr Allard does not change his mind.

Shop assistants had their own slang. A position in a shop was 'a crib'. To 'swap' was to leave for a position elsewhere; to be 'swapped' was to get the sack. John Lewis had been swapped. In H.G. Wells's novel, Kipps, too, gets swapped, and is advised by a fellow worker: 'Go straight up to London, get the cheapest room you can find, and hang out.'

That is what John Lewis did. He was swapped on a Saturday. That evening he wrote: 'I decided at once to go to London.' On the Tuesday, he took the train, and a very slow train it was: 'May 6: I left Liverpool at 7.45 and reached London at 6.30 pm.' He may later have told Spedan that it was planned just as a short trip, but he seems to have prepared the ground.

He walked from the station to Peter Robinson's shop on the corner of Oxford Street and Regent Street – 'saw Miss Prothero in the window, went in, and spoke with her'. (Perhaps she was a former colleague from Liverpool.) He then headed south to Vauxhall, where Aunt Hippisley lived – his mother's married sister Sarah – and where his cousin Percy Godfrey, now training as a solicitor, was visiting. William Speed (another uncle) turned up, 'and I walked home with him'. John had been corresponding from Liverpool with both Aunt Hippisley and Aunt Godfrey, who was lodging with her family in Holloway Road in north London. So he had contacts, and the cushion of family.

Next morning, 7 May 1856, he called at a drapery shop, Hodges & Lawson, on Regent Street, came to an immediate agreement with them, and 'entered' the following day. He had a new crib. His real life was beginning.

2

RETAIL REVOLUTION

Once in London, John Lewis wrote in his diary mostly about his adventures after closing time – visiting the Crystal Palace, seeing 'the Illuminations', patronising a 'singing saloon'. He was seeing a Miss Cox, whom he met playing cards at Aunt Hippisley's. Hodges & Lawson was not an inspiring shop and he was not improving his prospects by staying there.

So, 'I swapped', on 22 October 1856. He was getting in first, hearing a rumour that the boss 'intended to swap someone'. No notice had to be given on either side. He left in mid-afternoon. He now had to find somewhere to live. That night, 'Percy took me to show his bedroom at 4 Acton St' (off Gray's Inn Road), and he took a room in the same house.

The next day he applied to Shoolbred's, a long-established drapery on Tottenham Court Road. He saw the boss, 'but no go'.

He – and the aunts – already had it in mind that he should start up on his own, but he was only twenty, and needed more experience. He tried other shops, including Swan & Edgar on Piccadilly Circus. William Edgar was running a market stall when he met George Swan, and they had been trading on their Piccadilly site long before the creation in 1819 of Piccadilly Circus – previously just a crossroads – in the course of Nash's Regent Street development. Many of the early London stores, like Swan & Edgar – which, surviving takeovers, closed only in 1982 – were founded by young working-class men in partnership with a friend or relative, starting very small. They themselves were factors in the transformation of London and other big cities.

The economic climate favoured the young and hungry, although for every successful start-up there were unnumbered failures. And the future of drapery – in the sense of a small business selling only fabrics by the piece or by the yard – was doomed. There had always been some shops that diversified. In *Mr Polly*, H.G. Wells's second novel about the drapery trade, his eponymous hero is apprenticed 'in one of those large, rather low-class establishments which sell everything from pianos and furniture to books and millinery – a department store in fact, called The Drapery Bazaar'. Department stores ceased to be 'rather low-class' and the terms 'draper' and 'drapery' no longer correctly described either the entrepreneur or his enterprise. Yet the terms survived. John Lewis, on official documents, always described himself as 'draper and mercer'.

Big department stores were the future. There were not only Lewis's of Liverpool and Kendal's of Manchester, but their equivalents springing up everywhere, their very names becoming part of the identity of each town and city. In the last decades of the century, the amalgamations of small units incrementally acquired gave way to grandiose edifices, each apparently as permanent as a town hall.

Their golden age lasted for more than a hundred years, until takeovers, mergers and acquisitions unwittingly destabilised the sector. The department store founded by three Welsh brothers in London's Holloway Road had, above the main entrance of their new 1890s building, the words 'Jones Bros' carved in stone. Nothing, figuratively speaking, is carved in stone. The John Lewis Partnership acquired Jones Bros during World War II and in 1990, in the face of local protest, turned it into a Waitrose.

★

In the mid-nineteenth century, with the confidence of Empire and the profitable exploitation of the colonies, came the rise of a new, rich upper middle class whose requirements were increasingly met by department stores. The spreading railway network speeded up supply chains and brought people looking for jobs from the country into the towns. For women and children working, say, in Manchester cotton mills, it meant lives not far from slavery. For others, commercial expansion spelled *opportunity*.

Fabrics remained a department store's principal stock-in-trade, while sewing machines transformed dressmaking and tailoring. Ready-made garments, and garments made to order, became essentials to a department store. At first ready-made clothes were left with open side seams, to be fitted to the customer's figure. New synthetic aniline dyes allowed for silks and cottons to be produced in rich, bright colours. Previously, beyond twenty shades of black and fifty shades of grey, choice was limited to a spectrum of browns, fawns and muted greens and blues. (Scarlet was costly to produce and reserved for ceremonial and military clothing.) In John Lewis's young days window-dressing was limited by space and obscured by small-paned windows. In the last quarter of the century it became an art form. New glass technology allowed for electric lighting and large plate-glass windows. 'Window-shopping' became a pastime.

Once inside the doors, the customer was questioned as to her requirements by a 'shopwalker' – something between a doorman (to keep tabs on the customer) and a supervisor (to keep the shop assistants on their toes). In the first wave of this retail revolution, a customer might not wander around freely. She said what she was looking for, and accepted guidance whether it was to buy fabrics, foods, housewares, furniture, boots, shoes, hosiery, lingerie, furs, hats, blouses, mantles, handbags and suitcases, gloves, umbrellas, stationery … all under one roof, along with everything previously bought from the haberdasher's – tapes and laces, ribbons, braids and trimmings, ostrich feathers, artificial flowers, buttons and buckles, pins, needles and thread.

So John Lewis came of age professionally at the right time, even though in 1856 Swan & Edgar had no vacancy for him. He could have tried Marshall & Snelgrove, a long-standing family business, recently expanded into new premises on the corner of Oxford Street and Vere Street, and calling itself the 'Royal British Warehouse'. He might not have considered Harrods, on the site of the present department store in Knightsbridge, which originally opened in just one room. Charles Henry Harrod was an Essex boy. In 1824, aged twenty-five, he set up as a haberdasher and draper in Borough High Street, Southwark. He added grocery and tea deal-ing to his businesses, moving around, before settling for Knightsbridge. Both he and his wife – to judge, unfairly, from their photographs – were rough diamonds. In the year of John Lewis's birth, Charles Harrod was arrested for handling 112 lb of currants, stolen for him by the porter of a nearby grocery. He spent a year in prison and the porter was deported to Tasmania. It was Harrod's son, Charles Digby Harrod, who grew the business into an opulent department store, with an emphasis on high-class groceries.

John Lewis went back to Peter Robinson's shop on Oxford Circus, and perhaps Miss Prothero put in a word for him. After missing one appointment with Mr Robinson by oversleeping at his digs in Acton Street, he arrived in a cab at 9 a.m. the next day, and was immediately 'engaged for Mantles'. A week later he recorded: 'Mr R. in very bad temper.' Soon after, Peter Robinson 'told me he intended to make a draper of me. I was very mortified' – because he felt he was already a qualified draper – 'but he spoke satisfactorily of my service'. He was moved from 'Mantles' to 'Muslins', and by December he was in 'Silks', much more to his liking, and dressing the Silks window.

On Christmas Eve 1856 he went with Percy to a venue in Holborn: 'I danced with —— and intended to go home with her', but she went off with someone else. He had to work at Peter Robinson's for half of Christmas Day, changing his collar and brushing his hair before 'going upstairs'. Later he ate two Christmas dinners – of goose and then boiled mutton – in Tottenham Court Road with Percy, and drank a lot of brandy and water. He walked with Percy down to Haymarket feeling 'pretty miserable'. By eleven o'clock that night he was back in the dormitory at Peter Robinson's, feeling 'pretty unwell'. He and Percy determined 'never to spend another Christmas Day in London'.

He had bought his new 'Book for Diary' for 1857. But that went on Spedan's bonfire, along with all the others. With the end of the diary for 1856 we hear his young voice no more.

★

The mixture of dissipation and loneliness which John Lewis artlessly documented was the experience of hundreds of very young, badly paid shop workers, and of hundreds of very young, badly paid clerks in public and private offices. These unconsidered legions kept London's commerce running. The novelist Anthony

Trollope was one such, working as a clerk in the Post Office. Charley's off-duty life in Trollope's *The Three Clerks* (1858), based on his own experience, was much like John Lewis's twenty years later, though Trollope's background and education were superior, and less sustaining: 'I had no friends on whom I could sponge regularly,' as he put it in his autobiography. John Lewis was supported by his aunts in London, and Aunt Christian and his sisters back in Somerset, all keenly interested in his progress.

He struck lucky with Peter Robinson, who was then in his early fifties. A Londoner, Robinson had opened a linen drapery three years before John was born, in a little shop with small-paned windows on the north-east corner of what came to be called Oxford Circus, in a terrace of similar shops with frontages of no more than twenty feet. Robinson expanded his business by buying up the leases of adjacent shops, and converting a number of small units into one big one. In 1840 he branched out with a 'Court and General Mourning House' on Regent Street. Black was seen as mandatory by respectable people for varying periods following the death of a spouse or family member. The transitional 'half-mourning' was grey or mauve. Since death is certain but the time of death uncertain, and since it was not done to keep mourning garments in the back of the wardrobe in anticipation of the next one, new mourning garments and accessories had to be acquired at short notice.

The black dresses were run up by the shop's dressmakers in rustling silks for the better-off, and for the rest in bombazine (a silk and wool or cotton twill), and trimmed with crinkly black crepe. It was good business, and a year after the opening of what was known as 'Black Peter Robinson's', to differentiate it from the parent shop, a rival appeared on the opposite side of Regent Street. Jay's was modern. Prices were clearly marked on all goods, a practice hitherto considered inadvisable. Jay's advertisements in the public prints were eye-catching: 'SUDDEN MOURNING', in heavy black majuscule. John Lewis, when he came into his own, always refused to advertise. Quality and service, he insisted, should speak for themselves. But then, he would always remain resolutely behind the curve.

He was with Peter Robinson for eight years, by the end of which his confidence and his knowledge of the trade had increased enormously. John Lewis became the youngest Silks Buyer in London, ordering for Peter Robinson from the wholesalers and importers clustered around St Paul's Churchyard and the back-streets off Cheapside.

★

The male, unmarried assistants in the big drapery or department stores could not always afford to venture out in the evenings. Many were farmers' sons, from the West Country and Wales. They would sit, smoking cheap little cigars, in the dank gas-lit eating-rooms, where they ate and talked. John Lewis never lost his Somerset accent, but some shop workers were barely educated and few would have been to a grammar school. No one had enough information about the conditions of their existence, or about anything much at all, which did not stop them elaborating vehement if fantastical social theories; and those who were not functionally illiterate joined a lending library, as John Lewis did, and read the newspapers.

In H.G. Wells's *Mr Polly*, the dingy eating-room is the shop workers' 'smoking room and common room' – a reference to the university life of their more privileged coevals. It is where Mr Polly learns 'the joys of social intercourse'. There is talk about swapping, and crib-hunting, and what the future might hold. Shop assistants get chucked out when they get old, Mr Polly is told. 'Don't they get shops of their own?' he asks. How can they, comes the answer: they have no capital, they just have to 'stick to cribs' until they are past it. 'I tell you we are in a blessed drainpipe and we've got to crawl along it until we die.'

Acquiring a shop of one's own was in any case perilous. For those who took a lease on what Wells in *Mr Polly* called 'a small, unnecessary shop', the outlook was bleak: 'Essentially their lives are failures … a slow, chronic process of consecutive small losses which may end if the individual is exceptionally fortunate in an impoverished deathbed before actual bankruptcy or destitution supervenes.' There is a sad example of this in Emile Zola's 1883 novel *Au Bonheur des Dames* ('The Ladies' Paradise') based on the Paris department store Bon Marché. On the other side of the street is a narrow, old-fashioned drapery shop, with just two samples of drooping cloth in each of its two small windows. There are few customers. Beyond the shop counter, the family living room is lightless, its single window leading on to an interior courtyard, 'sodden and filthy' like 'the bottom of a well'.

Across the street is the new department store, with brilliant electric lighting illuminating phantasmagorical window displays around which excited passers-by stop and gather. The proprietor of the little drapery may look across at it with scorn, but his days are numbered. In British cities and towns, too, the small, tradi-tional specialist shops were dying. Canny survivors would become unutterably exclusive, giving new meaning to the (French) words 'niche' and 'boutique'.

John Lewis started small, doing what his mentor Peter Robinson had done many years before. On the other, west, side of Oxford Circus stood a similar row of narrow-fronted terraced shops. He acquired the lease of one pokey little unit, previously a tobacco-nist's, and opened for business in April 1864.

He was twenty-eight years old and had learned his trade. He could 'read', with a glance and a touch, the quality and value of cottons, woollens and silks, in all their strangely named multi-plicity of weave and weight and finish. He knew his wholesalers and suppliers. He calculated his profit margin even as he fingered the flow of satin loosened from the sample bale. He had the necessary capital. He deposited £783 in the Westminster Bank on smart Cavendish Square just behind his shop, soon transferring his account to the National Provincial, conveniently opposite him on Oxford Street.

There was vitality in this family, along with some unpredictability inherited from their father. Three of John's sisters also moved along, and away from Shepton Mallet. In the late 1850s they took themselves off to Weston-super-Mare on the Bristol Channel, twenty-seven miles from Shepton, and stayed there for the rest of their lives.

It was an astute move. Weston was a tiny village which grew as a resort, though was never so fashionable as Bognor Regis or Brighton. Day-trippers descended at Weston Junction from south Wales, Bristol and the Midlands. Weston-super-Mare was a favourite with manual workers on their annual outings from factories and mills. New villas and terraces were springing up.

With their ageing Aunt Christian Clark, whose husband had died in 1858, Elizabeth, Mary and Eliza opened as Lewis & Lewis, on the High Street. They lived over the shop. Lewis & Lewis was a 'Berlin Wool shop'. Berlin wool work was the craft of embroidering on canvas, with motifs supplied. Later, in the 1870s, Lewis & Lewis added 'Fancy Drapery' to their letter-heading: 'Also at 132 & 288 Oxford Street, London' – the metropolitan connection was impressive, and John gave advice about suppliers. His own letterhead then was announcing John Lewis & Co. as 'Silk Mercer, Draper, and Fancy Warehouseman'.

Two of the surviving family members were missing from Weston-super-Mare. Aunt Ann, the widowed Mrs King, who had lived in Castle Cary, disappears from the record. And it was Maria, the second eldest, who made it possible for John to open a shop of his own. About two-thirds of his £783 was supplied by Maria's savings, and the rest from his own. Not only did Maria give her brother her money but, aged thirty-four, she gave up her safe job with the drapery in Bath and joined him in London. For the first six years, and irregularly for another decade, Maria was behind the counter while John did the business and went out to do the buying.

Two years after John Lewis & Co. opened, there occurred the 'Panic of 1866', one of those international economic crises within financial institutions which result in increased unemployment and lower wages. That only helped John Lewis, never keen to pay anyone more than he had to. He knew where to go for the best value stock, and sometimes travelled to Paris and Lyons, bypassing the City silk wholesalers. He rented a house in Marylebone Road, on the edge of Regent's Park, with room for himself, Maria and three employees. And he fell in love.

*

She was Eleanor Breeks, two years older than himself, known as Nelly, and was leading an uneventful life. She and her extended family came from the extreme north of England, another world, where the very place names would sound strange to John Lewis – Mealsgate, Maulds Meaburn, Shap, Flass, Crainset Beck, High Ewbank, Skirsgill – and Warcop, a name he would remember. She had a rich hinterland, where Dents, Breekses and Wilkinsons were intermarried. John Lewis probably met her through one of his suppliers, Dent & Co., traders in tea, spices and silks from China – a firm created in the previous generation by a slew of Dent brothers from a farming family in Cumberland, three of them making their fortunes in Canton, Shanghai and Hong Kong.

The mother of the entrepreneurial Dent brothers was a Wilkinson. Nelly Breeks's mother was a Wilkinson. Nelly was born in the village of Warcop, in the beautiful Eden Valley in Westmorland, on the edge of the Lake District and bordering on Cumberland. The Breeks family were numerous in and around Warcop over many generations. There were few big estates in these sparsely populated counties, and many small farms held on secure tenancies. Nelly's grandfather, Richard Breeks, was one of these farmers, known locally as 'yeomen' or 'statesmen'. Her father, also Richard Breeks, married to Elizabeth Wilkinson, was described in the census as 'gentleman' and as 'farmer'.

The Dents made money and lost it, regrouped, prospered, went under again, but all came out of it very comfortably off and with an ongoing business. Thomas Dent was head of the China operation until his brother Lancelot took over. Lancelot was an opium dealer (as were they all), trading between Calcutta and China. A warrant for his arrest issued by the Chinese authorities played a part in triggering the Opium Wars. The youngest brother and partner, Wilkinson Dent, 'retired China merchant', built for himself the Palladian-style Flass House in Westmorland but lived mostly at 8 Fitzroy Square in London until his death in 1886. He had also been a partner in a sugar plantation in British Guiana, receiving generous compensation from the British government following the Slavery Abolition Act of 1833.

Nelly Breeks lived as companion to her unmarried maternal uncle, Robert Wilkinson, 'retired merchant' and formerly a partner in Dent & Co., in his imposing residence, 22 Cumberland Terrace on the east side of Regent's Park. The brass memorial to Nelly in Warcop church – of which more later – states that she spent her early years in Warcop at Eden Gate. This is the neo-classical villa built by another maternal uncle, William Wilkinson, who became Sheriff of Westmorland. Nelly's father died when she was in her teens, so seemingly Uncle William took Nelly and her siblings into his household.

In London, Nelly had relatives equally affluent. Her elder sister Agnes was married to George Moore, a philanthropic millionaire thirty years older than herself. The son of a Cumberland 'states-man', Moore was a draper's assistant in that county before moving down to London to join a firm of lace wholesalers; he married the boss's daughter, and over the years made a fortune on his own account in the lace trade. In 1861, after his wife died, he scooped up Agnes Breeks, the young woman from back up north. They lived in the mansion he built for his first wife on a double plot in Kensington Palace Gardens. He then acquired the Whitehall Estate near Mealsgate, where he was born, and built another considerable house.

A photograph of John Lewis at the age of thirty-three – four or five years older than when he knew Nelly Breeks – shows a bright and bold-faced young man, clean-shaven, and with crisp dark hair. For Nelly, cooped up in her Uncle Robert's house and not getting any younger, the attraction is not hard to see. For John, Nelly Breeks might seem quite a catch. That was not the point. They loved each other. They wanted to get married.

Her family were appalled. John Lewis was just a little draper, a shopkeeper, way down in the pecking order from wealthy merchants. His West Country provenance was alien and he had no connections, nothing and no one behind him. He was not good enough for Nelly; it was just not on.

So they parted, or were parted. She gave him her photograph.

Nelly remained with her Uncle Robert Wilkinson until he died in 1887, leaving her the house in Cumberland Terrace and £5,000. She was financially secure. She went back up north, settling in a house called Ash Bank in Penrith, which she shared with a widowed aunt, Elizabeth Weston, and a niece.

Her rich sister Agnes Moore died widowed and childless at the age of fifty-five, leaving a will so detailed as to constitute an inventory of every picture, piece of furniture and household item, all her clothes and bed linens, and every trinket and treasure that she possessed – not to mention the money. Her personal estate was valued at £85,446 15s. 11d. Among a long list of beneficiaries, she left £5,000 to her sister Elizabeth, who had shared Ash Bank with Nelly, and £5,000 to her youngest sister Mary, plus £2,000 to Mary's daughter, along with important items of jewellery for them all.

Her sister Eleanor – our Nelly – was bequeathed just £500 and, in Agnes's 'Letter of Wishes', 'the sapphire and diamond marquise ring, my ivory-backed brushes and everything for toilet of ivory'.

This legacy was derisory in comparison with what Agnes left to her other sisters. Nelly had money of her own. More significantly, she was becoming a casualty, and a family liability. Nelly's wasted life is a novel waiting to be written, and there were surely hundreds like her.

In 1899 a sister-in-law recorded: 'Nelly gets more and more imbecile.' Nelly had taken to the bottle. The following year she was consigned to Tower House, 'Mrs Theobald's House for Inebriates', in Leicester, for 'Ladies only, of the upper middle classes, two-and-a-half to four guineas a week'. It is to be hoped that Nelly had one of the four-guinea rooms, and a dressing table on which to lay out Agnes's ivory-backed brushes. She was a long way from home, but Leicester was a centre of the temperance movement, and Mrs Susan Theobald was an ardent campaigner and public lecturer for the cause. She was brave, openly making the connection between male alcohol abuse and domestic violence, a topic rendered taboo by shame.

Nelly left Tower House after some months for a trial period, staying in lodgings with her sister Elizabeth at Keswick in the

Lakes, not far from home. It was no good, and she was soon back
at Tower House. She died there, aged sixty-four, in January 1903,
leaving an estate of around £13,000. Her body was taken back to
Penrith for burial in Beacon Edge Cemetery, not far from her
home, Ash Bank.

That is not the end of this story. John Lewis did not forget
Nelly Breeks.

★

If John Lewis had other attachments in the two decades after he
opened his shop, moving from youth to middle age, there is no
way of knowing about it. His mind was on his business. Sales in
1864 were a remarkable £5,000 p.a., and £25,000 six years later,
and more than £100,000 by the 1880s. He bought the lease of
another shop in the terrace (but not next door), and then two
more unconnected units, and then the units on each side of his
original shop and, after acquiring a shop on a corner site, he
bought leases of two residential buildings on Holles Street,
between Oxford Street and Cavendish Square. There was a lot of
running out of one door and into another.

He could afford to do all this, not only because his business was
profitable, but because he banked all his profits. As his elder son
Spedan wrote, money for John Lewis spelled 'not spending-power
but safety'. He did not reinvest in his business. He did not bother
with carpeting the wooden floors of his showrooms, nor with
improving the ventilation and lighting. He did not develop all his
selling space, using upper floors for storage or just leaving them
empty. One thing he did spend money on was property, being
particularly proud of leasing buildings in Cumberland Place,
Regent's Park – Nelly Breeks's territory – and in Rathbone Place,
near Wilkinson Dent in Fitzroy Square. But he also bought at
auction over the years quantities of rubbishy properties in

unpromising areas, which he neglected to oversee and which remained unprofitable. He spent as little as possible on himself, on the wages of his employees, or on the conditions of their employment or accommodation. He did not go in for lavish, eye-catching window displays. Yes, he said, that might attract a crowd, 'but so it would if he stood on his head in his corner window' – an argument which seemed, to John Lewis, conclusive.

His sons Spedan and Oswald were startled to discover all his vagaries when they joined their formidable father in the business. He always stressed the importance of meticulous accounting. Yet his methods were eccentric. He was not a team player, being extremely secretive. No one else in John Lewis & Co. was allowed to sign a cheque. Spedan thought that his father's trading policies did not evolve from the day he opened his first small shop until the end of his long, long life, and that his mind was focused on a theoretical customer base of limited means, 'the world in which he had spent his childhood'. He was energetic and able, but his mind-set did not transcend that of a small-town draper as the world changed around him. He was irascible and had what was then called 'an excitable brain'. He was not physically strong either, and tired easily.

Yet however clear-sighted and even brutal Spedan was about his father's limitations, he had respect for his father's trading policies, and internalised them. The first was 'an extremely high standard of probity'. No deceit, no trickery, and prompt payment of suppliers. John Lewis's other key concepts were 'value' and 'assortment'. 'Value' meant cheap goods for ready money. John Lewis preferred to sell quantities of second-grade goods cheaply rather than a smaller amount of better quality goods at a higher price, and liked to undercut his competitors.

John Lewis rated 'assortment' even more highly than good value. It meant a wide choice. A customer should be able to find whatever she wants in stock, even if the particular item is asked for only rarely. 'Assortment' also means that the customer not only finds what she wants, but that she sees – and buys – something that she had no idea that she did want.

This policy had consequences. A wide assortment risked a serious proportion of stale stock. When Spedan first joined the firm, he had the notion of checking the reserves of a certain kind of sewing silk: 'I found that we were carrying one hundred and twenty shades in boxes of a dozen.' He had the whole lot brought out on to a counter, the boxes of same colour piled on top of one another. Of the popular colours, there were only two or three boxes. Of the slow sellers, there were as many as twenty. The buyer, when running low on the popular colours, had just been reordering the whole range. This was assortment gone mad and very poor stock control. An associated weakness was that the selling staff were not required to keep a record of what they sold each day.

'Fate had given my father an occupation which did not really suit him,' wrote Spedan. 'His abilities, especially his industry and thrift, had enabled him to make a very considerable fortune. But his achievement, great as it was, was very far short of those of some of his contemporaries.' Spedan mentioned in this context 'Mr William Whiteley, Mr Frederick Gorringe, and Mr Owen Owen of Liverpool'. His father, he thought, was 'supremely ill-equipped to succeed in that form of competition that similar retailers have tended to develop'.

John Lewis was temperamentally unequipped to ride with the second wave, when department stores proliferated and the top ones became exciting places to visit, and acceptable destinations for unaccompanied women – unaccompanied, that is, by a man. Their fathers, husbands and brothers had always had the freedom of the streets, and of clubs, chop-houses, music halls and so on.

Hitherto for women, there had been only the church, visits to one another's homes, and the workplace. The absence of public conveniences for women meant that in towns they were limited in how long they could be away from home on any excursion. The department stores were slow in exploiting that obvious need. Harry Selfridge would be the first to install women's toilets in his shop, well into the twentieth century, and allegedly to facilitate the suffragettes, who needed to be out and about all day on their campaigns.

Women were gradually improving their position through better education, through campaigning for entry into the professions and for the franchise. It may seem counter-intuitive that liberation also seeped in with the flurry of consumerism activated by the department stores. But, however indirectly, it did.

The most evolved department stores were, for their overwhelmingly female customers, palaces of dreams. That is the socio-sexual message of Zola's *Au Bonheur des Femmes*, freighted with descriptions of avalanches of lace, clouds of gauzy underwear and cascades of seductive silks. Its flagrant eroticism is somewhat ludicrous when rendered in English (and only a little less so in French). This was a man's fantasy, not a woman's, though Zola does voice a perception that in such an environment a woman could fall in love with herself and with her own possibilities – empowerment, if you like, of a particular kind. This was not John Lewis's style at all.

He like most of his competitors did, however, in the 1890s invest in a great rebuilding. The new John Lewis & Co. stretched all the way from his original little shop to the corner of Holles Street, incorporating his leased houses on the west side of that street. The new building included a basement and three floors of retail selling space, with a notional wholesale operation on the fourth floor. There were two oak staircases and even a lift –

though he considered this as an indulgence for the old and disabled, chivvying his customers to use the stairs.

His profits increased in the new premises, though as Spedan noted, 'not so impressively as his competitors'. William Whiteley, the first department-store mogul Spedan cited as amassing a bigger fortune than his father, was the son of a Yorkshire corn dealer, and left school at fourteen. Five years older than John Lewis, he served his apprenticeship with a draper in Wakefield, and came down south in 1851 with £10 in his pocket to see the Great Exhibition, which proved his inspiration – so many goods, artefacts and products, all under one roof. He saved enough to finance his own business a year before John Lewis started his, with a Fancy Goods shop at 31 Westbourne Grove, employing – typically for these start-ups – two 'girl assistants', one of whom he later married, and a messenger boy. In 1889 the 'Fancy Goods' shop became a department store. Whiteleys' glory days came after the turn of the century.

Frederick Gorringe, from Sussex, opened his small drapery shop in Buckingham Palace Road in 1858. Because of its proximity to Buckingham Palace, his shop was patronised by the ladies of Queen Victoria's household. His business expanded into three further shops and blossomed into a department store specialising in custom-made school uniforms for the upper middle classes. He was as conservative in his practices as John Lewis. It was his unique location, and his upmarket customer base, that made him so rich.

Spedan's third exemplar, Owen Owen, was a Welsh hill farmer's son, a decade younger than John Lewis. As a motherless young boy, he had helped out in his uncle's drapery shop in Bath. This uncle paid for his education and taught him the trade. In 1868 Owen Owen, with a float from the uncle, opened his own emporium in Liverpool. He was only twenty. He was a dynamo. Within five years he was employing 120 people. Unlike John

Lewis, he cared for the well-being of his staff. He was the first employer in Liverpool to give everyone a half-day off during the week, and he set up a fund to provide pensions for their retirement.

Spedan could have reeled off, had he chosen, his father's other main competitors. He did not even mention Selfridges. That was too painfully near home and near the bone. Debenhams was earlier on the scene, developing out of an old draper's shop in Wigmore Street. Debenhams remained in tune with the times, opening provincial branches in Cheltenham and Harrogate, and ended up with a nationwide empire. Derry & Toms originated as a small drapery shop opened by Joseph Toms on Kensington High Street in 1853. He was joined by his brother-in-law, Joseph Derry. By the 1870s they had bought up seven of the surrounding shops. Woollands was established by a family of brothers from Devonshire in 1869, bang opposite a long-standing linen draper, Harvey Nichols, at the top of Sloane Street in fashionable Knightsbridge. By the 1880s Harvey Nichols too had morphed into a glamorous department store. Arthur Gamage, son of a Herefordshire farmer, began with a watch repair shop and ended up with more departments than in any other store, a successful mail-order business, and a different trading emphasis, specialising in hardware, toys, sports goods, photographic equipment – with fashion, carpets and furniture crammed on the upper floors. Gamages became an institution, its annual catalogue of Christmas gifts popular with families, and it survived on its massive Holborn site until 1972. Then there was D.H. Evans, which opened a stone's throw from John Lewis & Co. on Oxford Street in 1879. Dan Harries Evans was another Welshman. By 1883 he had taken over three adjoining stores; in 1893 he moved into better premises and became a limited liability company, listed as having capital of £202,000.

It would be tedious to enumerate more, although there are more. The first point is that John Lewis & Co. was an integral part of the transformation of retail. It was by no means a British phenomenon. Department stores were springing into existence all over the Western world, spearheaded in the US by Marshall Field in Chicago and Macy's in New York.

The second point is that John Lewis, though a 'sole trader', had, in common with nearly all his peers who succeeded, a rural background and a strong family network. Uncles and elders in the trade gave the next generation a leg-up, and cousins, nephews and in-laws were accommodated in the businesses whenever possible. All businesses were family businesses, just as all farming was organic, by default. The phrase 'family firm' had visceral significance. There was a responsibility, within the extended family, for its members' economic survival, and an assumption that the next generation would carry on.

John Lewis's elder sisters had always looked out for him and, as he prospered, he looked after them. When Aunt Christian Clark died in 1875 she was buried next to her husband in the cemetery at Shepton Mallet. John was responsible for her memorial. This would have involved at least one visit to Shepton to make the arrangements. He had identical flat stone slabs laid over the two graves, engraved with dates of their births and deaths and, on hers, these words: 'She lived for others rather than herself.'

The following year he provided for the retirement of his sisters. Elizabeth was just over fifty, the others in their forties. But life expectancy for women in 1880 was between forty-five and fifty. (Aunt Christian, who lived until the age of eighty, was phenomenal.) John gave them pensions, and a new home – the freehold of a house on rising ground in Weston-super-Mare, on the corner of Arundell Road and Lower Bristol Road. It had, then, an uninterrupted view over the bay. The household was headed up by his beloved eldest sister, Elizabeth. Maria was there, finally leaving all responsibilities in Oxford Street, and Mary and

Eliza. In London, he himself moved to restricted quarters in Harley Place, off Harley Street, occupied mainly by mews (stables, with living quarters above) just north of Cavendish Square, so close to the shop.

John Lewis gave his sisters' house an invented name – 'Spedan Ham'. This is mysterious. 'Ham' is a common suffix to English place names – as in Birmingham, Farnham, Saxmundham – meaning a settlement. A 'hamlet' is a small 'ham'. It is not usual to have 'ham' separated from its identifying place name. Perhaps it celebrated, in his mind, the settlement of his sisters on the three acres that came with the house, making them self-sufficient in vegetables, eggs, fruit and firewood. Perhaps it was a reference to the little place simply called Ham, and its surrounding woods and steep lanes, around which he chose to tramp on his nostalgic visit to Shepton in 1893. 'Spedan' is even more mysterious and John Lewis was to use it twice more, for personal purposes – his own family home, and his elder son.

One summer in the early 1880s, John Lewis took a holiday – a cruise on the Caledonian Canal, the sixty-mile waterway between Inverness in north-east Scotland and Fort William to the south-west, through spectacular scenery. If his aim was to get as far away as possible from the stresses of Oxford Street he could not have chosen better. He went on his own. He found congenial fellow cruisers, and among them the young woman who would become his wife.

3

A WIFE AND TWO SONS

John Lewis made friends on the cruise with a fellow draper, Mills Baker, five years older than himself. With Mills was his much younger half-sister Eliza, always called Ellie, in her twenties.

Like John Lewis, Mills Baker came from Somerset, and they had much in common. Mills Baker's father, Thomas, was a draper in Bridgwater who went bankrupt, as had John's own father, and as did countless small traders unable to pay their debts. It was nevertheless something to keep quiet about – hence Ellie's cagey letter to her son Oswald, when he asked her for details of his West Country credentials.

Mills Baker and a brother, another Thomas, left Bridgwater for Bristol and found work as drapers' assistants. By 1860 the Baker brothers had their own business and paid off their father's debts.

When John Lewis met Mills Baker he was already a prominent Bristolian, living with his wife and five children in a fine modern house, The Holmes, at Stoke Bishop. Baker & Baker Co. occupied a prominent site on the corner of Wine Street and the old cheese market, with the Baker brothers' eldest sons already partners in the business.

Ellie Baker was born in West Bower – a small village just outside Bridgwater – in 1854, the year in which John Lewis took his first paid job as assistant in Nicholls & Co.'s drapery in the same town. He told Oswald for his 'Notes' how he remembered Ellie's mother bringing her into the shop, he all unknowing that she would be his future bride. She can have been no more than an infant, since he was only in Bridgwater for a couple of years. It's a nice story. Ellie was the younger daughter of Ann Tiver, bankrupt Thomas Baker's second wife. Thomas died when Ellie was three, after which her prosperous half-brother, Mills Baker, the eldest son of the first marriage, became her guardian.

In the year that Oswald compiled his 'Notes About My Father', he also wrote up 'Notes About My Mother', after her death, from information provided by her elder sister Mary. Ellie's early schooling was with the Misses Gore in Bridgwater. She was a bright little girl, and when she was fourteen Mills Baker sent her to a Miss Heywood's boarding school in Richmond. According to Mary, she was 'remarkable for her memory while at Richmond. She had a trick, even as quite a small girl, of using long words but was full of fun and not in the least conceited of her abilities.'

Mills Baker thought Ellie should have a university education. When she was seventeen he sent her for a year to the North London Collegiate School for Girls – the most progressive girls' school in England, whose headmistress, Frances Mary Buss, was an educational pioneer with a mission to give girls the same opportunities as boys. Mills Baker transformed Ellie's life without severing her from her immediate family; it was her mother who, in December 1871, signed the application form for the North London Collegiate, while he paid the bills.

Miss Buss was a friend of Dorothea Beale, another champion of education for women and the future principal of Cheltenham Ladies' College. This formidable pair inspired the anonymous quatrain:

Miss Buss and Miss Beale
Cupid's darts do not feel.
How different from us
Miss Beale and Miss Buss.

Miss Buss's mother had run a small school where she herself taught before founding, at the age of twenty-three, the North London Collegiate, in a small house, 46 Camden Street, in Camden Town. By the time Ellie Baker entered, the school had moved to larger premises in Camden Road, with an upper and a lower school. The fees were six guineas a year for the upper school. (Miss Buss later founded the Camden School for Girls, for those whose families could not afford the North London Collegiate.)

Miss Buss's aspiration for her pupils was that they should go on to one of the universities – London, Oxford or Cambridge. It was a new thing for women, and, even when they qualified for entry, and however well they performed in their final examinations, they were not awarded university degrees. Ellie went to Girton College, Cambridge – except that in her first year it was not yet Girton College, nor yet in Cambridge.

Emily Davies was a co-campaigner with Miss Buss and Miss Beale for women's education and women's rights. Miss Buss was one of Miss Davies's supporters when, in 1862, she set up a residential college for women in Hitchin, Hertfordshire, some thirty miles from Cambridge. Up to a third of the Hitchin students came from the North London Collegiate in the 1870s.

Miss Davies's entrance examinations were properly stringent. According to an 1872 report, Part I tested candidates in arithmetic, grammar, history, and physical and political geography; Part II required candidates to choose two subjects from Latin, Greek, French, German, algebra, geometry, experimental physics, chemistry, botany, music and drawing, of which one must be a language. Successful candidates, in their chosen subjects, followed the curricula of Cambridge undergraduates.

Ellie Baker, for practice, took the Oxford Higher Local examinations and came top, which won her a scholarship to Bedford College in London, the first higher education college for women in Britain. Then, the youngest of twelve candidates, she took Miss Davies's entrance examinations, passed second top, and in 1872 entered the college at Hitchin with a scholarship.

At the end of that year, the college moved to a purpose-built house on sixteen acres in the village of Girton, on the north-west outskirts of Cambridge, and became Girton College, with Miss Davies as its first mistress. In 1873 Eliza Baker was one of Girton's signatories to an unsuccessful petition to the Senate of Cambridge University requesting that instead of just being awarded a 'Certificate of Proficiency', female students should be admitted as candidates for a Cambridge Tripos examination.

So, Ellie was more than adequate intellectually, and involved in her new academic community and its issues. But something went wrong. The social pressure may have been too great. Girton's early students were mostly middle-class, the daughters of professional men. According to her sister Mary, 'during the first year she made little progress, as after the first term she broke down and had a serious illness which nearly culminated in brain fever and resulted in her missing the second term altogether'. 'Brain fever', an obsolete diagnosis, often related to an emotional crisis or, in women, to mental 'over-exertion', was believed to result from inflammation of the brain. In any period there are frequently occurring illnesses unheard of before or since, which express contemporary anxieties, and 'brain fever' – which Ellie only 'nearly' contracted – was one of these.

She took four rather than the normal three years to gain the equivalent of an 'ordinary degree' in political economy and history, coming through triumphantly as 'top of the roll'. An honours degree equivalent was not even open to women; and in her day women had to be chaperoned to lectures, admitted on sufferance, with some lecturers declining to admit them at all.

After Cambridge, Ellie Baker's first job was as assistant mistress at Highfield School in Hendon, in company with Fanny Metcalfe, her Girton contemporary, who stayed on at Highfield and became the headmistress. But Ellie had to leave, or chose to leave. At least two of her Baker half-brothers had gone out to South Africa to establish a business. One of these returned home an invalid, and Ellie gave up work to look after him. Once released, according to Oswald's 'Notes', she became second mistress back home, at Bridgwater High School for Girls. Ellie and her sister Mary were planning to start a school of their own. That ambition was scuppered when another half-brother died suddenly in South Africa; Mary sailed for the Cape to help look after his family. When she came back in July 1884, Ellie had already come to an understanding with John Lewis.

With her academic achievements, and with Girton as a springboard, Ellie Baker could have become one of those many remarkable women of her generation who revolutionised girls' education, influenced social policy and campaigned for women's suffrage. But family came first. It always would, for her. She was blessed with high intelligence. She was not blessed with particular beauty. Fashionable women in the 1880s wore their hair curled and piled on top, often with a fringe over the forehead. Ordinary women, including John Lewis's sisters and Ellie Baker, scraped their flattened hair back behind the ears into a tight bun. This is not a flattering style. She was very short – under five feet – and to her tall sons she liked to refer to herself as 'little Mama'. But then John Lewis was short too. He would not have chosen a wife taller than himself.

Whether Cupid's dart did or did not strike Ellie Baker on the Caledonian Canal, it was not love at first sight for John Lewis. Spedan, reading their father's diaries before burning them, reported to his brother a 'dramatic entry' about admiring a young lady who got on the same London bus, and having the feeling that he had seen her somewhere – and discovering, when she moved into the next seat, and started talking to him, that he had in fact met her, six years before. 'Had those two people not got into that bus, or being there had said nothing to each other, you and I would I suppose never have been born.'

Ellie resigned, before ever taking it up, a new appointment as senior mistress at the Bedford High School for Girls. She and John were married on 1 November 1884 in the parish church of Stoke Bishop, the home of Mills Baker and his family. The bride was thirty, her bridegroom forty-eight.

★

Miss Buss, apart from academic entrance tests for the North London Collegiate, required candidates to produce, on a piece of cloth, a neatly crafted buttonhole. It was 'a rule of the school that no girl should enter who couldn't make a buttonhole'. Emily Davies of Girton was careful how she addressed women's accepted primary function as wives and mothers. What was the object of university education for women? 'Many persons will reply, without hesitation, that the one object to be aimed at, the ideal to be striven after, in the education of women, is to be good wives and mothers. ... But having made this admission, it is necessary to point out that an education of which the aim is thus limited, is likely to fail in that aim.'

In the same book (*The Higher Education of Women*) Davies wrote: 'What is really wanted in a woman is that she should be a permanently pleasant companion. So far as education can give or enhance happiness, it does so by making the view of life wide, the wit ready, the faculty of comprehension vivid.' Like many like-minded women of her generation, Miss Davies never married. The average Englishman felt threatened by feminism. His domestic supremacy, and his comforts and convenience, were at stake.

Ellie Lewis became a wife and mother. It is all that she became. That is not nothing. Emotional intelligence became her currency. She was not timid, and was to have no qualms about speaking in public. But she would be channelling her aspirations into the lives of her sons and husband – certainly 'making the view of life wide' in the case of Oswald, destined in her mind for success in all he attempted. It is a bit startling to read Spedan's assessment of his mother. He paid tribute to her goodness and loving kindness, saying 'that if everyone were like her, there would be no sorrows in human life except for accidents and illnesses' – but also that she did not exercise her intellectual abilities, to such an extent that he was 'unaware of them'.

The new couple's first home was Number 1a, Park Square, on the edge of Regent's Park, in the area Lewis had made his own over the years, always within easy walking distance of the shop. There, on 22 September 1885, their first son was born, and named John Spedan, always known as Spedan, pronounced 'Speed-ann'.

Ellie can have had no part in the choosing of her sons' names. This is the second time that Lewis had used the name Spedan.

Another son arrived on 5 April 1887, by which time they had moved up to Hampstead and what would be the family home for the rest of their lives. It was called Branch Hill House. Lewis renamed it Spedan Tower.

Where on earth did this name 'Spedan' come from? It has occurred as a surname, rarely, in Cumberland and Westmorland, which might suggest some connection with Lewis's first love, Nelly Breeks, though none has been found. Spedan's own explanation of his name has passed into the official record. His belief was that it was a veiled tribute to his father's aunt Ann Speed; he even called a Partnership yacht launched in 1952 the *Ann Speed*. Only a month before his death, Spedan wrote to Amanda (Lewis) Cornish, a young kinswoman, that his name: 'is, I suppose, unique among all the world's millions, for it is an original coinage by my father in warm gratitude to Miss Ann Speed, an aunt who filled in his childhood the place of his lost parents and whose kindness he never forgot'. The photograph he had of her was that of a 'truly magnificent old lady'.

This aunt, born in 1789, was the fourth of ten siblings of which the eldest was Aunt Christian Clark and the youngest Aunt Julia Collett. The only thing known about Aunt Ann Speed is that John spent some time with her in Castle Cary, when she was already Mrs King. A search of the deaths of women called Ann King born in 1789 throws up dozens, and it seems impossible to identify her. She could have remarried, changing her name again, and moved away.

Unlike kind Aunt Christian and beloved sister Elizabeth, Aunt Ann was not mentioned at all in Oswald's 'Notes' about his father. She is not mentioned in any of the surviving family correspondences. The photograph to which Spedan referred is now thought to be of his Aunt Christian. Perhaps Ann Speed made some magical and indelible impact on the small boy John Lewis. If Spedan, as would be quite natural, asked his father about his name, the answer would have been by word of mouth, and unrecorded. Spedan never said. The explanation may have been confided to one of the burned diaries. It remains a mystery.

John Lewis named his second son Oswald Speed. Around the same time, he moved his sisters from Spedan Ham to another house, nearer the Weston town centre – 8 Quadrant Square, which he named 'Oswaldene'. Ellie cannot have liked the name Oswald. She always called her younger son Peter, or Pete.

Father called the shots in this family. John Lewis was eighteen years older than Ellie. He had been running his business and his own life for twenty years and was used to having his own way. He was obstinate, irrational in argument, and given to sudden agitations and rages – the result of his 'nervous energy' and an 'excitable brain'. His physical health was uncertain and gave rise to endless anxiety, not least to himself. He needed tactful handling. That was Ellie's main job.

Spedan Tower, solid and solemn in appearance, built in the late 1860s, was approached by a long drive from a gate lodge on Branch Hill, just a stone's throw from freedom – the ponds and woods and wildness of Hampstead Heath, which became the boys' playground. A bit of West Heath had even been incorporated into the five-acre gardens, which sloped steeply downwards away from the house. There were stables, a coach house and an ice house.

It was only a short walk to Hampstead Underground Station, once that opened in 1907. Not that John Lewis took the Tube. Until he acquired a motor car, he was driven to and from Oxford Street daily by his coachman in his own brougham drawn by two horses – a 'carriage and pair'. The coachman lived over the stables. There are no known photographs of the interior of Spedan Tower, a fact entirely in keeping with Lewis's secretive nature. He and

Ellie would have furnished it from scratch in the mahogany-heavy styles of the 1880s, with curtains and carpets from the shop.

The Lewises never modernised Spedan Tower, though they did get the telephone. By the time John Lewis died there in 1928, the house was a Victorian survival, the plumbing and heating systems archaic. There was never more than one bathroom, in spite of, in early days, a family of four plus cook, parlourmaid, housemaid, and a nanny for the children, all living in. And a trained nurse in residence for times of serious sickness. People of means might go into a nursing home, but not go into hospital. To be fair, a single bathroom for such a household remained standard until well into the twentieth century.

Ellie created a warm world for her sons. She was in charge of their early learning and brought them along effectively. They each had multiple nicknames which survived into adulthood. Oswald was not only Peter or Pete, but Oddie, Buffles, Blogs and, to Spedan, Black Blogger. Spedan was Spedie or Spoushie/ Spouchie. They were trained young to call their parents Mater and Pater, but they were Mother and Father, and Father was also Dad, or Pa. As children, they were made to keep diaries. Oswald's childhood diaries have survived, and he kept the practice going all his life, with a few gaps. Spedan's childhood diaries have not survived, and he kept none in adult life – though he was to dispatch daily such a flood of letters and memos that virtually every action and passing thought was recorded somewhere, to someone.

The family at Spedan Tower kept themselves to themselves. John Lewis lived and breathed the shop. He and Ellie had few acquaintances, let alone friends, outside their families and the business. 'Our private circle could hardly have been smaller,' Spedan later wrote of his boyhood. 'My knowledge of life was very narrow. My father practically never entertained at all, and my brother and I had hardly ever stayed in any house but our own home and the house of our aunts in Weston-super-Mare.'

★

Oswald and Spedan were educated to be gentlemen. The first step was a private boarding school, preparing little boys for the entrance examinations to one of the great and ancient public schools – Eton, Harrow, Winchester, Westminster, Charterhouse, St Paul's. Spedan, when he was nine, was swiftly expelled from his first prep school for being 'scandalous, idle and disobedient'. An unruly, naughty boy, then, and not a conformer. He moved on as a day boy to Heddon Court on Shepherds Walk in the heart of Hampstead, owned by its headmaster Henry Stallard, and known familiarly as 'Mr Stallard's school'. (Heddon Court later moved out to East Barnet on the northern fringes of London.) Oswald joined his brother at Mr Stallard's school when he too became nine – but was taken away before the end of his first term, suffering from earache and headache; and he was losing weight.

Oswald had been a dangerously delicate baby and remained a delicate child. Parental anxiety was not misplaced, in that illnesses and infections carried off young children all too easily. The treatment recommended for him by the two doctors consulted was bracing sea air, so in mid-December 1896 Oswald, his mother, and the nanny took the train to Brighton, the luggage following by road 'on one of Pater's carts'. An apartment was taken, and Ellie left Oswald with Nana to spend endless chilly mornings on Brighton beach, with rather few visits from his family. He did not even come home for Christmas, though he got sent his presents.

In the new year, Ellie moved Nana and Oswald to a seafront house in Margate, a quieter resort on the Kent coast. She found a retired teacher to give Oswald his lessons, and he did a good deal of reading. He finally came home in May 1897 and returned to school. But no, it was not finally after all. At the end of the summer holidays Oswald was back in Margate with Nana. All in all, he missed out on several years' schooling, though the retired teacher obviously did a good job, and Nana must have been a capable, loving young woman, and not overprotective – for young Oswald was the first in his family to experience the future, in January 1897: 'Had a ride in a motorcar in the morning. It was such fun. We went along at a splendid rate, and as I was on the front seat I could feel the wind blowing hard in my face.' Later, Nana married, and sent Oswald birthday greetings annually so long as she lived, and he gave her a 'small pension', according to his son Peter.

So there was Nana, and there was Mother, for Oswald. His childish diary entries are uncomplaining (he knew that his parents would be reading them) though he expresses 'much grief' at the departure of Ellie after one of her rare visits. She did what she could. Duty to a husband trumped duty to a child, no question. John Lewis could not be left. And then there was Spedan.

But Oswald was always her favourite, her darling, her 'sweet beloved', and she made no secret of it. There is perhaps some overcompensating for his early exile in her constant and emotionally charged expressions of love. On his eighteenth birthday, she wrote to him of her 'eager hopes for my beloved boy, so often nearly lost, so hardly reared and therefore so doubly and trebly dear … you must have a delicate little creature of your own if you are ever to know how the sight of my fine manly son rejoices my heart …'. Indeed, Oswald grew even taller than his elder brother. Both were well over six feet, towering over their parents.

Ellie again, seven years later: 'Well sometimes I fear there is some little grain of truth in Spouchie's oft repeated asseveration that "Black Bloggy" was always Mother's favourite because he was the "mangy one" – so flattering, isn't it? But never the less it is true that my little ailing Peter, my delicate, suffering and most winning little child, did win his way to a special little shrine of his own which no doubt all mothers keep in their hearts for the dear frail blossoms that are year-in year-out in danger of vanishing from their sight.'

While it was not in his nature to respond to his mother's endearments in kind, Oswald derived from the maternal love showered upon him a lifelong sense of entitlement. Setbacks in adult life surprised him; he remained artlessly convinced that he could have and do anything he wanted – especially if one knew the right people, or threw enough money at a problem.

Spedan meanwhile, in 1899 at the age of fourteen, took 'the Challenge' for a scholarship to Westminster School. He won a Queen's Scholarship, coming fourth in the list of twelve in the election for that year. These scholarships were awarded for merit, not parental need. Whatever about being 'scandalous, idle and disobedient' when he was nine, Spedan was clever.

There has been a school in the precincts of Westminster Abbey since long before the Reformation, when it was dissolved, and refounded by Queen Elizabeth I – head of the Church of England but no bigot. She permitted the non-Protestant use of Latin in the school's prayers and services, and ordained the annual production of a play in Latin, to be written and performed by the Scholars. (The Lewis boys never took part.) Queen's Scholars had historical privileges, such as access to the Strangers' Gallery at the House of Commons, and on Sundays were allowed to walk on the Terrace of the House. They had seats in Westminster Abbey at the coronation of a new monarch and their shouts of 'Vivat Regina!' or 'Vivat Rex!' formed part of the order of service. Spedan was present for the coronation of Edward VII in August 1902, interrupting the family summer holidays; the Lewises always took a month away at the seaside, or in Scotland, or visiting the capitals of Europe. They travelled by train first-class, and stayed at the best hotels.

A Queen's Scholar had all his tuition and half his boarding fees waived. Spedan's parents wanted the boys home at night, so he, and soon Oswald, were 'home-boarders', and made by omnibus the six-mile journey to and from Spedan Tower. This did not mark them out as different, since home-boarders were in the majority.

Reginald Airey, a Queen's Scholar who left the school only three years before Spedan arrived, published in 1902 a volume on Westminster in a series 'The Great Public Schools', thus a unique source for what it was like when the Lewis boys were pupils. The school had taken over the monks' old quarters and spilled out along to Great College Street. The boys, in their uniforms of Eton jackets (short-fronted tail coats), wearing or carrying gowns, clattered between their classes through carved medieval doors and archways and along vaulted, stone-flagged passages. There is direct access from the school into the abbey, through the cloisters. In the Lewises' time the school was a largely unreconstructed architectural conglomeration spanning eight centuries – neither comfortable nor convenient, and an extraordinary survival. The gymnasium was contrived by roofing over the gap 'between the Chapter House and the crypt beneath the schoolroom, approached from the Dark Cloister, through a vaulted entrance, the piers of which date back to the time of the Confessor' – i.e., the eleventh century. Every architectural style was represented, up to the contemporary – which meant, in the year that Spedan entered, the rebuilding of the house called Rigaud's in what seemed at the time a jarringly raw red brick.

For Spedan's first two years the headmaster was William Rutherford, a distinguished scientist and classicist. Oswald passed the Westminster entrance examinations, but did not win a scholarship, and when he joined Spedan in the summer term of 1901 the new headmaster was William Gow, a classicist, and member of an artistic family.

More significant for 'Westminsters' – as the pupils are known – than the headmaster was his housemaster. Westminsters are divided into houses, most of them clustered around Little Dean's Yard. The Lewises were both in Grant's, the oldest of them all, rebuilt in the mid-eighteenth century to a design by Christopher Wren, himself an 'Old Westminster'. Attached to Grant's on one side was the house of the master of Queen's Scholars, and on the other the newly built Rigaud's. Their housemaster was Ralph Tanner, who taught classics. In May of 1901, noting the arrival of their new headmaster, the school monthly magazine *The Elizabethan* also remarked on the two new boys in Grant's: 'O. Lewis and A. Boult' – the latter being Adrian Boult, the future conductor.

Although Westminster School and Westminster Abbey were, in Airey's words, 'one collegiate entity', John Lewis was a radical in politics and a militant atheist. He did let Ellie, a committed Anglican, take the boys to church at St John-at-Hampstead on Sundays, but had not allowed them to be baptised. She arranged this surreptitiously, taking them in 1900 for a holiday in Whitby on the east coast of Yorkshire; and while there she achieved her purpose. Spedan and Oswald were baptised in Whitby.

Oswald was reluctantly confirmed in his last year at Westminster, unimpressed and unconvinced. 'What a farce it all is!' he wrote after taking Holy Communion for the first time alongside his mother in St John-at-Hampstead. Neither the Church of England, nor any other Christian denomination, ever meant much to either boy. Spedan's approach was quite sophisticated. He argued in a debate on the 1902 Education Act, that 'in a National School preference should not be given more to one form of religion or doctrine rather than to another'.

This was in the school debating society, which admitted a maximum of twenty-six members, sometimes sinking to as few as six, and in 1901 was 'in as bad a way as it ever can have been', with a very low standard of speaking, according to *The Elizabethan*. Spedan joined in autumn 1902. Late in life he told his confidante, Eleanor McElroy, that: 'I sat in the School Debating Society for a whole term without ever speaking at all, but then directly I began to speak, I began to be given jobs that were kept for the star performers.' That is an overstatement, but he was a lively participant. The first time Spedan spoke was against the motion: 'That in the opinion of this House a system of fixed stopping places should be adopted for London omnibuses' on the grounds that it would be less hard on the horses than continually stopping and starting, and that 'people would learn to get on and off between the stopping-places while the bus was moving'. This indicates – and who knew, nowadays? – that horse-drawn omnibuses could be stopped anywhere, as if they were cabs; and that Londoners had not yet conceived of queuing at bus stops. On another occasion he proposed, vehemently, a motion against the pastime of motorcar racing on public roads, a new thing. Motor cars that could travel at 80 mph, he said, could never be used on British roads. People would get killed. Perhaps, he suggested, within a hundred years motor cars will be superseded by flying machines. 'The great bulk of the people are pedestrians, and the roads are there for the people.'

Westminster boys were quite rough. There were frequent and violent playground fights, and being good at games had more status, and made a boy more popular, than academic distinction. *The Elizabethan*, even though it was edited by whoever was captain of the Queen's or (after the death of Queen Victoria) King's Scholars, carried more column inches on team lists and impassioned accounts of school and inter-house matches than anything else. Cricket and football were the chief sports, played on the fields half a mile away on Vincent Square. Westminster and

Charterhouse, another ancient London foundation, claim to have influenced the evolution of Association Football back in the 1860s, by persuading the nascent association to adopt the offside rule. As for cricket, a peculiarity of Westminster in the Lewises' time was that while house rivalry was intense, the school teams did not play other schools apart from Charterhouse; they rather grandly played London cricket clubs, Old Westminsters, Old Boys of other public schools, Oxbridge colleges, and private gentlemen's teams.

The colour for sporting distinction at Westminster is pink. Spedan and Oswald did not get to wear much pink. They were included, but infrequently, in the second or third school teams for football – Oswald played in goal – and not at all for cricket. Neither shone. This hurt. In middle age Spedan wrote that, 'a principal desire of my boyhood was to be good at football. For years at my prep school, and for years again at Westminster, I never found in this way my feet – and in the footballing world was a nobody.' But then, he claimed, he was given a chance in an important match, 'and jumped in that one game from being a nobody to being a real top-notcher'. This is not apparent from the sports pages of *The Elizabethan*. Compensatory fantasy sustained Spedan. Many of his tales are about early difficulties transformed into successes. Looking at the bigger picture, it has a poetic truth. Only the details are apocryphal.

All their lives, Spedan and Oswald longed to excel at sports and games – football and cricket at school, then tennis, golf, fishing and, in Oswald's case, hunting and shooting. Spedan did not shoot, and in the school debating society proposed a motion strongly deprecating the preservation of game birds on the grounds of cruelty. The opposition's case was that 'shooting is about the only sport indulged in simply by gentlemen', and Spedan's motion was defeated.

After their schooldays they could always afford the very best sporting kit, and the best coaching. It was to little avail. Neither of them was really gifted. Oswald carried on regardless, and as a grown-up man wrote long hole-by-hole accounts of his rounds of golf in letters to his elder brother. But Spedan, who had a short fuse, and 'excited brain' like his father, would fly into rages at his lack of success on the golf course or the river bank. Tennis was a bit different. Tennis was social. Tennis involved girls. To be good enough was good enough.

Throughout his life Spedan was to have many valued acquaint-ances, but few close friends outside the business. He and Oswald coincided with interesting characters at Westminster – not only Adrian Boult but the author A.A. Milne, the troubled mathe-matical brothers R.K. and A.S. Gaye, and Saxon Sidney Turner, who, like the Gayes, proceeded to Trinity College, Cambridge, and became part of the circle around Lytton Strachey, Clive Bell and Leonard Woolf.

Spedan retained just a few lifelong friends from Westminster, one of them being Donald Robertson, who had been with him at Heddon Court, and was a year ahead of him at both schools. Robertson's temperament, and his trajectory, were very different from Spedan's. He became an academic, a Fellow of Trinity College, Cambridge, and Regius Professor of Greek. Spedan remi-nisced how Robertson was bullied at Westminster, and how the bullies, 'seeing me come into the same House with a scholarship and the special dress [of a Queen's Scholar] … and knowing that I came from the same school in which, like Robertson, I had left at the top, had every inclination to give me an equally bad time'. There follows an involved story about how he, Spedan, ingen-iously foiled a plot to beat Robertson up for 'the sin of declining in summer to exchange his top hat for a straw'. Decades later, he was fighting and winning old battles as if they were yesterday.

Spedan and Donald Robertson were friends out of school. Spedan Tower was not entirely hermetic. School friends did come up at weekends to play cricket in the garden, mess around on the heath, and add to the Lewis boys' immaculately annotated collections of moths, bugs and beetles. Towards the end of his life, Spedan was recalling to Robertson: 'the clearest memory of sitting on the gate at the bottom of our drive to watch for you coming at the beginning of a Sunday afternoon into view, and remember a particular Sunday when tenacious hope slowly faded'. And again, about an occasion 'sixty years ago when you and I spent a day in collecting water beetles from horseponds'. Sorting old correspondence in his retirement, he came across a cache of 'delicious letters' from Robertson. Would Donald like them back? Donald asked him to destroy them, and they went on the bonfire, even though 'to me they seem charmingly light-hearted, lively and kind, and I am glad to have had that renewal of one of the chief happinesses of what, as I look back, seems to have been quite a happy boyhood'.

Natural history was Spedan's passion. He read a paper to the school's Natural History Society on 'The Effects of Sexual Selection as compared with the Effects of Natural Selection'. There were frequent visits to the Natural History Museum and the zoo in Regent's Park. His father, recognising this powerful interest, made him a present of life membership of the Royal Zoological Society on his eighteenth birthday. (Oswald at the same age was given life membership of the Royal Institution, founded to promote scientific education.) Spedan would later claim with justification to apply the mind-set of an ecologist to the management and structure of the Partnership.

In retrospect, Spedan had little gratitude to Westminster School. He felt it let him down 'dreadfully'. In a memo of 1947 to the first 'Partners' Counsellor' about the importance of helping along newcomers to the firm, and maintaining frequent personal contact, he said that at his prep school he had been 'kept well up to the mark', ending up 'top of the school'. But at Westminster: 'One interview a term with the headmaster was the whole effort that was made henceforward to prevent my slacking to such extent as reasonably bright boys can do without encountering inconvenient consequences. If my housemaster had spent a very few minutes even once a month in talking to me about my place in the form and so forth, I should have continued to work not laboriously but tolerably hard.'

It annoyed Spedan to see others getting ahead of him, but not enough to make him work, nor to make him 'really unhappy', except on prize days. 'I have always thought that, as far as the happiness of my boyhood went, the extreme inefficiency of my housemaster was for me a very great misfortune.' He blamed Mr Tanner for 'letting me fall away in my work'. This resentment remained a lifelong refrain, along with others. Someone or something was always to blame for Spedan's failures or setbacks. Since his housemaster Ralph Tanner was also the classics master, and Spedan was on the 'classical side', it may be that Mr Tanner understood more about Spedan than Spedan appreciated. Or Tanner possibly lost interest in him when it was decided that he was not going on to university.

'The aim of the average Westminster's life is to obtain election to either Trinity, Cambridge, or Christ Church, Oxford,' according to Reginald Airey. Three or four Westminsters were guaranteed election to both or either every year, with an accompanying grant. Others could qualify by examination. As a King's Scholar, Spedan would have been a shoo-in. But as they moved up the school, it became unlikely that either Spedan or Oswald would be following the approved path. Father, in his sixties, in poor health, was not expected to live long. In the interest of continuity and the conservation of the family fortune, it became accepted that Spedan would go straight into the family business. The effect of this decision on Spedan is understandable: 'I let my temperamental tendency to take my own line and to find boring anything prescribed by anybody else caused me to do no more work than comfort required.'

It was university-educated Ellie, rather than John Lewis himself, who most favoured this plan. The alternative, if Father were to die soon, or become incapacitated, would mean either selling up, or taking on a partner from outside the family. It is also possible that Ellie did not want to be left alone with her difficult husband without the support of her sons.

John Lewis was becoming increasingly unpredictable and Ellie was suffering from her 'nerves'. She had reason. In the middle of the summer term of 1903, sixteen-year-old Oswald wrote in his diary a long account of a cricket match and then, like an afterthought: 'Father was sent to prison today for contempt of court and is now in Brixton Jail.'

4

PRISON INTERLUDE

John Lewis, by now white-bearded and – apparently – a solid citizen, had become involved in local politics, elected in 1901 to represent the Marylebone West division, within which his shop was situated, on the recently formed London County Council (LCC). He stood as a Progressive, one of the group that formed the majority on the LCC. The Progressives were radicals, many of them from working-class backgrounds, and affiliated to the Liberal Party.

There were significant figures among the Progressives, among them John Burns, representing the division of Battersea. He became a friend and ally of Lewis, though a generation younger. Burns was a self-made engineer, one of sixteen children in a single-parent family and happy to claim that his mother was a washerwoman. He was a big man in every way and, as a militant socialist and trade unionist, had his own bruising brushes with the law, including imprisonment.

Both Burns and Lewis, like most other Progressives, were to lose their seats on the LCC in 1907, when the Moderates, affiliated to the Conservatives and rebranding themselves the Municipal Reform Party, gained control. By then Burns, an impressive politician, was already the MP for Battersea, aligned to the Liberals and, becoming more moderate himself, would later hold government office and become a member of the Cabinet as President of the Local Government Board.

Lewis himself was a very selective radical. He was every inch a capitalist and held no socialist principles. What he believed in fiercely was 'justice', which he interpreted to suit himself. He was a single-issue crusader. In his own years on the LCC he campaigned for leasehold reform, also becoming treasurer of the Town Tenants League for reform of the land laws. So when he came into conflict with his own landlord, he was more than ready to make it public, and a test case. The political became personal and vice versa.

He had been a leaseholder of the Portland Estate, which comprised 192 acres of Marylebone, ever since he opened his first little unit on Oxford Street in 1864. After he bought the leases of two residential properties on the west side of adjacent Holles Street, he moved the main entrance of John Lewis & Co. round the corner. The family started speaking of 'going down to Holles Street', rather than to Oxford Street. Holles Street, linking Oxford Street with Cavendish Square, and his properties, numbers 16 and 17, were up near the square, one of them right on the corner.

The priority of the Portland Estate was to preserve the social distinction and architectural integrity of Cavendish Square and its environs. Lewis had an agreement with the estate that he could use the houses for commercial purposes, but that the interiors should be ordered in such a way as to allow them, at some possible future date, to revert to private dwellings. Under the terms of his leases, he was not permitted to make changes to the Holles Street façades. He was perfectly aware of this when he moved his main entrance round the corner. He transformed the interiors into showrooms and changed the fenestration. His policy always was to sign any covenant or agreement while having no intention of abiding by it. And so began a dispute which would drag on for three years – and that was only the first round.

★

In 1899 the Portland Estate was inherited by Lord Howard de Walden, known as Tommy, the grandson of the fourth Duke of Portland. Now staggeringly wealthy, he was only nineteen years old; so essentially, when the estate, with its chief surveyor backed by batteries of accountants and lawyers, made objections to Lewis's development of the Holles Street houses, this white-bearded shopkeeper was doing battle with someone not much older than his own children.

Lewis's argument was that he had in fact reached an agreement with the estate to make the changes, but that the papers had never been signed due to an oversight. Fuelling his lack of compliance was his entrenched conviction that a landlord had absolutely no right to interfere with the arrangements of a long-standing lease-holder who had always paid his rent. Tommy de Walden himself had no experience in negotiation, and Lewis was not interested in negotiating. In the end the estate obtained a formal court order requiring Lewis to restore the houses to their original state.

He duly signed the court order. But then over more than two years he defied the order and did absolutely nothing about restoring the frontages. He boarded up his new windows and covered them with placards printed with anti-landlord protests and a banner: 'An Appeal to the Court of Public Opinion'. Howard de Walden was a decent, serious and unusual young nobleman. The child of a broken marriage, he was uninterested in the flummery of rank, though he was much interested in the flummery of the Middle Ages, and in the arts, in engineering, and in high-powered motor cars and speed boats. His instincts were humanitarian. He had no appetite for taking Mr John Lewis to court again. However, he applied to the court to have the court order enforced. Failure to apologise and comply would mean either a prison sentence or a fine for Mr John Lewis.

The case came up before Mr Justice Cozens-Hardy, Lewis's contemporary and a Liberal MP before he was appointed to the Bench. With a reluctance equal to the young landlord's, he committed John Lewis to prison for contempt of court, with the provision that he could 'purge his contempt' at any time by expressing regret and undertaking to restore the Holles Street houses to their original state.

Because of the prominence of his department store and his position as a local councillor, John Lewis was a well-known figure in Marylebone, but still the 'little man' – just an elderly shop-keeper, with no clout in comparison with his wealthy landlord. Lewis wanted a public showdown, and he got one. His blood was up. He was relying on his LCC supporters rousing the Liberal Party to take up his cause, to make representations in Parliament, and get the law changed in favour of the rights of leaseholders. It did not quite work out, not this time.

His diary entries during the drama of the summer of 1903 are, fortunately, among the sparse extracts copied out by Kenneth Hudson before the diaries went on Spedan's bonfire. So we know that on 16 June the police called upon him at the shop, and explained that the Sheriff's Officer would be arriving to accom-

pany him to Brixton Prison at 2 p.m. When Lewis emerged from
the Holles Street entrance, there was a crowd so dense that he
found it hard to get through to his waiting brougham, with his
coachman – 'a jolly good fellow' – at the reins to drive him to
Brixton Prison.

Once at the prison: 'I had to turn out my pockets and take off
my garments to be weighed, the fellows were somewhat rough
and I requested them to be civil.' In his cell, 'the mattress and
pillow were so uncomfortable that I could not sleep'. He 'wired'
Ellie – that is, he sent her a telegram – and she sent down a better
mattress and pillow the next day. She also ordered his meals to be
sent in from specialist caterers, who were supplying four or five
equally exigent prisoners. The food was served to him on 'a
miserable little table less than 2ft square'.

Lewis behaved as if he were in a substandard hotel, demanding
frequent interviews with the prison governor, demanding more
visits and letters than were normally permitted, and a different
newspaper. (The governor, Colonel H.B. Isaacson, happens to
have been the governor of Reading Gaol when Oscar Wilde
arrived to serve his sentence in 1896.)

Lewis followed the daily routine – prayers in the chapel, and an
hour's exercise in the yard, 'I and a few others by ourselves, away
from the other prisoners'. Supper was at 5 p.m. and then the cell
was locked up until morning. On the first night, 'as I felt cold I
paced up and down and the warder called out at 8 p.m. that I must
go to bed'. The prison doctor checked him out, twice, 'and was
very pleased'. He did not feel humiliated. He was on a crusade,
expecting the affair to go national.

The family at Spedan Tower were distraught, or at least Ellie
was. Oswald's diary still consisted mainly of sports reports, but on
3 July he wrote: 'The situation with regard to Pater is getting
simply horrible. His mind appears to be weakening. Today he had

a terrible row with the Governor of the prison … Mater's nerves are getting bad again.' Ellie had visited her husband during the day, and on her return found 'a telegram from Mr John Burns MP requesting an interview with her at the House of Commons tonight'.

John Burns too had been to Brixton Prison that day, according to Lewis's diary, 'by special permission from the Home Secretary, the Governor having advised me that he had sent a telegram'. This was gratifying. But Burns knew his LCC colleague felt that John Lewis did not have a leg to stand on, legally, and would not come out to support him. 'He [Burns] did all he could to persuade me to apply for my release and after his strongly expressed opinion that the Liberal Party could do nothing in face of my having signed the undertaking to carry out the Order of the Court … I consented to see Lithgow.' Samuel Lithgow, with offices in Wimpole Street in Marylebone, was Lewis's solicitor. In his early forties, he had founded the Institute for Working Men and Women, and was also a property developer; he would have done the conveyancing for Lewis's random property purchases.

'Mr John Burns MP has persuaded Pater to give in,' recorded Oswald. Not so. On Saturday 4 July, Lewis wrote: 'Lithgow and the Commissioners came and I signed the apology but no sooner had I done so I wired him not to part with it until I had seen him on Monday.'

He had changed his mind. He would not apologise after all. And on Monday 6 July, when Lithgow brought the document back, 'I tore it up without remorse.'

Lewis's next delusion was that the Home Secretary himself would intervene and order his release. Ellie was frantic. John Burns and the Liberals were relying on her to make her husband come to his senses, which says a lot about their high estimate of her capabilities. Unable to persuade her husband to change his mind, she took the initiative. Three days later Lewis wrote in his diary: 'Sir Charles Ritchie came to see me at E's request.' Ritchie, later Lord Ritchie, was a high-flying Conservative MP, a previous Home Secretary, and currently Chancellor of the Exchequer – a very eminent visitor to a prisoner in Brixton and, seemingly, an unlikely contact for the Lewises to have.

But Ritchie, a man of Lewis's own age, also headed up his family firm, William Ritchie & Sons of London and Dundee, East India merchants, jute spinners and manufacturers. John Lewis & Co. may have done business with William Ritchie & Sons over the supply of floor coverings. And Charles Ritchie, when President of the Board of Trade, had implemented the recent setting up of the LCC. Lewis could have known him in either or both contexts. 'He [Ritchie] came into my cell and reasoned with me and assured me that the Home Secretary could not release me being a civil not a criminal [sic], so that at length I said I would instruct my solicitor to take the necessary steps for my release.'

Lithgow drew up a second apology. Lewis signed it. And on the evening of 10 July, Ellie and Lithgow arrived bearing the Order of Release. 'And with the assistance of the officers I soon bundled up my clothes and bedding together and departed feeling sick of the confinement but still willing to remain in prison if the Liberal Party could or would make capital out of my imprisonment. E was beside herself with joy at my liberation.' Of course she was.

Lewis had been in prison for three weeks. Back home, the next day, he wrote: 'The impression from such strange experiences is surprisingly little, it passes away like a dream.'

It hadn't turned out as he imagined. Three days later, before going into an LCC meeting, 'I attended [a] meeting of the Executive of the Land Law Union and was warmly received,' while he expressed to them his disappointment 'that the Liberal

Party had not made better use of my imprisonment'. He sacked his solicitor Samuel Lithgow, perhaps because he had been insufficiently strenuous on his client's behalf. Lithgow subsequently flourished, serving on the LCC, becoming a governor of the North West London Polytechnic, and ending up with a CBE, which is more than John Lewis ever did. Meanwhile Lewis took all his business to the prestigious firm of Charles Russell & Co., which remained the family solicitors over generations.

Lewis did not, as he had undertaken to do as part of 'purging his contempt', reinstate the original frontages of the Holles Street houses. He simply left his Holles Street windows boarded up, for years, and his relationship with the Portland Estate continued to fester.

★

And yet – this intractable, irascible John Lewis was also the irrationally heroic John Lewis, and the man who never forgot his first love, Nelly Breeks, and had a sentimental streak. He was also, or became, a cultivated man. The Lewises may have been socially isolated, but in the boys' teenage years the family, including Father, went at least once a month to the theatre, to the opera and to classical concerts. They were all serious readers, Oswald keeping an impressive record of the books he read in every year, and what he thought about them.

John Lewis had a personal devotion to the poet Lord Byron which was all his own, although embraced by Ellie. It is on the face of it an unlikely pairing. In his first year in London as a young draper's assistant, he joined a lending library. He mentioned in his diary only one book: in July 1856, 'In all evening reading the Life of Byron.'

The early books about Byron were by friends and acquaintances, celebrating or exploiting their connection with the famous romantic rebel. Although Byron's poetry caused a stir, the extent and nature of his sexual extravagances were revealed only later. It was not Byron the libertine that inspired Lewis, it was Byron the libertarian – the radical, the champion of the underdog, the freedom fighter – not that Byron fought, though he subsidised the struggle of the Greeks against the Ottoman Empire with large chunks of his fortune. Byron spoke only three times in the House of Lords, but used that place to attack the exclusion of Dissenters and Roman Catholics from public life, and to defend the Luddites and frame-breakers who feared, with reason, that the new technology would result in their unemployment, as happened in Shepton Mallet. Byron's long satirical poem against exploitative landlords, 'The Landed Interest', was now even more pertinent.

Byron's supposed birthplace is 24 Holles Street. There was a memorial tablet on the wall placed by the Society of Arts, who protested against its disappearance during Lewis's redevelopment. Lewis went one better. In 1900 he commissioned a bas-relief plaque of Byron in profile, one hand cupping his chin, a pose copied from Thomas Sully's popular portrait of 1828. He had it set up over one of his new display windows. He would know too Byron's 'The Landed Interest', which added a frisson.

A Byron Club had been formed in 1876, meeting in the Crown & Anchor pub in the Strand, where Byron had first met with the London Greek Committee to discuss supporting their cause. Later meetings were held just round the corner at the Temple Club in Arundel Street. The club gained momentum on the centenary of Byron's birth in 1888, and flourished until World War II. (It was revived in 1971.)

The Lewis family were all members of the Byron Club. In October 1910, Ellie reported to Oswald: 'The Byron Club Dinner went off with great éclat on Saturday – and a little speech by little

Mama was received with extraordinary enthusiasm – even old Spoushie positively flowing forth on its merits. ... He spoke very well, as usual.'

Spedan's enthusiasm for matters Byronic was, however, moderate. His father made a representation of the Byron plaque the registered trademark of John Lewis & Co., and had a sketch of it printed in miniature on the letterhead of his business stationery. Four years after he joined the firm, Spedan had this 'scrapped', as he expressed it to Oswald. But he maintained the connection in the naming of the firm's internal clubs and societies – the Byron Football Club, the Byron Cricket Club, and so on. This increasingly obscure association lasted well into the twentieth century, and the plaque remained *in situ* until destroyed in a German air raid in 1940.

★

The Brixton Prison episode may or may not have been an embarrassment for John Lewis's sons at Westminster School. Spedan, though he wrote a lot about his father's character and behaviour – in *Partnership for All*, in letters, and in memos to managers – never mentioned his father's incarceration at all. Reported widely in the national press, it would surely have heightened their profiles at school. When, in the autumn of 1903, most of Spedan's cohort moved on to Oxford or Cambridge, the writer of 'Grant's House Notes' in *The Elizabethan* reported: 'We are glad to say that J.S. Lewis [and two others] have all decided to stay on for another year ... J.S. Lewis has been appointed a House Monitor.' The following spring Spedan played football twice for the Third XI, enough finally to get him his school colours, entitling him to wear a pink and black blazer. But as Grant's House Notes added, 'he will have left before next season', and maybe never bothered to get the blazer.

Grant's House Notes again, in August 1904: 'We regret to record the absence of J.S. Lewis through serious illness', but that he was making a good recovery. 'We hope that Lewis will have been back for some time when this appears.' Spedan's illness is not documented. Maybe he was simply depressed, marking time at school to little purpose when his friends had left for university. He did come back and left, finally, at the end of the summer term. He was by then nearly nineteen, and after the holidays began going down to the shop.

Working with his father was a startling experience. It was a startling experience for his father as well, accustomed as he was to being the unquestioned boss, his methods and policies un-challenged, for forty years.

Spedan had no specific job or brief other than familiarising himself with the life and routines of the shop and getting to grips with the different departments and the way they were organised. He was young, educated, imaginative, and naturally thought in terms of changes and improvements, which his father saw as assaults on his authority. Spedan fell ill again in his first year in the firm. He went to convalesce in a hotel full of clergymen and 'derelicts' on the Mediterranean, whence he wrote to Oswald: 'Nothing can, so far as I can see, interfere permanently or even seriously with my reformation of the whole of the business house-keeping' – citing the vagaries of stock control, the low calibre of the buyers, and the old-fashioned showroom displays. There was no way that this was going to run smoothly.

Oswald joined the debating society at Westminster as soon as Spedan left – opposing the introduction of the decimal system on the grounds that the number 12 was more easily fractured than 10. In a debate in February 1904 on Chamberlain's fiscal policy, Oswald complained that the society was 'prejudiced in favour of Conservatism', and that there was 'no reason to abandon Free

Trade'. Many people, said Oswald, 'blindly voted for Protection, gulled by Chamberlain's cleverness, without really knowing what it was'.

A fellow debater that evening, H.I.B. Hallett, who went on to become a member of a higher talking shop, the Oxford Union, pointed out, with approbation, that 'every tradition of Westminster was Imperialist'. Oswald opposed the new Cadet Corps; in June 1905 *The Elizabethan*, while commenting on an 'eminently satisfactory year' for the debating society, singled out O. Lewis, negatively, for pouring 'his usual scorn on the Cadet Corps' and for deprecating 'the almost exclusively Conservative tone' of the debates. The vice-president of the society opined that 'Mr Lewis's condemnation of the Corps was only a reflection of his ignorance.' It sounds as if Oswald's interventions were informed by evening discussions with his radical father. Once out of range of paternal tutelage, Oswald would modify his views.

Oswald did not resent Westminster as Spedan did. He respected, or accepted, the education he received, and in his first years worked hard to catch up because of the gaps in his earlier schooling. He distinguished himself academically rather more than Spedan, winning some maths prizes. One of the masters introduced him to photography, lent him a camera and the apparatus for developing and printing from plates. Photography became and remained a serious hobby. As an Old Westminster he was a more faithful attender than Spedan at reunions, dinners and sporting events, and nurtured, in the furtherance of his professional life, the contacts he made there.

In 1905, the year he became eighteen, the question arose as to whether Oswald should stay on another pointless year – as Spedan had, pointlessly and unhappily. Oswald wrote in his diary that his career at Westminster, 'though very varied in the past, has become somewhat stereotyped and dull now. My failure to retain my place

in the First XI and Dad's eternal worry about my homework have
proved powerful factors in my present state of boredom. If I
prolong my stay after September I may become a monitor and I
might do something in the 1906 sports.' He was still playing in
goal for Grant's and, sporadically, for the school Second XI (who
generally lost, even a match against Old Westminsters Second XI
in which 'O. Lewis kept goal well and was much safer than usual').

It was his mother who made up Oswald's mind for him. She
wrote him one of her long, intimate letters, advising him to leave
school and join the firm, so as to keep in his father's good books
and – tacitly – to bring him up to par with Spedan in their father's
favour. Oswald, his mother's darling, had long felt that Father
came down too hard on him, and that his relative indulgence
towards Spedan was unfair. Spedan was temperamentally very like
his father, though that brought its own problems.

The financial security of the family was locked into the success
of John Lewis & Co. Father was getting old and would surely be
needing help from his heirs and successors in running the business. So Oswald left school that summer. In a final summing up of
his school career he wrote that he 'wished he had been more
popular'. His diary entry for 12 September 1905 says simply:
'WENT INTO BIZNESS!'

Before Oswald went into 'bizness' there was a family holiday for
the whole of August in Scotland, at the imposing Dunblane
Hydro Hotel in the Perthshire countryside, with accommodation
for 200 guests. Hotels, like the important department stores, had
shot off the scale in terms of opulence and magnitude. Ellie was
'taking the waters', as was Cousin Mabel, who accompanied
them.

Cousin Mabel was the daughter of John Lewis's Uncle Alfred,
who had a dim drapery shop in Fore Street in Taunton, back in
Somerset. It was currently managed by Mabel's brother, Colston

Murray Lewis. Ten years older than Oswald, Mabel was his confidante and he would often stay with her at her house in Minehead. An able and attractive woman, she never married. She was always a good friend and supporter of Ellie's as well, in spite of being a Lewis, not a Baker.

At the Dunblane Hydro Hotel there were orchestral concerts or dances. Oswald had a ball in all senses. As a tall, good-looking young man, he was decidedly 'popular', as he stressed in his diary. He danced with Mabel – but also night after night with a 'young actress' called Connie Hengler, and her sister Irene – 'deucedly pretty' – and with another pair of sisters, Ethel and Nellie Constant. 'I am getting spoilt. I score here tremendously as the other boys, though some of them dance well, are not well mannered.' He and Irene Hengler 'sat on a seat in the grounds (in a retired position) for one hour and twenty minutes'. But then: 'A certain Miss Hollis (pretty and notorious) has arrived … must get myself introduced.' By 19 August, 'I like Miss Dora Hollis best of all the girls here.' The next day he had 'eight hours' with her. He took her to church, took six photographs of her, 'sat in a cosy corner with her', sat next to her at the evening concert, 'and got her name in my birthday book'. If Spedan was on this holiday, he is not mentioned in Oswald's diary.

It did not end well for Oswald. At the fancy dress ball, Miss Hollis 'behaved shockingly to me. I only had three dances with her out of twenty.' He found her flirting in the drawing room with 'a confounded soldier'.

Back at Spedan Tower, Oswald developed and printed his portraits of Dora in the pantry that he had set up as a dark room. 'Three of them are absolutely splendid.' End of story. He never saw her again.

5

'HELL OF A TIME'

n 1906, with both boys in the firm, John Lewis branched out. Mr Peter Jones, founder of a department store on the corner of Sloane Square and King's Road, fell ill. King's Road in Chelsea was composed of artisan cottages and small shops, with streets running off it down to the Thames. It was fashionable in a bohemian way, with a few fine old houses surviving from more rural times. The store was well placed, on the fringes of an area across the square being developed for the prospering classes.

Jones's trajectory was typical. Six years younger than Lewis, and the son of a Welsh hatter, he too had served his apprenticeship in draperies in his home area before coming to London, working as a draper's assistant, setting up his own little shop in 1871, and then expanding by acquiring leases on adjacent small units. These small units became twelve, and in 1890 his emporium was rebuilt with

all the contemporary grandeur expected by the carriage trade –
carpets, palm trees, and much marble. Peter Jones was the first
shop in London to be lit by electricity throughout. Mr Peter Jones
described his business as: 'Silk-mercers, Costumiers, and Complete
House-furnishers'.

By the turn of the century Jones was employing 300 people,
and floated his company on the Stock Exchange. His board then
made a policy decision which turned sour. Instead of stocking
top-quality merchandise to bring in the upper middle classes of
Sloane Street, Cadogan Square, Eaton Square and the area called
Belgravia, the showrooms were piled high with tacky bankrupt
stock, and there were constant price-slashing sales, all in pursuit of
instant profits. The plan backfired and the business, like its
founder, was failing. Mr Peter Jones died on 1 September 1905.

John Lewis had never yet expressed any wish to expand his
business by opening a 'branch'. But now, in his seventieth year, he
walked, it is said, the two miles or so from Oxford Street to Sloane
Square to meet with the executors, with £20,000 in his pocket
– probably just twenty £1,000 banknotes, 'white notes' as they
were called, printed in black on tissue-thin white paper. These he
slapped down on the table. The £20,000, plus a bit more, bought
him 50,000 shares out of the total of 80,000, giving him a
controlling interest. As the majority shareholder, he joined the
board and soon had Spedan and Oswald appointed directors,
along with Cousin Mabel's brother, Murray Lewis. Thus Peter
Jones became part of the family business, with the four Lewises,
after time, dominating the board.

Both boys were living at home, where pleasure was restricted
– few visitors, no alcohol, no smoking, and changing into formal
evening clothes for dinner. John Lewis rarely strayed beyond the
boundaries, apart from family outings and his legal forays. He was
not likely to suffer the scandalous fate of his rival William Whiteley

of Bayswater, the 'Universal Provider', with whom he had a run-in over the 'three-mile rule'.

This was an agreement by which a buyer, changing jobs, would not pass on to the competition, within a radius of three miles, any information about his previous employer's suppliers, rates of pay, profits, or any other business secrets. Mr Whiteley had lured away Mr Yearsley, John Lewis's Silks Buyer – John Lewis & Co. being famous for their silks. Lewis took Whiteley to court, and won. Mr Yearsley returned to Oxford Street. William Whiteley was shot dead in his store in January 1907 by a young man claiming to be his illegitimate son.

Also in 1907, for her health and his, Ellie went on holiday with Spedan to Deal, in Kent, where Spedan did some intensive and ecstatic butterfly-hunting. Given the claustrophobia and increasing tensions at Spedan Tower, getting away did the family members a power of good. Ellie was always anxious that her sons should stick together and be good friends, though she did not believe that they could ever live or work together. Her loving promptings were surely behind the way in which Spedan had written to 'best beloved Bloggs' when Oswald was away the previous summer: 'I miss you much more now than in the Margate days ... I am taking Susie [Cole, a girlfriend] to the Zoo.' Spedan liked girls as much as Oswald did. And now, from Deal: 'In my daily life I may perhaps have good friends, some one or two, but never another brother – and such a brother.' He added that he really needed more income and was just 'scraping by'. Spedan was a big spender.

In September, John Lewis took Spedan's place with Ellie on the Kent coast for a break. The couple got on best in these situations, away from the business, 'like two nice comfortable old tabbies', as Ellie wrote to her 'Pete': 'Dad is contented and happy.' So they were, sometimes, quietly happy together. Their increasingly frequent holidays also kept Lewis away from Oxford Street for a few weeks, enabling their sons to make what changes and improvements they dared. Spedan was reorganising the showrooms. Oswald, in the Counting House, kept his father in touch with 'the biz' by letter. This was not plain sailing: 'By the way darling,' wrote his mother, 'you are *most* wise to write to Daddy so frequently, and such nice long letters too.' They both felt, Ellie continued, that he had it in him to become 'a really good writer', but. ... This was all about Oswald's handwriting. It was only, Ellie said, a matter of 'varying the stature of the capitals'. And – again, just 'by the way' – 'Daddy detests abbreviations (such as "I've" for "I have"). ... All you do in the Counting House gives him *huge* satisfaction.' Perhaps.

Both Spedan and Oswald had two styles of handwriting – one childish, neat and upright, just joined-up print; the other cursive to the point of abstraction, slanting sharply to the right as if flattened by a hurricane. In letters to each other, they sometimes used the two different scripts in different paragraphs. Oswald's cursive script was virtually horizontal and, yes, pretty illegible to the unpractised eye.

According to Oswald's 'Review of Progress' for 1908: 'The year began with uneasiness and closed with open strife.' In the Counting House he was acquainting himself with his father's arcane accounting methods, discovering that the chief cashier had been cheating the firm for years, and sorting out his father's portfolio of mismanaged properties. Oswald was not allowed to sign cheques for John Lewis & Co. because his father said his signature was not good enough. Spedan cunningly evolved an official signature which was just like his father's. It made no difference. He was not allowed to sign cheques either. (Though they both signed vouchers, 'without Dad seeing'.) It was not really about handwriting, it was about control.

★

Shortly before Christmas 1908, Spedan dropped a bombshell. He just 'mentioned' at breakfast that he had proposed to his secretary, and she had accepted his proposal. The young woman had been working with him in the partners' private office, and her name was Margaret Lynette Phillips Griffith-Jones, known as Nettie.

Exploding with fury, John Lewis told Spedan that if he married Miss Griffith-Jones he would cut him out of the family business – and Oswald too, because he always treated the two alike. All that year the brothers had been playing the field, going out together and separately in the evenings and at weekends with a series of fanciable dancing partners, and comparing notes, competitively, on their successes. The Lewises having no social circle, they got to know girls at their own friends' parties, in dance halls, and at stage doors. Susie Cole had been Spedan's most regular girlfriend that year.

Nettie Griffith-Jones was a very different kind of person, and five years older than Spedan. Lewis may not have liked her very Welsh background. Her grandfather had been Mayor of Aberystwyth and a local wholesaler. Her father did well as a solicitor in his home town, and thought to better himself by coming to London and becoming a barrister. This did not work out, and the family was in financial difficulties. That is why Nettie Griffith-Jones was going out to work at John Lewis & Co.

John Lewis was behaving towards Nettie just as Nelly Breeks's family had behaved towards him. His relationship skills were rudimentary. His response to any challenge was to dig his heels in and refuse to budge. But he was not stupid. Spedan was actually not ready for marriage, to anyone.

Spedan could be volatile, with sudden violent tempers. He could not bear to be teased, and on one such occasion lost control and went for Oswald with his fists. 'I became afraid that his nerves were so overwrought that he might go into delirium,' wrote

Oswald. Spedan complained to their father about being tormented by Oswald, and Father took Spedan's side. 'Dad declines to see that Spedan's nerves are in a very bad state, and blames me entirely.' Spedan would only get worse, 'if he is allowed to excite himself so, and rather praised for doing so'. He suffered chronically from an ulcerated throat, other unspecified malaises and, according to Oswald, this tendency to 'delirium'. The term comes up frequently in connection with Spedan and was another way of expressing the 'excited brain' – inappropriately extreme reactions, and a tendency to lose all control: traits he shared with his father.

For moneyed patients, a rest-cure abroad was the standard treatment for almost anything. At the beginning of 1908, Dr Acland prescribed for Spedan a sojourn in Switzerland, a plan which his father flatly refused to entertain, again threatening to throw him out of the business. So Spedan stayed at home, partly so that the plans for Oswald's imminent coming of age should not be thrown out by such a crisis, and all went smoothly. 'Dad gave me £50,000 and a partnership (one quarter's profits), also a gold watch and chain,' wrote Oswald. He got the interest, but the capital sum remained under Father's control. Spedan had received the same amount of capital under the same conditions at his own majority, and a gold watch and chain, and now both were partners in the firm.

Their partnerships in John Lewis & Co. were informal – 'partnerships at will'. There were no legal documents drawn up, just personal letters. The day after his twenty-first birthday, Oswald, who did not trust his father an inch, 'took the letter Dad gave me stating that he had given me £50,000 to the Nat. Prov. Bank and there deposited it'. Then he went out shopping – for a new top hat and a gold matchbox to go with his new gold watch-chain. He ordered a new suit, offered sixty guineas for a horse, and bought a frame for a photograph of Spedan 'for my room'.

As for Spedan's engagement to Nettie, the main obstacle was Father's 'views', as Spedan told Nettie's father. Nettie was a feminist and a suffragist. She was interested in improving the position of working women. Her views were not John Lewis's.

Oswald confided almost nothing about Spedan's engagement to his diary. No one would have known much about it, had Oswald's son Peter not been contacted, many decades later, by Nettie's family, who thought he might be interested in seeing the correspondence in their possession. Nettie, her letters demonstrate, was intelligent, serious and level-headed. And her father, though a loser in John Lewis's eyes, wrote to Spedan in a strikingly kindly manner when the engagement was finally broken off.

Ellie, with her husband and elder son locked in conflict, and with her husband's rants spilling out all over her in private, completely collapsed. She could not take any more, although there would always be more to take. A nurse was engaged to look after her. The atmosphere at Spedan Tower went from bad to toxic. In early 1909 the brothers took drastic action – more drastic than most sons would ever have contemplated, let alone pulled off. They kidnapped their mother.

According to Oswald: 'Father continued to behave in what seemed to us all a perfectly intolerable manner, and we decided to leave the business, home, and him. Mother was ill in bed with a nervous breakdown when the day came to depart, but with the assistance of the hospital nurse we got her away safely' – to a flat at 10 Queen's Gate in Kensington. There they camped out for several weeks with Ellie, and one hopes the nurse too, while negotiations with their father were conducted through solicitors.

In the end, Spedan decided to go back to Spedan Tower, though he would now be spending most weekday nights at a gentlemen's club, the Fly-Fishers' Club on the corner of Swallow Street and Piccadilly – an eccentric choice as he was not (yet) a fly-fisher. Oswald took the lease of a flat on his own account: 69 Bickenhall Mansions, off Baker Street, a high, red-brick block of comfortable 'mansion flats'. Ellie moved in with him – but then she too returned home to Spedan Tower.

Spedan ended his engagement, writing to Oswald: 'Broke off Nettie. Shocking row.' Naturally there would be. But Nettie regained her equanimity. She knew, she wrote, that people would say he had done it to save his partnership in the family business, but that was not what it was about; she told her sister that 'it is doubtful with our *two very* strong wills we should have carried it off in the long run. He is very young, and an absolute genius, and I could never converse on the very many things he loved and knew much about.'

Nettie never married anyone. She lived life to the full and to a ripe old age, loved by her extended family. Spedan returned to his life of casual social and sexual activity with a variety of partners.

Oswald would never live at Spedan Tower again. He had not been enamoured by the prospect of a lifetime running John Lewis & Co. with his brother. His father had thoroughly unnerved him only a few months after he first entered the business, travelling down to the shop in the brougham, telling him that he and Spedan could never work together and that he himself should 'clear out of the business at once and for good'. Afterwards, it was as if this conversation had never happened.

Oswald had borne enough of his father's threats and moods. He was thinking of a career in finance or politics, and became properly energetic in his own interest. He joined the Eighty Club. ('Spedan got Hon Charles Russell [the family solicitor] to propose me.') Strongly affiliated to the Liberal Party, the Eighty Club was a good way of meeting people and getting himself known.

In November 1908, Oswald got himself elected in the Liberal interest to Marylebone Borough Council, his father's former stamping ground. Since there was no vacancy, he went to see the town clerk to find out whether any councillor 'could be dislodged', and was told there was one 'who would do anything for a consideration'. The consideration, securing a resignation, was £50. This transaction is pure Oswald – just practical common sense as he would see it – and at the resulting by-election he was elected. He had a piece of luck here, as not only Liberals but Conservatives voted for him in order to keep the Labour candidate out.

His parents were away on another of their holidays, this time in Italy, when his father read in the newspaper that Oswald was standing for the Marylebone vacancy. His mother wrote to him: 'As you might expect, his first words were, "But the Boy ought certainly to have consulted me before taking such a step as this."' Ellie did not take sides. She continued to wear herself out trying to make peace within the family, defending and explaining the sons to each other and to their father, and vice versa. This letter to her 'darling Peter', from Italy, covers many pages: 'There is no doubt that the older he gets and the less effectively strong he feels the more sensitive he becomes about his own personal position and about being treated with deference. ... So we must do all we can to smooth things for him, and try to make the inevitable changes that time *must* bring ... as little painful to him as possible'. They must be 'loving and gentle' with him. And never forget 'that it is to him we owe our fortunate position'. She believed that 'with a little tact' they should be able now to 'keep him away from the business a very great deal'.

She ended up: 'I need scarcely say that I am doing everything to keep him comfortable and contented.' This was not easy. For a wedding anniversary present, she had commissioned two watercolour paintings of the gardens at Spedan Tower. He just 'grumped', and she was disappointed. The only thing that seemed to soothe him was when she played the piano to him in the evenings. A cynic might surmise that this was the one occasion when he had to keep quiet.

Ellie did understand her husband. Lewis's shock and confusion following the flight to Queen's Gate elicited her pity, and guilt. She was not a woman to abandon a husband. Whether she loved him or not is largely irrelevant. He was simply there, dominating their lives, and those comfortable lives depended upon him, as she had implied to Oswald. To put it crudely, she and they knew which way their bread was buttered.

Ellie's conciliatory policy had little traction. Later in the month, she wrote from Paris: 'I have had 2 or 3 pretty bad returns of the irritation and excitement', still on about Oswald's standing for the Marylebone Borough Council, and about his handwriting: 'If you love your little Mama, *do do do* write more compactly in your letters to Dad', with the 'letters taller and less "stretched out"'. ... Do try to realize how wearing it is for poor Ma to have this on the tapis, morning, noon and night.'

In early 1909 Ellie was helping Oswald to furnish his new flat, and engaging two live-in maids to service it and him. Oswald had no intention of going back into 'the biz', and he wanted to get his £50,000 capital out, and more: 'and as Father would not pay me out, I proceeded against him and S[pedan] to have the business wound up'. In his quiet way, Oswald was ruthless. He was suing both his father and Spedan as a co-partner. His own solicitor retained the top barrister Edward Carson, KC, to represent him. The case came up in court and was adjourned 'in order for me to obtain another affidavit'. Meanwhile Ellie begged Oswald to accept a compromise.

John Lewis caved in. To be taken to court by one's own young son was not to be borne. Before the case came up again, he offered, in Oswald's words, 'the £50,000 with interest and profits to date, and half the value of the house properties, shares etc standing in the names of S and myself [worth about £34,000]. I offered to waive all claim to goodwill.' Another £10,000 was added to the package. Ellie implored Oswald to 'try to be as good and friendly a brother as you can to dear old Spoushie. He will always want you more than you will him.'

Oswald, now out of the family business altogether, was mollified, as well he might be. He now had more than £60,000 in the bank to spend or invest, plus whatever the interest and share of profits were to date, plus the prospect of half the value of Spedan Tower, and other bits and pieces.

He was a rich young man, nowhere near on the scale of Howard de Walden, but rich. But he felt disadvantaged in his social and political aspirations by the lack of a university degree or any professional qualification. He decided after all, a bit late in the day, to go to Oxford. He contrived this by going to see his old headmaster, Dr Gow, who activated Westminster's connection with Christ Church. Oswald passed the entrance exams after paying for some coaching, and was awarded an Exhibition (a minor scholarship) to read law and jurisprudence. At the same time, he ate his statutory dinners in London at the Middle Temple, sat the Bar exams, and in January 1912 was duly called to the Bar and photographed in wig and bands – not that he ever practised as a barrister.

★

'Poor old Dad's condition is absolutely deplorable. He seems crushed with sorrow – what I would give to see that a compromise had been arrived at to end the present state of things.' That, on 2 March 1909, was not about Oswald's defection, but about Lewis's renewed battle with his landlord. The Holles Street windows were still boarded up. The estate was content for business to be conducted within the houses, but still insisted that the façade be reinstated. Lewis, in his turn, insisted on retaining his plate-glass windows for display purposes. Deadlock.

The windows issue was particularly galling for Lewis because of the explosion on to the scene in 1908 of a new department store at the other, western end of Oxford Street, hitherto the 'quiet end'. It was a department store such as London had not yet seen. Harry Gordon Selfridge was from Chicago, and his building was designed by the architect of the famous Chicago store, Marshall Field.

Mr Selfridge was everything that Mr Lewis was not. His department store was more Zola's sensual, sensational evocation of Paris's Bon Marché than John Lewis & Co. Selfridge believed in aggressive marketing and extravagant, fantastical promotion. His advertisements and announcements flooded the front pages of the newspapers. He compared the 'act of shopping' to going to the theatre, and his window displays were the first act of the drama.

On opening day, 15 March 1909, the silk drapes over his shining expanses of plate glass were theatrically drawn back and revealed marvels. A visit to Selfridge & Co. was an adventure, and 'the customer is always right', as the advertisements proclaimed. Mr Selfridge offered free rail tickets to anyone from out of town who spent £5 in his shop. After Blériot's first cross-Channel flight that summer, his monoplane was put on exhibition inside Selfridges, attracting huge crowds.

There is no record of anything that the Lewis family had to say about this terrible, wonderful phenomenon. To bring it up at the dinner table at Spedan Tower, or in the Partners' office at the other end of Oxford Street, would be to invite trouble. Spedan and his father already quarrelled constantly over the running of 'the biz'. In the month that Selfridges opened, Spedan wrote to Oswald, from the office: 'Hell of a time. This blasted place is worrying me out of my mind. ... He's taken to examining all the vouchers himself, and he still signs all the cheques. I'd sacrifice my share of the profits to get him to stay away.'

Spedan's evenings, however, were his own. In April 1909, again to Oswald: 'Achieved last night another step on the ladder of vice.' This ironic laddishness was how they communicated about their private lives.

★

Sometimes an accident is just an accident.

Sometimes it is a protest against a situation which is too hard to manage. However it was, in May 1909 Spedan was riding down to work from Spedan Tower on his own horse, as he often did, intending to leave it in the stabling belonging to John Lewis & Co. in Weymouth Mews. Coming out of Regent's Park, he was thrown from the horse. Were it not for this accident, there might have been no John Lewis Partnership.

He was hurt and bruised but thought little of it. Within days, he was seriously ill, with a high temperature and in great pain. He had damaged his right lung in the fall. Fluid and pus built up between the lung and the chest wall. This condition is called empyema, and the spreading infection and inflammation render it life-threatening.

Spedan Tower became a home-hospital. Oswald was just sitting his Oxford entrance exams when Ellie wrote to him on 4 June:

> Dear Spedan is having a shocking time, such pain and weakness with great restlessness. Sir Thos Barlow [the Royal Physician] came for his second visit this evening. Dr Turtle sleeps here every night and the two nurses are doing their utmost – in fact we are all simply living for the dear boy. Dad has driven back this morning to sit with him at intervals. The pain in the lung is very bad and the oppression in the breathing. ... Poor darling – such an illness

is indeed a calamity and is likely to last longer than Spouchie is at all aware of … do write to Spouchie, he is awfully fond of you.

Sir Thomas Barlow arranged for Sir Watson Cheyne to operate. It was a question of draining the pus and fluid and clearing the site of infection. The risk of putrefaction spreading and of sepsis (fatal) was high. Bacteriology was not mainstream in 1909, and most surgeons saw no reason even to wash their hands before operating. But Cheyne had worked with Joseph Lister, the father of antisepsis in Britain, and like his mentor he applied carbolic acid (phenol) to the wound. Spedan lost the use of the lung, but he came through.

In that same summer of 1909, while Spedan was so ill, John Lewis, in a burst of desperate energy, produced his own wild kind of window display, as the estate's solicitor was renewing the demand to remove the hoardings from the Holles Street windows. Lewis took a leaf out of Mr Selfridge's book and sought maximum publicity. In September he unboarded the Holles Street windows, sticking on to the hoardings huge posters covered in words attacking Lord Howard de Walden, his 'wicked young landlord, that *Monument of Iniquity*'.

Again, he did not have a legal leg to stand on, but the political wind was blowing his way. The Liberals were in government. In his 'People's Budget', Chancellor of the Exchequer David Lloyd George proposed 'a tax of 20 per cent on the unearned increment of land values'. In an incendiary speech in London's docklands, Lloyd George excoriated the London landlord as 'a gentleman who doesn't earn his wealth. … His sole function, his chief pride, is the stately consumption of wealth produced by others.' Even better for Lewis, Lloyd George's case in point was that of a department store owner, Mr Gorringe of Buckingham Palace Road, who, on the expiry of his lease, had his annual rent increased by the Duke of Westminster from a few hundred pounds to £4,000, plus a premium of £50,000 for a new lease.

Lewis, deliberately provocative, could not claim that Howard de Walden had abused his position financially, but had he not contrived to have a blameless elderly shopkeeper – himself – sent to jail?

> In the Holles Street Drama the young baron is discovered behind the curtain pulling the wires for the imprisonment of his old tenant …
> Can it be right that the prudent citizen who builds or buys his house can do nothing to improve it without being blackmailed in solicitors' fees to get free from arbitrary restrictions which ought never to have been imposed?

And again:

> It is a great hardship upon those who by the cultivation of their business have created a value in the property which it did not possess before that they should be liable to be thrown out of that property.

He addressed his landlord directly as one who,

> stepped into enormous unearned wealth, created entirely by the community in general and the occupier in particular. The Duke of Portland said ownership had both pleasures and duties; of the pleasures indeed you with the energy of your youth have tasted freely, as witness your lovely villa in Monte Carlo, your steam yacht, your motors, your racehorses, your palaces in London and the country.

And more in the same histrionic vein. Lord Howard de Walden, insulted and with his reputation compromised, decided he must sue for libel.

John Lewis threw money at the case. He retained in his defence his solicitors, Charles Russell, who instructed two heavyweight barristers – Sir Edward Carson, KC (whom Oswald's solicitor had instructed against Lewis himself in the matter of the £50,000), F.E. Smith, KC, later Lord Chancellor and Earl of Birkenhead – and two rising stars, Theobald Matthew, later a leading criminal prosecutor and Director of Public Prosecutions, and Raymond Asquith, son of H.H. Asquith, the prime minister. Picking Raymond Asquith was mischievous. The Asquith family lived in Cavendish Square, and H.H. Asquith retained his lease when he moved into 10 Downing Street. So the prime minister, like John Lewis, was a tenant of Lord Howard de Walden.

It was to be another eighteen months before the case opened. Spedan, when his father's posters went up, was miles away from London, convalescing at the Albion Hotel in Eastbourne, under the care of a nurse. Bored to death but still weak, he proceeded to the Swiss Alps around Christmas.

During the boys' childhoods, it had been Oswald whose delicate health had given constant anxiety. Now it was the other way round, and Oswald seemed robustly set up for a splendid career. When Oswald went up to Christ Church in the autumn of 1909, Ellie was thrilled: 'My hardworking, able Son!' He found the college rooms allotted to him not to his liking. He had his eye on something better, and his mother encouraged him: 'If you find you can secure those nice rooms permanently by an extra outlay, I certainly should not study expenses.'

Spedan did have to study expenses. The hotels where he and the nurse stayed had to be paid for. Although he was potentially richer than Oswald in the long run, contingent on the profitability of John Lewis & Co., and on his presumed succession as sole proprietor, his current income was not enough for him. He had conceived, while mouldering in Eastbourne, what seemed to him a good idea. As Ellie put it to Oswald: 'Spedan wants me to transfer the rest of my money from you to him, as he says you have difficulty in finding satisfactory investments for your own capital and are therefore only *burdened* by mine! But would it be "expedient?"'

Ellie owned a quarter of John Lewis & Co.'s shares, at least some of it in cash. It is characteristic of her to have passed some capital on to Oswald for him to invest, because she loved him so much. On his twenty-first birthday she recalled his birth – how the 'sweet white bundle was laid in my arms, as I rested gently, between life and death' – and from that day on he had been his mother's 'pride and joy and comfort'. When he was placed in the second class in Prelims – the first-year Oxford examination – she congratulated 'my precious, precious darling'. She liked him having her money at his disposal 'for contingencies'. Oswald was such a wealthy young man that it is hard to see what contingencies he would be unable to cover.

Though meticulous about keeping his accounts and comfortable with figures and balance sheets, Oswald rarely, if ever, had success with his investments, which he managed himself – a misfortune which caught up with him late in life, when his capital was running out. Spedan was more cavalier about his money than Oswald, from whom he now proceeded to try and borrow.

Spedan became outstandingly, even overwhelmingly, fluent and persuasive when communicating his ideas and desires. Oswald, as a public speaker, though always well prepared and articulate, was ponderous in his delivery, without an innate ability to charm and amuse his audiences as well as to impress and inform them. Ellie went to hear him speak at the Oxford Union, the university's debating society, and the training ground for many a career in public life. Ellie's verdict was encouraging but, by her standards, moderate: 'I firmly believe you will have great weight as a practical politician and attain conspicuous success early in life.'

'My career at Oxford ended in a great disappointment,' Oswald wrote in his diary at the end of his three years. He – and Ellie – presumed he would get a first-class honours degree. He got a (perfectly respectable) second. He – and Ellie – presumed he would be elected President of the Union. This did not happen. Maybe, he thought, it was because he stood for office 'unduly early'. Or because not many Christ Church men bothered to join the Union, so he had few friends there. And 'my being older than the ordinary run, while it gave me the benefit of experience, made me rather out of touch with my audience'.

He was surprised, and saddened, that he had 'failed'. He had not failed. His expectations were unrealistic. This is poignant and not his fault. Unconditional love of a mother for her child is one thing. Uncritical and constantly expressed adulation do the child no favour when the time comes to engage with the wider world. Oswald was a dogged young man and proceeded to advance his standing in the Liberal Party, joining both the National Liberal Club and the Reform. Having left Marylebone Borough Council when he went to Oxford, he was re-elected to the LCC to represent Hoxton, standing for the Liberal-backed Progressive Party.

John Lewis, in his mid-seventies, had become more comfortable about spending some of his money, though none of it on improving the wages or the living and working conditions of his employees. Lord Howard de Walden had his 'steam yacht' and 'motors'; Mr Selfridge of course had a motor car, Mr William Bourne of Bourne & Hollingsworth had a motor car. In May 1910 John Lewis ordered a motor car. 'What do you say to a

Rolls-Royce?' Ellie wrote to Oswald. 'Price £1,280. My word! What swells we shall be!'

Spedan accompanied his parents on a test drive in a chauffeur-driven Rolls, as Ellie reported to Oswald, 'through Bond Street, Piccadilly Circus, Strand, Kingsway and Oxford Street to see if we thought the size and length of the car a drawback in thick [horse-drawn] traffic, but it simply went in and out between the vehicles and turned sharp corners with absolute ease, and is undoubtedly far more manageable for town than a carriage and pair of horses'. And it was 'the very best of English workmanship'.

John Lewis never drove the Rolls himself. They always had a chauffeur at Spedan Tower, the stables converted into garages. Spedan never drove himself either. Oswald bought his own first motor car – a 15.9 hp two-seater Vulcan, with a folding hood like a pram – in the same year that his father bought the Rolls. He drove it himself, trashed it almost immediately, and thenceforth he too always employed a chauffeur.

It was not just convalescing in expensive hotels, and wining and dining the Rosies and Susies, that depleted Spedan's bank balance. While Oswald was still a Partner, the two of them planned to acquire land for playing fields for the employees of Peter Jones Ltd and John Lewis & Co. The company had rented playing fields in Acton, but these were not good enough. There were already various leisure activities organised by John Lewis & Co., including the Byron Sports Day, and musical entertainments in hired halls. This provision for recreation outside business hours, and much more, was becoming normal good practice among substantial retailers and manufacturers. After the murder of William Whiteley, £1 million of his money, as he had instructed in his will, had gone to the building of Whiteley Village, near Walton-on-Thames, as retirement homes for the staff.

The Lewis brothers were ambitious. They wanted to create a country club, with cricket and football pitches, tennis and golf, boating and fishing. When Oswald left 'the biz', Spedan nursed the project, and found what seemed to him the perfect place.

Grove Farm was in rural outer suburbia, at Greenford in South Harrow. The farmhouse was big enough to be adapted one day into a clubhouse and social centre and, meanwhile, provided a retreat for himself. Grove Farm's sixty-three acres could accommodate all possible sports and outdoor activities, and also fulfil Spedan's passion for botanising and bug-hunting. The price was £7,000.

Spedan did not have access to his £50,000 capital. There seemed no point in trying to engage his father's cooperation. So he persuaded his bank manager to let him buy Grove Farm on an overdraft, in view of his future prospects, the bank holding the title deeds as security.

Completion of the purchase went through shortly after his riding accident, when he was at his most dangerously ill. Grove Farm had to be put on hold while he convalesced, returning to work at the shop in early 1910. Though he kept on his room at the Fly-Fishers' Club, he organised the Byron Sports Day at Grove Farm, and began to spend time there at weekends. Grove Farm became the place he loved most, and where he became happy. It was where he worked out what he wanted to do with his life, and with the family firm.

6

FATHER TRIUMPHANT, OSWALD ASCENDANT AND 'AN EXCELLENT NURSE'

Autumn 1910, and an atmosphere of 'suppressed crisis' at Spedan Tower. No surprises there. Spedan's ideas for transforming the business were shot down by his father who clung on to control of everything that mattered and most of what did not. Spedan, exasperated, stopped going in to work altogether.

Ellie urged Oswald to 'have a talk' with Spedan: 'Dad has been bad for over a fortnight, and has rung the changes from terrific outbursts of furious rage to periods of morose gloom. ... So my sweetheart it makes such an extraordinary difference to me having dear you to think about and rejoice over. ...' She kept, she said, Oswald's photograph 'propped up on the elephant clock' and kisses it as she passes. Oswald did have a discussion with Spedan, Ellie warning him that his elder brother was 'depressed, and feeling the nervous strains of our circumstances. So intolerably trying, that I begin to wonder what will happen next.'

The upshot was that in February 1911, Spedan sent his father an ultimatum, issued through the solicitor. He gave his father three options, summarised thus by Ellie, who thought it an 'excellent letter':

> Execute a deed of partnership acceptable to both and for Spedan to return to the business.
>
> State when and how he would arrange to pay out Spedan's capital.
>
> State on what terms he would hand over the business to Spedan and himself retire.

Dad, when he read it, 'of course pished and pshawed over it a good deal, but I think when he has had time to simmer down he will answer it'. Spedan was not prepared to turn up either at Spedan Tower or Holles Street till the matter was settled. Ellie played the piano. 'Without that, Dad would have been awfully grumpy last night.'

Only a few days later, the Rolls-Royce was to be delivered and Lewis told Ellie to fix a day with Spedan to take a spin with them, in order to give his opinion, as if they were the best of friends; and Spedan, as if they were the best of friends, accepted with alacrity. 'Funny pair, aren't they?' Ellie commented.

Spedan's ultimatum was let lie, because John Lewis had something else on his mind.

The libel action brought against him by Lord Howard de Walden came up in court in that March, 1911. The two barristers retained by Howard de Walden were sufficiently eminent by any standards, but not so waspishly formidable as Lewis's. He himself prepared the ground, canvassing the tenants of Cavendish Square to send in letters declaring that they would have no objection to his modern shop fronts on Holles Street, even though one of the houses involved was right on the corner with the square. The prime minister, whose barrister son Raymond Asquith was acting for Lewis, wrote from 10 Downing Street to say that he had no objection. That was a coup for Lewis.

The case was tried before a 'special jury'. Either party – it was probably the estate – could opt for a 'special jury' by paying a fee. A 'special jury', as opposed to a 'common jury', was composed of gentlemen and 'men of substance'. Sir Edward Carson, for John Lewis, cross-examined young Howard de Walden with a barrage of short, sharp questions to which he mostly answered yes or no. John Lewis took the stand on the second day. He had the best platform he would ever have.

Lewis had been well advised, and did not bluster or lapse into personal abuse. He declared that he had no animus against the plaintiff: 'I have the greatest respect for him and regard him as a man more sinned against than sinning.' His quarrel, he said, was with the board of management of the estate, maliciously pursuing purely technical rights. He quoted from his own pamphlet on leasehold reform, written in Brixton Prison, reminding the court how he had chosen to go to jail in order to publicise the injustice of the land laws, presenting himself as the fearless champion of the public good. F.E. Smith, KC, summed up for the defence with a confident claim that the posters were fully justified and that no 'honourable man' in Lord Howard de Walden's position would have vetoed the new windows.

The presiding judge, Lord Chief Justice Lord Alverton, was not impressed. His summing-up amounted to a vindication of the estate, as being entirely within its rights, and a denunciation of John Lewis as a deliberate troublemaker who had never had any intention of complying with the terms of his covenant with the estate. He reminded the jury of how Lewis's posters insulted and defamed the plaintiff. Things looked bad for John Lewis.

Sure enough, the 'special jury', after only twenty minutes, returned the verdict that John Lewis was guilty of libel. They awarded damages against him – of just one farthing (representing one-quarter of one penny).

Technically, he lost. Morally, he had triumphed. He shook Lord Howard de Walden by the hand and said he hoped that they might now be friends. The case was reported fully in the press and made the front-page illustration of the *Daily Graphic*. *The Times* opined that the great landlords of London would do well, in view of public opinion and the threat of crippling taxation, to think of breaking up and selling parts of their estates since the leasehold system had become dysfunctional.

Howard de Walden grasped the nettle and, with equal impulses of philanthropy and self-preservation, evolved in the ensuing months the 'Marylebone Scheme', by which he would offer his tenants 999-year leases, virtually freeholds, which gave them security, independence, freedom to arrange the properties according to need, and addressed most of the issues which inflamed John Lewis.

Lewis, not unnaturally, took the credit, writing to *The Times* endorsing the scheme and praising Lord Howard de Walden's 'splendid lead'. The conflict, he added, had cost him over twenty-three years more than £40,000 and three weeks in Brixton Prison. His 'sacrifices' were well worth it in view of Lord Howard de Walden's proposals.

'What do you think of the *Freehold* victory?' Ellie asked Oswald. 'I see it as a great result of all the long years of fighting.' But Spedan had his own preoccupations. In early 1911 he told Oswald: 'I am building and planting at Harrow [Grove Farm] with my usual hare-brained energy.' In the summer, however, he had a setback. On holiday on the Norfolk Broads, he had trouble with the scar on his chest. Oswald was not to tell Mother. The scar was opened by a local doctor who found that an abscess had formed in the seam. 'I have had rather a time of it.'

Mother had to know, because Spedan needed another operation, again performed by Sir Watson Cheyne, and another period of recovery at Spedan Tower with a Dr Attlee in daily attendance. It was a whole month before he was able to walk downstairs unaided. Ellie to Oswald, towards the end of October 1911:

> Oh! Pete darling! Do take care of your precious self for the sake of your little mother. It breaks my heart to see poor Spoushie as he is, and my one bright spot is the joy of knowing you are well and strong. … It is four weeks to the day since the operation, and the wound persists in healing over at the top leaving a hollow underneath which at all costs must be prevented, consequently the doctors keep snipping away the new flesh at the top with scissors, and then cauterising it with caustic and this of course is most painful and uncomfortable. I try not to show it but in my heart am frightfully anxious about the poor Boy.

She wondered 'where it will all end', though 'his excellent Nurse tells me he could not be better fed or done by in any way'. But perhaps Spedan would not survive. Perhaps Spedan would remain for an indefinite period an invalid at Spedan Tower.

Spedan had not lost the will to live. During the weeks of pain and inactivity, he read, and thought, and he talked to his nurse. Even though, he said, he did not believe he would live beyond forty, he knew what he wanted to do and how to put into practice his ideas – which made no sense at all to his father. So after another month, he took his life into his own hands.

Ellie to Oswald, 17 November 1911, a Friday: 'Spoushie suddenly announced this morning that could *not* endure the status quo any longer and would drive out to Harrow with Dr Attlee this afternoon, but *remaining* there! Which he did!' He was driven over to Grove Farm in the Rolls with the doctor and the 'excellent Nurse'. Father took the news of the 'flitting', reported Ellie, 'wonderfully quietly'. The house felt lonely, but 'of course it was best to bring such a state of friction to an end'.

★

The 'excellent Nurse' who accompanied Spedan in his flight to Grove Farm was Eleanor McElroy. She lived with him for the next twelve years.

The relationship between patient and private nurse was intimate. She was on duty twenty-four hours a day, sleeping in an adjoining room. During Spedan's second ordeal, Eleanor McElroy dressed his wound, supervised his diet, dealt with bedpans, washed and shaved him, dressed and undressed him – and listened to his plans for the future.

A nurse was an employee. If Ellie wondered over the years about the precise nature of Spedan's relationship with Miss McElroy, she suppressed speculation. Oswald, who spent many enjoyable weekends at Grove Farm, never called Eleanor by her first name even though, when he or Spedan gave their luncheon parties – usually at the Savoy, followed by a matinee – she would always come too. Oswald's wife, in later years, apparently rolled her eyes at the mere mention of Miss McElroy.

They were an odd couple, Spedan in his mid-twenties, and she rising forty. He, well over six feet tall, recalled her, when she came to assist Sir Watson Cheyne with the second operation, as the 'minuscule nurse'. Her own description of herself was 'square and squat'. The few photographs of her, looking like a mushroom in a round flattish hat, bear this out. In one of them, taken at Grove Farm, she stands – wearing the hat – at a wicket, wielding a cricket bat. No extant photograph reveals her face clearly.

While she would always monitor Spedan's precarious health, she became his housekeeper, secretary, collaborator, confidante and companion. They worked together, played together, travelled together. His nicknames for her were 'Bill' and 'Podgers'.

Eleanor McElroy was a trained hospital nurse, born in 1872 in Bootle, on the estuary of the River Mersey, close to Liverpool. Merseyside was brimming with Irish McElroys, some first-generation arrivals and some longer established, mostly working for shipping companies. Eleanor's branch was from County Wexford, where there was a substantial family farmhouse, Springfield, at Tullycanna. Like most of her family, Eleanor was a devout Roman Catholic.

After Spedan married, he and Eleanor wrote to each other at least once a week until she died, unmarried, aged eighty-nine. Only the last twenty years of their correspondence has survived, somewhat culled. Reminiscences in Spedan's late letters convey some flavour of life at Grove Farm. When Spedan and his wife had a weekend visit from Percival Waterfield – an Old Westminster – Spedan showed him a moth in his collection which they had captured together long ago at Grove Farm, and he reminded Eleanor of the evening when 'in getting two of them on a certain hedge, he and I had made ourselves late for dinner and had thoroughly incurred your displeasure'. Playing patience in his widowerhood, he recalled how he and Eleanor 'used to get great fun out of racing each other at Miss Milligan. On several nights that practical research into the Laws of Chance kept us up until after midnight.' ('Miss Milligan' is a long game of patience played with two packs of cards.) In his last letter, aware that Eleanor was near death, he said he could hardly believe he had known her so long, recalling old days when her 'idea of a really good evening was to sit by some pigsties shivering with excitement while ill-advised rats got in the way of the contents of my .419 cartridges'.

His tone throughout the correspondence is one of affection, with no tinge of erotic nostalgia. That proves nothing either way. A basis of their relationship, however, may be deduced by the way he likened her to one of his long-serving secretaries: 'Phyllis has the same quality of perceptive sympathy, like you she gets out of being useful to other people the satisfaction that a real musician might get out of playing music.' That is a graceful way of express-ing not only emotional intelligence but the selfless devotion that Spedan inspired in, and exacted from, his female assistants.

That said, he had respect for Eleanor's abilities, assuring her that if she had been born thirty or forty years later, 'you would have been one of the most eminent and possibly the most eminent woman doctor in the world', or the matron of a hospital, or the headmistress of a school – someone 'with influence'. As it was, she was never given 'the scope or chance'.

Perhaps not. But her background was more interesting than Spedan's, and her connections intriguing. Hugh McElroy, Eleanor's grandfather, was the son of an immigrant farm worker in Netherton, outside Liverpool on the Leeds to Liverpool Canal. Hugh himself prospered sufficiently to buy Maghull Hall, a mansion a few miles up the canal from Netherton. Spedan wrote of the exceptional 'vitality' that he and Eleanor shared, and 'which raised your grandfather and my father to the success which they reached'.

Eleanor's parents were William, son of prosperous Hugh McElroy of Maghull, and Mary Hannah Chaloner – from Liverpool, but related to Chaloners who had lived at Gisborough Hall in Yorkshire since the sixteenth century. Two Chaloners had held high office in Ireland under Elizabeth I. Eleanor's kinsmen at

Gisborough Hall were landed gentry, and she liked the tenuous connection.

There was more. Writing about her love of London, she noted: 'I take after my illustrious ancestor the Lord Chancellor of England. He is called "the cockney saint", he loved his London.' This 'illustrious ancestor' was Sir Thomas More, executed by Henry VIII. A bit far-fetched? Eleanor's maternal uncle, Vincent Chaloner, married Rebecca Ullathorne, descended from a John Ullathorne who married into Thomas More's direct line in the eighteenth century. The connection, if even more tenuous, was genuine.

She had interesting first cousins from Merseyside. After the death of Father Richard Alphonse McElroy, a Canon Regular of the Lateran, a much revered prior of St Mary's Priory in Bodmin, Cornwall, Eleanor wrote to Spedan: 'He and I were the last of our large family to bear the name' – because the others were girls who married. Prior McElroy was predeceased by his brother, another Hugh McElroy, who in 1912 was appointed chief purser on the maiden voyage from Southampton to New York of RMS *Titanic*. When the *Titanic* struck an iceberg and sank, Chief Purser McElroy was among the 1,500 or so people who lost their lives.

Eleanor also had a lively French connection. Her sister Mary was married to Athanase Perreur-Lloyd, from an Anglo-French family living in France. Eleanor was close to the Perreur-Lloyds. Two gorgeous red-haired nieces, Marcelle and Odette, spent frequent holidays at Grove Farm. Marcelle married Serge Poliakoff, the Moscow-born modernist painter. Mary Perreur-Lloyd, as a widow, lived in Eaton Square, a stone's throw from Peter Jones, where her son Alexis, Eleanor's nephew, worked for a while for Spedan, as did the red-haired girls.

The extended family of Eleanor McElroy was entertaining for Spedan, and much more fun than his own. A whisper, trickling down to Oswald's son Peter, has it that Spedan did propose marriage and that she declined, on the grounds that she was too old for him. Her Catholicism may also have been an issue. When one of Prior McElroy's sisters married a non-Catholic, she was ostracised by her family.

No one can know the complexity, or maybe it was the simplicity, of her relationship with Spedan Lewis.

★

Spedan was in debt. It was not just the interest on the bank loan for buying Grove Farm, but the money splashed out on building, landscaping, planting trees, and creating a cricket pitch, a football pitch, a tennis court and a golf course. Close to the farmhouse there was a croquet lawn and a roughish bowling green. The property being his, not the firm's, he thought to recoup his funds by charging rent to Peter Jones Ltd and John Lewis & Co. for their employees' use of the facilities. This proved difficult. He was more than £11,000 in the red, and chose, in February 1912, to reveal the state of his overdraft in a letter to his father wishing him a happy seventy-sixth birthday.

'Alack! Alas!' wrote Ellie to Oswald. 'Of course a sort of earthquake, volcano, and bomb arsenal all rolled into one, and this cheerful document was handed to me directly I came in to breakfast. It's an enormous help that S is so far away.' For, seeking to forestall his repeated throat infections, Spedan and Eleanor were spending the winter in hotels in Switzerland, Italy and France, presumably racking up more debt.

But a few weeks after posting the bombshell birthday letter, while at the Hotel Albion in Menton, and shaky after six days in bed, Spedan heard from his bank manager – and reported to Oswald – that 'J. L. & Co. have paid into my a/c £11,300. This is the result of four weeks' correspondence between Father and me. If he intends to drop the cheque question, he has certainly behaved as handsomely as anyone could have done.' The 'cheque question' was Father's threat to withhold Spedan's monthly remittance. But that too came through.

Lewis had behaved handsomely because no businessman whose reputation depends on his sound finances wants it known that his son, a partner in the family firm, is in trouble with his bank. Also, and curiously, he and Spedan always seemed closest to one another when they were fighting, as if that were the restricted code of their affinity. Spedan understood this. He wrote in *Partnership for All* how everything he knew about business he learned from his father. He evolved his very different idea of how a business should be run, but acknowledged: 'We were well-matched. I was very much a chip off the old block.'

He returned to work, spending more time at Peter Jones in Sloane Square, and conceived the idea of taking it over and running it independently of Oxford Street. Father was bored by Peter Jones, and it was making a loss.

This possibility became a subject of fresh arguments, with Spedan telling his father that unless he made the transfer, or retired, he would withdraw from 'the biz' altogether, just as Oswald had. Lewis then banned him from Spedan Tower – as he had banned Oswald – and collapsed into melancholy. He was 'ageing rapidly before our eyes', wrote Ellie, 'and bitterly resents the disabilities which old age brings'. As for herself: 'I stand at my post resolutely … Daddy makes it well-nigh impossible for any living soul to exist where he is. The boy [Spedan] must in self-defence avoid him all he can. Nurse [McElroy] is an inexpressible comfort, and relieves me of the necessity of playing two parts and trying to be in two places at once.'

It was 'bliss' when her husband went on his own to Weston to see his old sisters, and Spedan could visit and spend the night, bringing Miss McElroy: 'I sent her and Spedan off in the car, with lunch, and all requisites, and here I stay, I contend with Dad day after day, so glad that there's someone to care for Spoushie and keep him safe and happy elsewhere.'

★

Oswald was now even taller than Spedan, and handsome, with a fine moustache. At school he had opposed the introduction of a cadet corps, but signed up for the Officer Training Corps at Oxford. He now joined the Westminster Dragoons, a part-time, Territorial (home-based) cavalry regiment. Oswald volunteered for enough courses to obtain a commission: Lieutenant Lewis.

The Westminster Dragoons were a super-smart regiment and Oswald's commanding officer was none other than Tommy Howard de Walden. Ellie was quite excited. In October 1912 Howard de Walden visited the shop, with a surveyor and a solicitor, in his determination to reach a peaceable compromise over the windows. 'All fine,' she wrote to Oswald. 'Spedan was there, and Lord H de W said he knew Mr L's other son. So you see, he does know who you are!'

Oswald, along with other young officers, was a guest of Howard de Walden, newly married, at Seaford House in Belgrave Square. Ellie was thrilled: 'My word! You are going it!!' Even Dad, she said, was impressed, listening eagerly as she read out Oswald's account of the evening. Oswald was introduced to Lady Howard de Walden, and proud Mama 'did not fail to tell him [Dad] that Lady Howard de Walden certainly had something to look at when you appeared on the scene in full dress uniform!' It may have been on an earlier occasion that the shop-windows issue came up; Lady Howard de Walden remembered 'Lewis's son' telling her husband (as she recalled in *Pages from My Life*) that: 'If you ever let him have his way over this, I really fear the old man might die, for he so enjoys being angry with you!' Those days were over now, and Lewis did not die.

Lewis, 'most unwisely', as Ellie wrote, invited Spedan to dinner at Spedan Tower to discuss Peter Jones Ltd, where Spedan had as yet no designated authority. In the drawing room, after dinner, Lewis asked Spedan what it was he had to complain of.

'Oh dear! He got more than he bargained for and all in the plainest English.' It was 'appalling' to listen to 'such an indictment of a father from his own son. Dad remained as unmoving as a stone. Self-satisfied as ever! Blind, absolutely blind, incapable of apprehending any of the facts laid before him. ... S. became really frantic and lashed him with his tongue. I thought I would have died of fright.' Ellie had been up to Grove Farm the following day for lunch and tea: 'They seem very comfortable out there, and Speedie looks better as regards physique, but his eyes show a deal more excitement and anxiety than I like to see. ... He is still keen on PJ.'

The dinner debacle would be just another row, and not worth noting were it not that Ellie's account demonstrates the dynamic of all the family rows, so apparently destructive, but dangerously exciting, and by this time addictive, with everyone playing his or her customary role. Oswald was nowhere in this choreography. He had not seen or spoken to his father since he left the business. He was the essential audience, the recipient of dramatic playbacks from his mother and brother.

Spedan always said that Oswald had 'all the luck' – he began a letter to him 'Dear Ascendant One' – and Oswald might not have demurred. In early 1913 he wrote Spedan a strong letter of advice and warning: Spedan should not think of throwing his own money away on Peter Jones and getting into debt, when he could be making useful contacts among the Liberal leadership, and laying the foundations of a distinguished career and a place in the great world, away from the business.

'Socially my position has been enormously improved,' Oswald had noted in his diary, 'by the severance of my connection with the business.' He was saying to Spedan, without actually saying it: 'Why don't you do as I do?' Spedan's response highlights the difference between their values and attitudes.

'I believe you are wrong,' he replied. 'I do not think I am capable of achieving social or political distinction without some special motive force such as a specific cause, or an ambitious wife.' In the life he contemplated at Grove Farm his chief enterprise was 'a little working community' and 'the building up of a little model of what should be a quite satisfactory life if everyone was of my type'. He was not interested, he said, 'in public honour or entrée into any *grand monde*'. He had no time for 'social duties', which interfered with his 'actual work' and with 'reading and music and gardening and idling in the open air. I can better do without the personal acquaintance of the Party Leaders than I can without any others.'

Oswald in the same letter warned him officiously that 'people were talking' about Spedan's ambiguous private affairs. Miss McElroy shared his domestic life, and was he not meeting up with other women as well? This must have been most irritating, from a younger brother. 'I see no lady friends,' replied Spedan, 'except R[osie] once a week, and that barely for a matinée or something of that sort, and Eleanor. I imagine you do not think her living here ill-advised? The principal neighbours are all very friendly. What *are* these accounts from "all society" that you hear?' And he was *not* in debt.

★

Suddenly Ellie had something to do that took her away from Spedan Tower. In 1913 Oswald was adopted as the Liberal parliamentary candidate for North Dorset, a constituency held by the

Conservatives at the last election by a tiny majority; young as he was, he stood a good chance. His constituency agent, Mr Beer, was optimistic, and Oswald threw himself into the cause, nursing the constituency, meeting people who mattered, speaking whenever and wherever he could, placing articles in local papers, and even buying a small local printing business, the Wessex Publishing Company, to print his campaign literature.

His mother was his most active supporter, and campaigning for 'Pete' gave her a rush of new life. 'Nerves' were forgotten. Ellie demonstrated hitherto unused capabilities, travelling down to the constituency frequently, staying in the rooms they retained in the Digby Hotel in Sherborne. Escorted by Mrs Beer, the agent's wife, she mustered 'lady supporters', addressed women's meetings, opened garden fetes, attended fund-raising sales of work in village halls, and she made public speeches. She loved every minute of it, once spending a whole week down in the constituency without Oswald and, in London, often lunching with him at his flat in Bickenhall Mansions to discuss strategy.

She and Mr Beer between them gave Oswald tactful advice about his public speaking. As in the debating society at school, as at the Oxford Union, Oswald was articulate. No one could be more articulate. Oswald was well informed. No one could be more well informed. And Oswald could be really boring to listen to. Not that Ellie would ever put it that way. Mr Beer, she told her son, was pleased with him. 'He thinks you are so admirably throwing off the academic style and getting real hold of your hearers.'

Outside the constituency, Oswald's life was outwardly rather proper. However many times he took young women out, or they visited him in his flat at Bickenhall Mansions – and there were many – their first names were not confided to his diary. He took girlfriends to Grove Farm for weekends and to play tennis. He discovered the joy of travel, and with married-couple friends fished for salmon in Norway and cruised on the Mediterranean. He – and Spedan too – went skiing in Switzerland. Oswald's liaisons were serial and not serious. 'Avoid intimacy!' was a jokey mantra he shared with Spedan. He bought a new car. He had his own horse, Venus, and went hunting with it in Dorset and Sussex. He attended a 'shooting school', country-house shoots being on his aspirational agenda.

Oswald took dancing lessons, in the company of a 'Mrs Holmes'. She was Eva, the wife of Stanley Holmes, a chartered accountant and a fellow Liberal member on the LCC. This couple became his cronies. He stayed with them at their hospitable house in Maidenhead, the riverside town favoured by well-heeled London weekenders with motor cars due to its discreet island hotels and racily convivial Thames-side society. He took the Holmeses to Grove Farm; he watched top cricket matches with them at the Oval; he played bridge with them, and shared theatre and dinner parties. Stanley Holmes was good company, socially secure and politically ambitious – the sort of person that Oswald thought Spedan should be getting to know.

Oswald's uncle Tom Baker gave him much-needed advice on investments; his capital had declined from more than £60,000 to just over £40,000, but that was still a whole lot of money. These were good times for Oswald.

The rapprochement between the Lewis family and the Howard de Waldens grew ever warmer. Tommy Howard de Walden was something of a romantic idealist, and an unaffected eccentric. He painted and acted and liked dressing in medieval costume. He wrote poetry, essays and plays. He fell in love with Wales, and in 1911 bought a lease on medieval Chirk Castle, in Denbighshire, as one of his family homes (he and his wife were to produce six children). He became a passionate supporter and nurturer of

Welsh culture, offering an annual prize for the best new play on a Welsh theme, whether in Welsh or in English. He set up the Welsh National Drama Company, in support of which he took the New Theatre in Cardiff for a week in May 1914. The programme included a play written by himself, *Pont Orewyn*, about Llywelyn the Great.

John Lewis, hitherto unenthusiastic about his Welsh origins, threw himself into this enterprise. On Sunday 8 May, he and Ellie went to Cardiff by train to hear Lord Howard de Walden give a lecture on the Welsh drama. On showing a letter from 'the Secretary', they were given seats in the front row. When Lady Howard de Walden stepped down from the platform where she sat beside her husband, Lewis introduced her to Ellie, and she expressed the hope that Mrs Lewis would come back to Cardiff on Friday for the last night. Lewis recorded these social transactions with gratification.

On learning that tickets for the play were not selling well, Lewis determined to micromanage the situation. After returning from Cardiff that evening he wrote in his diary: 'Decided to send Morris down to Cardiff tomorrow. And to do all I can to fill the theatre on Friday night.' On hearing from Morris that attendance was poor, 'E and I started for Cardiff at 11.30 a.m. In the afternoon I had an interview with Captain Vaughan and offered to buy up a lot of tickets for Friday night, but he was worried about Thursday. I however was more concerned about Friday as Lady H de W had pressed E to come. ...' He nevertheless bought a lot of tickets for Thursday.

He and Ellie were staying at the Park Hotel, from where she wrote to Oswald on Friday afternoon telling him they were expecting 'a lively evening': 'Lord and Lady de W and Lloyd George, and many other bigwigs, are due at 6.35, on the train from Paddington.' They would be staying in the same hotel. She and Dad were invited with the bigwigs to the 'large dinner' to be given by Lord Howard de Walden after the performance.

Chancellor of the Exchequer David Lloyd George, while paying lip service to women's suffrage, had been dragging his feet on the issue and was thought by activists to be insincere. An irate woman leapt into his reserved carriage on the Cardiff train at Paddington, and was led away, leaving Lloyd George 'greatly amused', according to the *Western Mail*.

Cardiff was braced for an invasion of suffragettes, and, Ellie wrote, cars were being driven around randomly, 'for the suffragettes must not know which car the Chancellor is in. Dad has been buying tickets *wholesale* and having them given away so as to fill the theatre, and his coming here has made quite a sensation and the local newspapers are full of it.' The *Western Mail* reported that he had purchased more than a hundred circle tickets to be distributed to local schools, to 'inculcate an interest in Welsh drama in the rising generation'. A quantity of these were scooped up by the suffragettes – an unintended consequence of his largesse.

Mr Lewis 'was accorded quite an ovation' when he and Mrs Lewis took their seats in the stalls, and there was 'a remarkable burst of enthusiasm' when the Chancellor entered his box to the right of the stage. Plain-clothes policemen and stewards in evening dress were seated among the audience. Lloyd George, the 'Welsh Wizard', made a speech; Lord Howard de Walden made a speech too. There were then three consecutive plays, Howard de Walden's *Pont Orewyn* coming last.

At the end of the first play, 'suddenly from the circle came the strident tones' of a suffragette. 'Mr Lloyd George,' she began, 'is it right for you to come to the play when women are in prison?' Her 'feeble protest' was of short duration, as she was removed by stewards.

Lloyd George seemed 'very little concerned' and was soon

John Lewis in his thirties.

His future wife Ellie Baker, aged 24.

Shepton Mallet, John Lewis's birthplace, in 1850.

The row of narrow shops where John Lewis opened his first business.

Ellie with her sons, Spedan and Oswald, in 1897.

Spedan Tower, Hampstead, the Lewis family's home for 42 years.

Peter Jones,
Sloane Square, 1920.

Nelly Breeks,
John Lewis's first love.

John Lewis's youngest
sister Eliza.

The Silk Room at John Lewis.

John Lewis & Co., Oxford Street, 1890.

Spedan Lewis dressed to join the family business, 1904.

Oswald Lewis, dressed to join the family business, 1906.

The exterior (above) and interior (below) of Peter Jones, with heavy, dark-varnished wood displays and fittings, both photographed around 1900.

Eleanor McElroy, Spedan's housekeeper and companion, at the wicket at Grove Farm (below).

Leckford Abbas in Hampshire, on Spedan's first country estate.

enjoying the 'broad humour' of the second play, after which, the mood of hilarity in the theatre was such that further interruptions by the suffragettes only added to it. As the curtain fell on this play, another woman rose, pointed at the Chancellor and exclaimed: 'That is the villain of this piece.' Just then, 'the lights went up and revealed the features of Lloyd George wreathed in smiles. The people were convulsed.' Other women attempted to speak but were not heard above the hubbub. Eight suffragettes were ejected and detained by the police, but no charges were brought.

The *Western Mail* carried, as well as this lively report, a picture of 'Mr John Lewis, owner of the well-known Welsh draper of Oxford Street, London department store, outside the New Theatre' with 'his secretary' – a pleasantly goofy-looking young man identified as 'Mr Maxwell'. The caption also refers to a 'long-existing feud', in spite of which Mr Lewis 'is doing all he possibly can to make Lord Howard de Walden's movement ... a complete success'.

Lewis perhaps felt he had overstepped the mark – or more likely, as after the court case, he was milking the situation to the last sweet drop. The *Western Mail* published a letter from him on 19 May: '... I wish you to understand that I merely shine with a reflected glory. My name would never have appeared in connection with this movement at all but for the work of Lord Howard de Walden, and all I have done has been to endeavour to second his public spirited efforts to give it a good start.' No one seems to have mentioned, or minded, whether Lord Howard de Walden's play was any good or not.

Mr and Mrs John Lewis had a wonderful time, if exhausting for Ellie, who then returned to her campaigning in Oswald's constituency, writing from the Digby Hotel in Sherborne: 'You can't *think* how I am enjoying being away on my own for this little spell!'

Then everything changed. On 4 August, Britain declared war on Germany and its allies. The scheduled general election was postponed (and Oswald's candidacy with it); there would be coalition governments for the duration of the war. The Westminster Dragoons were mobilised and Oswald reported to barracks. He had to provide two chargers for his own use in the field and took his hunter, Venus, and another, called Robert, given to him by Tom Baker. The Dragoons and their horses sailed for Egypt as part of the force mustering to defend the Suez Canal against possible annexation. 'Write often to Mama,' Spedan urged Oswald. 'She lives for your letters.'

7

SPEDAN'S PARTNERSHIP

S pedan was medically unfit for military service. His battles remained familial.

Oswald was away at the war, and Ellie's involvement in his political career was over. Stuck with her ageing, raging husband, she lapsed into depression, and became physically ill. Spedan urged her to see Dr Attlee, but she wouldn't, because Father was against it. Father – while carefully logging his own symptoms, such as 'My hands cold until lunchtime' – did not like doctors. What follows is a summary of a gleeful blow-by-blow account from Spedan to Oswald, covering two closely written sheets of foolscap on both sides:

Eleanor, 'the little brick', becoming worried about Mother, visited Spedan Tower and found that Ellie had been running a temperature of 104 for the past two days. She went straight down to the shop, found Spedan and his father in the Partners' office and, 'with tears in her eyes', said that Mrs Lewis must see a doctor, and have a trained nurse at once in order to get her temperature down, or she might not survive another twenty-four hours.

Father 'off-handedly denied it was serious, refused to call Attlee and absolutely declined any alternative second opinion or agree to a nurse being obtained'. In the ensuing shouting match, Father became 'completely frantic', as Spedan warned him that if he did not call Dr Attlee that evening – it was already after five o'clock – he would never speak to him again, 'and would bring the Public Authorities down on him'.

What happened next raises the question of whether, sometimes, in his frenzies, Lewis might have been violent towards his wife too.

'He slapped my face, threw the waste-paper basket – the big wicker one – at me, and followed that up with the telephone directory. I dealt easily with the basket, but caught the book behind the ear, exactly in the right place for a knock-out if it had been harder.' Had there been more effective weapons to hand 'we might both have ended up on the floor'.

The racket was audible outside the office and a customer ran from the shop 'in a state of agitation'. Since the 'artillery' had run out, Father went for Spedan with his fists, so Spedan pushed him down into his chair, 'in spite of the zeal with which he sought to kick my shins to bits', and held him down while he 'howled like the Fiend'.

In the end, which was some time coming, Spedan and Eleanor rushed out into the dark to find a doctor and were seen by Dr Horder at 141 Harley Street. Horder, 'a capital chap', quickly grasped the situation, promising to take entire charge by phone and to stand absolutely 'no nonsense at all'.

Mother had another version, also retold to Oswald: 'Luckily for me, Miss McElroy happened to drop in ... and knowing how difficult Dad is about doctors and nurses, she went down to Holles St and absolutely frightened Pa out of his skin, and reduced him to such an abject state of terror that I could have had a *dozen* nurses and *half a dozen* physicians.' Spedan let her believe that the waste-paper basket battle was only about getting a second opinion. In this version, it was gallant Miss McElroy who overcame Pa, while 'Dear Spoushie has been awfully good about coming to see me, and sending me flowers and grapes and new books.' She had been suffering, she believed, from 'fever and gastric influenza', and Dr Horder had 'at once ordered a nurse'.

They struck lucky with Thomas Horder. A physician in his early forties, he was at the top of his profession since attending on the late King Edward VII, as he would attend on all reigning monarchs for the rest of his long career. In 1918 he was given a peerage. Just as importantly, he was a draper's son from Shaftesbury in Dorset, so able to understand men like John Lewis.

There was a truce. In early December 1914, Spedan spent half an hour alone with his father, and agreed to return to both the shops. John Lewis ceded to Spedan the day-to-day control of Peter Jones Ltd and the chairmanship of its board.

That was not as good as it sounds. Lewis remained on the board of Peter Jones and, at a meeting which Spedan could not attend, took the opportunity to cancel the Greengrocery Department. A condition of the new arrangement was that Spedan must work at the Oxford Street shop until 5 p.m. each day. He then took a 'taximeter car' down to Sloane Square, and saw lots of people for a few minutes each, hiring and firing and scattering orders and memos. The shop shut at 8 p.m. 'I am working as I never worked before,' he told Oswald on the last day of January 1915. 'I stay till 7.30 but E[leanor] won't let me be later, threatening lunacy and heaven knows what.' Eleanor was properly alert to Spedan's 'excit-able brain'.

He needed to make sweeping changes, and fast. Peter Jones was a disaster. It was more than twenty years since its founder's major makeover, and had been sliding downhill ever since. Robert Bichan, who started in the Furnishing Drapery Department in Spedan's first year, found it 'an empty bucket of a shop' and was 'shocked by the cheap and tawdry stock'. Most of the other male assistants were illiterate, partly because so many young men were away at the war. John Lewis said that he used to recruit the sons of farmers, but now all he got were the sons of farm labourers. But then, Mr John Lewis was a notoriously 'rotten payer', as Bichan put it.

Peter Jones had no frontage on Sloane Square itself, and the King's Road façade still consisted of several separate entrances into different departments. The main entrance was in Symons Street, round the back. Attached to the shop, where King's Road meets the square, was a pub, the Star and Garter, which belonged to Peter Jones Ltd and was the only section of the company to be making a profit. Then came the Midland Bank, then a louche little cluster – a sweetshop, a tobacconist and, on the corner of Symons Street, a pawnshop, Millar & Fitch, 'with filthy cobwebby windows'.

Bichan was twenty-six, and his boss, Spedan, only three years older – 'and believe me', wrote Bichan, 'a more strikingly hand-some man it would be difficult to find'. Ellie consistently praised Oswald's appearance but did not dwell upon Spedan's, any more than she commented on his high intelligence. It was always Spedan's state of mind that exercised her, as in September 1916 when he was on holiday with both parents in Wales, and she reported to Oswald: 'I think S. is in a highly nervous and over-wrought state, but this is between ourselves. We are both extremely pleased to have him with us, dear old fellow.' Both sons were fine young men, with large, heavy-lidded dark eyes. Oswald's face was a little like their father's in his youth. Spedan's was oval, with full, clearly modelled lips, and an elongated chin.

Bichan, in the 1960s, recalled in the *Gazette* what Spedan achieved at Peter Jones Ltd, 'in a house already tottering on its feet, with a war on, and money trickling over the counters barely enough to cover the weekly commitments'. There was just one workroom, in the basement – with a flagstone floor, the only light filtering down from the pavement above. Here two carpet-sewers sat with three upholsterers. The selling staff mostly lived above the shop, in shared bedrooms. There was one washstand for three people in the men's quarters, and no running water. Spedan had hot and cold water piped into every bedroom and 'revolutionised the antique plumbing'. He did the same for the girls' quarters, and invited them to choose materials for new curtains, and their carpets, from the shop. The staff eating-room, which was 'like a Borstal refectory', was transformed by Spedan with small tables, bright paint and a new kitchen.

Somehow Spedan found time to take dancing lessons, both he and Oswald having long ago clocked that a man who danced well was popular with women. When renovating the staff dining room he had a sprung dance floor laid. And 'all the selling staff, men and girls, are being put into navy blue instead of black', he told Oswald. He was making 'exhaustive changes' in floor layouts and displays. He wanted to create an Estates Department and a Maids' Register, and was starting a Children's Department. He appointed Cousin Mabel's brother Murray Lewis as his general manager. This did not work out well. 'Murray is a dear but Oh such a fool', and most of the buyers were hopeless too. Robert Bichan shared his employer's opinion of Murray Lewis: 'This pleasant and like-able gentleman was a complete square peg in a round hole. He lacked authority, and was slow in making decisions.'

Spedan commissioned Oswald to get him exotic objects from Egypt, to sell in Peter Jones. Oswald sent cigarette-holders and umbrella handles made of ibex and buffalo horn, and these proved a success. 'I should be afraid of ostrich eggs,' wrote Spedan, 'too much like "cottagers' treasures" and too bulky and fragile.' What about more weapons? Spears, and other items 'sufficiently "native"'.

Spedan stocked his new Second-Hand Furniture Department by sending his buyers to make multiple purchases at Harrods' regular furniture auctions, resulting in 'a bustling trade' at Peter Jones: 'How quaint are the ways of men! Lords, ladies and nuts are buying the choicest products of Tottenham Court Road after a few years in each other's houses.' (He meant that the furniture, not the lords, ladies and nuts, went between each other's houses.) He had success with 36-inch red Axminster carpeting. The 'lords, ladies and nuts' bought it for runners down their front steps, to protect the parquet floors of their entrance halls.

So 'the Quality came in daily', according to Bichan. But really smart ladies were not buying their dresses and hats at Peter Jones. They found Spedan's service departments extremely useful for repairs and replacements, and they bought essential household equipment. They did not, yet, buy curtain material there for their own bedrooms, but for their maids' bedrooms. By the end of his first year Spedan had made most of his organisational changes and was finding 'hopeful evidence that my strategic concept is sound'.

Grove Farm was where his vision of Partnership germinated. His 'strategic concept' is glimpsed in action in his remark to Oswald that he was inaugurating 'a profit-sharing scheme for the Buyers'. In his time at Grove Farm with Eleanor he had been planning a revolution in retail, an experiment in industrial democracy.

By his own account, it began with his realisation that the Lewis family were taking annually more out of the business for them-

selves than the combined wages of the whole workforce of three
hundred or so. This was textbook capitalism. Employers took the
profits. Why else were they in business? They paid labour at the
going rate, or as little as they could get away with. That was how
Mr John Lewis operated.

It was not only the intrinsic unfairness of this which exercised
Spedan. He was not a Marxist, nor any kind of a Christian. He
saw that the gross economic inequality between the boss and what
he always called the 'Rank and File' must ultimately result in
unrest, strikes, maybe riots, and commercial catastrophe. The
trade union movement was on the case already. He was a pragmatist as much as he was an idealist.

He also knew that the reason why Father had made over such
large sums to himself and Oswald as each reached adulthood was
to protect the family fortune – the one thing he cared about –
from the threat of Lloyd George's redistributive 'People's Budget',
supertax, and inheritance tax. Spedan was not about to renounce
his own inherited wealth. He needed it for what he meant to
achieve. But unfettered accumulation was simply wrong.

Profit-sharing was his solution. Each employee, from the very
lowest to the highest, should receive an annual 'bonus' – a percent-
age of the profits in ratio to each individual's wages or salary, and
paid in shares or bonds. This made every employee a 'Partner'. In
the event, the terms under which shares could be realised, or sold,
evolved over time. The pathological secrecy which characterised
John Lewis's regime was to be reversed. Trading figures were to be
shared with everyone, and trading policy up for discussion. He
would establish a minimum wage, based on the cost of living
index.

Spedan had done his homework. 'I have read all the books,' he
assured Oswald. He knew about other experiments in industrial
democracy. He had read William Morris. He had studied Robert

Owen's management of the cotton mills of New Lanark as a 'model community', and knew of similar experiments in the United States and in Europe, and how his idea of Partnership would differ from the well-established co-operative movement.

'Community' was a central plank of his vision. His provision of sports and leisure facilities for employees was not original. Many companies, most of them family businesses, were doing the same, for the same mixed motives. Spedan went further. His experiment in industrial democracy had leisure and welfare at its core – not only sports but educational opportunities, and the drama and music clubs and societies which would proliferate, over the next twenty-five years, making for friendships across all levels within the eventual Partnership. The Partners' lives outside of working hours turned out to be so communal that many Partners were to find their life partners within the company, with their children following on in the next generation, making the Partnership a 'family business' in another sense. Everyone had a vested interest in the firm's success, since their annual bonus depended on it.

'Happiness' and 'cheerfulness' were among Spedan's favourite keywords when outlining his plan. Family life at Spedan Tower had only rarely been happy or cheerful. There was pragmatism here too: happy and cheerful employees worked more willingly, were more mutually supportive, more productive, and more likely to go the extra mile. This was and remains obvious.

Spedan had to wait and wait, elaborating his plans but unable fully to implement them. Only after the death of his father and after years of growing frustration could the terms and conditions of Partnership become codified.

Meanwhile, at Peter Jones, Spedan was making a start. There was one major flaw in his plans. In order to share profits, you have first to make profits. Right now there were no profits. The balance sheet was further unbalanced by Spedan's welfare improvements.

The idea of Partnership grew out of Spedan's passionate rejection of his father's relationship with the money and his uncaring attitude to the workforce. Yet, as he acknowledged, he learned everything he knew about the business from his father. He had no other mentor. And he respected, and adopted, wholeheartedly, his father's guiding principles of honesty, good value and a wide assortment. It was complicated. His father's probity within the business sat oddly with his unscrupulousness outside it.

In his 'bonfire' letter to Oswald of 1959, Spedan would recall a day in his first year at Peter Jones when Father came to lunch in the restaurant. They went up in the lift, but came down by the stairs, passing through the Millinery Room, where Father was confronted by the 'tremendous change from a large showroom in which there had been absolutely no stands at all, to one in which there were scores and scores: little ones all along the deep shelves against the windows and taller ones of various heights in groups about the floor'.

Father paused at the foot of the stair and Spedan waited for the storm to break. But Father just exclaimed: 'I told you I would not ...' and then stopped. Nor did he write anything about the occasion in his diary, which amazed Spedan, and disappointed him too.

Nevertheless, John Lewis was appalled by the financial losses, demanding that Spedan return the Peter Jones shares he had transferred to him. Spedan refused. But more cash had to be found. The Midland Bank would not extend his overdraft. Spedan in June 1915 did what Oswald had already done. Through a solicitor, he demanded from his father the release of the £50,000 he had been 'given' at twenty-one.

Lewis was prepared to give in, on condition that Spedan ceased to be a partner in John Lewis & Co. This meant that Spedan would lose his quarter-share in the annual profits. He wavered:

'Poor old Dad is very pleased. He didn't like the prospect of the scandal of his son giving up a fortune and thousands of pounds a year, rather than enduring a year or two more working under him.' Spedan however stiffened up, took the £50,000, suffered the diminution of his personal income, and had no further connection with the Oxford Street business. Soon afterwards his father was, by statute, struck off the board of Peter Jones due to repeated non-attendance at meetings.

★

Oswald had a short war.

In Cairo, his regiment saw no action. He longed to be back in political life, deciding to 'leave the Yeomanry' after the war, and was reprimanded by a Major Pitt for being absent without leave; he had gone off snipe-shooting. He dined at Shepheard's Hotel, scoured the bazaars, took Arabic lessons, went boating up the Nile to visit 'a friendly Sheikh', and to the races at Gezira.

In January 1915 he was thrown from his horse, Venus, while on parade, and a week later sprained his shoulder when mounting, reactivating an 'old trouble' incurred playing tennis at Grove Farm. Pain in his right leg, resulting from his fall, was more serious. Captain Avery, the regimental doctor, diagnosed sciatica and Oswald had 'electrical treatment' from an Egyptian doctor. In February 1915 the regiment moved to Ismailia, where he had hot sulphur baths, massage and more electrical treatment.

At the end of the month he was granted leave of absence, boarded a hospital ship, and was home by mid-April. His mother was waiting for him at his flat, and that evening they dined with Spedan, Miss McElroy and Murray Lewis at the Marylebone Station Hotel.

He went dancing again with Mrs Holmes, which proved 'unwise, as my leg was much worse afterwards'. He thought to

start an import business in partnership with an Egyptian acquaintance who would send back 'native artefacts', and set up an account
for the purchases at the National Bank of Egypt. The scheme
never got off the ground.

With his return came a reconciliation between both sons and
their father. The nuclear family dined together at Spedan Tower
for the first time in years, along with Tom Baker, whose presence
ensured a peaceable evening. Mother, Oswald thought, was showing 'the symptoms of another nervous breakdown', and at Father's
suggestion he took her to Harrogate where they both took the spa
waters.

One of Oswald's worries was what to do with the Wessex
Publishing Company, bought to promote his now defunct parliamentary candidacy; from Harrogate he wrote to Spedan asking
him to give the company a try at producing Peter Jones's 'illustrated circulars'. Spedan replied that 'our Advertising Manager
reports that he is very strongly of the opinion that your Printing
Business is not equal to our Autumn Catalogue'. Good graphic
design was already, as it remained, central to Spedan's notion of
what is now called 'branding'.

★

The octogenarian John Lewis found a new crusade during the war
years. He was vehemently opposed to smallpox vaccination. He
was not alone, with organisations such as the National Anti-
Vaccination League active in the cause. Lewis's campaign in 1914
centred on the medical profession's advice to make vaccination
compulsory for army recruits. He resorted to his favourite medium
– big, provocative posters on his shop window: 'Inoculation is a
dangerous superstition, a cruel, blood-poisoning operation!'

He obtained a private meeting with Asquith, the prime minister. It is a measure of Lewis's continuing visibility that he gained

such access. He summarised the interview, not entirely coherently
– in Hudson's transcription – in his diary. He spoke as if his opinion carried great weight in the world. He would lend his voice to
encouraging recruitment if compulsory vaccination were abandoned, and offered to 'do my best without regard to expense, of
course you realise that what I am doing is costly to me because
women are influenced by doctors as much as by priests'.

'Well, I will consider it, and write to you,' said the prime
minister.

Lewis's campaign achieved a livelier reaction at street level. He
circulated a printed letter to every Member of Parliament: 'On
Friday May 14 as I was returning from the inspection of new
buildings of mine in Bolsover Street, my clerk of works ran after
me to tell me that a man was destroying one of my posters. ... My
80 years prevented my quite catching him up but I managed to
bring down my umbrella handle on his new silk hat.'

You have to hand it to John Lewis. Where retail was concerned,
he was dead against eye-catching publicity. In publicising himself
and his causes he was a virtuoso. The man whose new silk hat he
bashed in was a Dr Cathcart. He took Lewis before the magistrates for ruining the hat. Lewis retaliated by accusing Cathcart of
destroying his posters: 'Let every Member write down the proposition for himself and look at it.' The proposition 'that to force
into the body of a healthy man the virus of a disease would make
him stronger to resist sickness' was, in Lewis's opinion, patently
absurd and wrong. The magistrates bound over both Lewis and
Cathcart to keep the peace. Little wonder that Ellie seemed to be
on the verge of breaking down again.

In September 1915, Oswald heard from the War Office that he
had not, as he had expected, been invalided out of the service and
was instead to be placed on half-pay for six months. So he took
himself off on holiday to South Africa. He packed some sample

ostrich feathers from Peter Jones, in case he could source something similar while away. He was gone for more than four months. Before he sailed for home, he heard from the War Office that he had an extension of another four months' sick leave on half-pay. When the Medical Board's subsequent report proved inconclusive, he was given yet another month. He put out feelers, through a contact at the Foreign Office, for a posting to somewhere warm, for the sake of his health.

Father intervened. Having no help now from Spedan in the running of John Lewis & Co., he invited Oswald back into the business. Spedan advised him to accept, on the grounds that if he did not, Father might take a partner from outside the family. Mother, obviously, was in favour. Her health, recorded Oswald in his 'Review of Progress' for 1916, 'gave us all grounds for anxiety … Father's health is never very good and I find he is greatly aged.'

It looked as if Father had not long to go.

Oswald accepted the invitation to return to the business. The very next day he was offered a position as military attaché at the British consulate in Seville. This he declined, and asked the War Office if he might now resign altogether from the service. They agreed with alacrity.

So, after seven years of distancing himself from what he saw as the social stigma of shopkeeping, Oswald went back into it on a Monday morning in May 1916, his hours 9 a.m. until 6 p.m., plus Saturday mornings. His father no longer went to the shop every day, but he hung on to his authority in a way that left Oswald with his hands tied. Ellie tried to prevent Oswald from complaining; he must realise 'that Dad takes an exaggerated view of the honour he confers by giving you (or anyone else) the power to sign cheques on the Firm'.

One of Oswald's first challenges was averting a strike which was 'about to take place owing to Father's suddenly ceasing to pay commission on sales' – one of Spedan's initiatives. Oswald thought he had solved the problem; but it did not go away and Oswald was not sufficiently alive to the growing unrest.

At the end of the following year, Oswald recorded that he had 'quietly but steadily strengthened my position in John Lewis & Co. My relations with Father are more cordial than ever.' He spent one evening a week at Spedan Tower, 'which undoubtedly gives great satisfaction to all concerned. … Trade has broken all records' and the structure of the organisation was 'strengthened'. He was making notes for a book about the 'System of the Business' in several volumes.

He made up his mind to stay on in the business, so long as Father lived, 'in order to give myself every opportunity to become qualified to manage the business by myself'. Trade was again 'breaking all records' and the business had been developed by opening the third floor for selling purposes and by making use of empty rooms in the Holles Street houses. And, with a regular income to supplement his own shrunken dividends, he was upgrading his flat at Bickenhall Mansions.

In the last year of the war, Oswald and Spedan began to engage in stately epistolary discussions about the future of the family business as a whole. Spedan wanted his brother to join him in the Partnership project. Oswald could be 'Viceroy', the (unspoken) corollary being that Spedan would be king. Oswald was not seduced. He had no faith in the project, telling Spedan that he really should have been able to make lots of money during the war.

Spedan was less interested in making lots of money than in setting up the culture and structure of his Partnership. In any case, he was not then, or ever, interested in exploiting the luxury trade. Three decades later, when he had long had control of both shops and many branches, he wrote in a memo to his general secretary

that he held to a policy of 'Quakerish elegance' and 'inconspicu-
ous good taste'. Those who wanted *grand luxe* were 'not our
public', and never would or should be. His ethos lived on. Patrons
of John Lewis stores always knew what they were good for, and
what they were not.

Spedan had been pouring his own money into both Grove
Farm and Peter Jones. That could not go on. His father could
have bailed him out, but chose not to. When – finally, finally – he
was near death, he told Spedan how sorry he was about the loss of
Grove Farm, and that he would have helped him, had he known
then that Spedan could not afford to keep his capital tied up in it.
The old man had completely forgotten that apparently Spedan
had 'almost gone down on my knees' to him; and Spedan, at the
end, did not remind him.

Grove Farm would have to go. The loss remained a lifelong
grief to Spedan. It was a bereavement. He tried to persuade
Oswald to buy it, and rent it back to him. When Oswald said no,
he sold it for £20,000 – to the caterers J. Lyons, who took over
house, farm and sports facilities as a club for their own workforce.

Spedan, with Eleanor, perched in an apartment near Peter
Jones, in Eaton Square, but smoky London did not suit Spedan
because of his lung problems. He leased Coombe House outside
the village of Balcombe in Sussex, the decision being clinched
when he heard that the area was particularly rich in moths. At
Balcombe, he became fanatical about golf. Spedan was hoping to
work in future years mainly from home. He deliberately never
took on any operational position in the company, aspiring to
create an organisation so smooth, transparent and well structured
that his physical presence should be seldom necessary.

Yet he was a control freak, and could never leave well alone. He
evolved at Peter Jones his way of communicating with senior
management through a relentless stream of memos; and with the

Partnership as a whole, at whatever level, through a weekly house magazine, the *Gazette*. This idea, like most of Spedan's ideas, was not in itself original. The house magazine of J. Lyons, *The Lyons Mail*, had been running since 1913, and there were others. The originality lay in how he used it. He had in view the sharing of 'Knowledge, Gain and Power' among all Partners, and the *Gazette* was to be their forum. It was also his personal forum. It was his tool. The first issue appeared on Saturday 16 March 1918, with a front-page letter from himself as chairman 'To my Fellow-Employees of Peter Jones Ltd', addressing them as 'Dear Ladies and Gentlemen'.

He wrote most of the first issues himself, since the magazine – which cost in its early days one penny – did not immediately catch on or attract contributions, and nearly foundered. The chairman was left in dialogue with himself, which did not bother Spedan as he always had a lot to say. Even after the participation of Partners became its central function and attraction, Spedan continued to pour out articles – explicatory, or inspirational, instructional, philosophical or just tetchy – sometimes unsigned. There was never doubt about the authorship of his pieces. He habitually applied initial capital letters to both common and abstract nouns, making everything momentous; and the high-energy prolixity of his style was all his own.

In the interests of transparency he had already made public each week's sales figures, department by department, posted up the staff staircase. Now they were published in the *Gazette*. No information was to be confidential to senior management, and he set up a 'Committee of Communication', whose members included both managers and the managed. Naturally the managed appreciated this rather more than the managers. Buyers, something of a caste apart, feared a loss of their authority. It was his suggestion that the pay rates of all Partners at all levels should be published in the

Gazette that set the ball rolling: this highly controversial notion jolted the magazine's Letters pages into life.

Over the decades, the Letters pages remained the *Gazette*'s most dynamic feature. Spedan was adamant that all letters and contributions from Partners would be published anonymously. This was counter-intuitive. His point was that Partners should be free to air grievances and injustices, make suggestions, criticise policy, and voice complaints about a more senior Partner. 'Anonymity makes possible quite harsh criticism without fear of consequences to ourselves or others.' Even the chairman's actions could be questioned, and sometimes were. Anonymity also 'safeguarded' those managers who were criticised from appearing to avenge themselves on their critics, or from bearing 'an even subconscious grudge'. There was to be no censorship of the letters. Freedom of speech, wrote Spedan, was a 'sham' unless it was taken as far as decency allowed. The general editor, answerable only to the chairman, was 'one of the Partnership's most important members' – though the chairman scrutinised every issue before it went to print.

Does that mean Spedan retained a veto? And it is hard to believe that there was never speculation about who had written what, though the larger the workforce, and the workforce was growing, the less likely this would become. It is equally hard to believe that there was never a letter so unhinged or incoherent that it was not fit to print, but such occasions are not documented, and it may be that cynicism is misplaced. With the *Gazette*, as with much else, Spedan walked a tightrope between the extremes of democracy and autocracy (which he would call 'Leadership').

★

The year 1919 was a better one for Peter Jones, and the Partners received their first bonuses, in two instalments, in the form of preference shares. But no one in Spedan's family believed in his ideas. Oswald wrote in his diary, repeatedly, that he did not think his brother would ever make a success of Peter Jones. Father wrote to Oswald in January 1919: 'I hope you will take care of Spedan bearing in mind that he is quite incapable of taking care of himself.' And in September that year: 'I feel much concerned about Spedan. Had he been more responsive to my affection for him in his youth, how different he and his affairs would be.' It is hard to know what to make of that last sentence, other than that it was the child Spedan, and not himself, who had failed, if failure there was. John Lewis was never in the wrong.

John Lewis was emotional and not all his emotions were negative, though the nature of his generous gestures suggests that he exercised money-power as a way of reversing a narrative and overcoming humiliations. Now he did something quite extraordinary.

As a young man Lewis had been wounded by rejection from the wealthy family of his first love, Nelly Breeks. In August 1919 he and Ellie were driven north in the Rolls-Royce to Nelly's home country, Westmorland. In Penrith, he called unannounced at Nelly's former home, Ash Bank, where a niece, Daisy Thomson, was living. Ellie stayed in the car. Was she in his confidence, up to a point? At Ash Bank, Lewis explained who he was, and how he had always loved Nelly, and that in memory of her, he intended to give a large sum as an endowment fund for St Columba's Church in her home village, Warcop.

The Rolls took Lewis the five miles from Appleby, where they were staying, to Warcop, where he visited the vicar. His proposed endowment carried one condition, which was that a portrait of Eleanor Breeks, his Nelly, should hang in the vestry of the church, for ever. Whether he had it with him already in the boot of the

Rolls is not recorded. It was – it is – a large photogravure made from a photograph of Nelly in middle-age, set in a carved oak frame measuring about four feet by three feet, and so heavy that it takes two people to move it.

There remain mysteries. Nelly Breeks died in Mrs Theobald's home in Leicester in 1903. There is little likelihood that Lewis would have been apprised of this by anyone at the time. Any letters from Nelly would have certainly gone on Spedan's bonfire, like the diaries. Even if he and Nelly had remained in sporadic contact, and he knew her circumstances, why wait a full sixteen years after her death before he made his move? How did he know about the house at Ash Bank? How did he acquire the photograph of Nelly from which the photogravure was made, taken at a later age than when he knew her? He still had the one she gave him when they were parted.

The answers may lie with the Vicar of Warcop, the Reverend Seymour Shaw. A West Country man from Teignmouth in Devon, he was educated at Truro in Cornwall, then went out to South Africa, where in his late twenties he was ordained. Returning home, he served in parishes in the south of England before becoming Vicar of Warcop in 1901. He was in 1919 a married man in his fifties with two sons. There is also the gratuitous fact that in 1907 he went to London to identify the body of a younger brother, an alcoholic doctor, who had died of a morphine overdose.

Nelly Breeks became an alcoholic, and alcoholics sometimes share their sorrows, when under the influence. Nelly's thwarted romance with young, penniless John Lewis, subsequently the prominent department-store owner, may have become known in the village and reached the ears of the Revd Shaw, or his wife Eva, and they saw opportunity. It may have been Shaw who first approached Lewis, and not the other way round. In this context, the big brass plate Lewis had put up on the west wall of the church sheds some light:

IN AFFECTIONATE MEMORY OF ELEANOR BREEKS DAUGHTER OF RICHARD BREEKS OF EDENGATE IN THIS PARISH AND THAT HER NAME MAY ALWAYS BE HELD IN REMEMBRANCE HERE WHERE HER EARLY LIFE WAS SPENT. A SUM OF FOUR THOUSAND POUNDS HAS BEEN ADDED TO THE ENDOWMENT OF THIS CHURCH BY ONE WHO LOVED HER, TO INCREASE THE VICAR'S STIPEND BEYOND WHAT IT NOW IS FROM OTHER SOURCES. THE SAME TO BE CALLED IN PERPETUITY 'THE ELEANOR BREEKS ENDOWMENT FUND'.

There follow the dates of her birth and death and a note of her interment in Penrith.

So the income from the endowment was not going towards the upkeep of the church, nor to benefit some local charity, but into the pocket of the Revd Seymour Shaw, and of his successors.

Edward Short, known as Ted, became a Labour MP, held ministerial office, and was raised to the peerage as Lord Glenamara. When John Lewis visited Warcop in 1919, Ted Short was a little boy of seven, the son of the village tailor and draper. In 1983 he published a memoir, *I Knew My Place*, about the Warcop of his youth, and devoted several pages to the vicar, 'Old Shaw', whose real passion, Short recalled, was for his numerous hens. Ted Short, in adolescence, worked for and with him for sixpence an hour, and grew to appreciate time spent with this 'tall, dignified and gentle' man.

The vicar certainly needed money. A village joke was that when the Shaws' donkey died, they ate the donkey. The Shaw boys went to the village school, 'an unheard of thing for gentry to do', though Short's point is that Shaw was not gentry, nor in the farmer and shopkeeper class, but somewhere in between. His stipend was £400 a year, according to Short, 'even after he persuaded a local lady to make a bequest to increase it'. (Writing in late life, he got the story wrong.)

For any large or unusual memorial in an Anglican church, a 'faculty', or permit, must be obtained from what are now the Church Commissioners. The faculty, then as now, was obtained at diocesan level. Yet we have the Revd Seymour Shaw travelling to London to clear the matter with the authorities, and staying at Spedan Tower. Both the vicar and John Lewis, for their different reasons, needed the arrangement to go through, and it did.

For John Lewis, it was mission accomplished, and an old sore soothed. Nelly's portrait is still in the vestry, hung high, with no identification label.

8

THE STRIKE

Spedan's idea of Partnership did not preclude a hierarchy. Since he wanted to live a life as much outside the office as in it, he needed heavy-hitting, reliable senior management – like-minded men who could share and promote his vision. One says 'men' advisedly. He liked women, and working with women, and he liked strong women, but he never had a woman on the board apart from his own wife.

In spring 1920 Spedan made a first experiment in a policy which was to be a hallmark of the Partnership project: the recruitment into senior management of highly educated high-flyers, mostly with first-class degrees from Oxford or Cambridge, and preferably some experience of the wider world. Working in a shop had never been a likely career choice for such as they. Working in a shop was low status. It was not a 'profession'.

The first high-flyer he persuaded to join him at Peter Jones was an Old Westminster, a contemporary of Oswald's. Percival – Percy – Waterfield was the visitor to Grove Farm with whom he had hunted for moths at dusk, making them late for dinner and incurring Eleanor's displeasure. Waterfield was a very able young man, and a devoted member of the Church of England, with the formal demeanour considered typical of a civil servant. He had starred as a classicist at Christ Church, Oxford, and come second in the open competition for appointments to the higher civil service. He had been working in the Treasury, the ministerial department responsible for the government's financial and economic policy, since 1911. In early 1920 Spedan enthused his friend with his project and enticed him to join Peter Jones Ltd, on terms that would make it worth his while.

Waterfield wrote an explanatory letter of resignation to the Secretary of the Treasury: 'I should be ill-advised to reject the advantageous offer which has been made to me to join a friend in a private enterprise, in which I hope that, in addition to greater leisure, and less risk to my health from overwork, I may still find opportunity for performing, in a humbler sphere, work of some value to society.' One can hear, behind these lines, the eloquence of Spedan encouraging Waterfield to take the plunge. He was appointed finance director of Peter Jones Ltd, his chief function to be Spedan's financial adviser. Spedan would have hoped that his friend's expertise would solve the firm's and his own cash-flow problems.

But Waterfield had made a big mistake (and so had Spedan). The arrangement lasted only a matter of weeks. Waterfield was immediately plunged into turmoil and crisis. Whiteleys, the department store in Bayswater – in comparison with which Peter Jones was a minnow – had offered to buy Spedan out, taking over his shares. Spedan was considering the offer seriously. Waterfield, knowing little of the sector or of the background and expected to advise, went in person to consult Oswald, not feeling up to giving an informed opinion himself. Oswald's diary: 'I said I thought Spedan would be well advised to sell his interest for 200,000 pounds if he can get anything approaching that sum which I understand he can.'

Spedan was fantasising about what he might do next, if the sale went through. He had various ideas, 'from buying John Barnes [a big department store on Finchley Road in north London] to chartering a boat and beating the heavens with wireless messages about the beetles of rarely visited islands'. This was a couple of weeks before the decisive meeting to make or break the deal. We hear nothing more. Whiteleys did not acquire a controlling interest in Peter Jones Ltd. They probably did not come up with a good enough offer.

Waterfield resigned. According to a biographical account by Richard A. Chapman: 'It is probable that he simply felt unsuited to commercial life and to the particular pressures of working with Spedan Lewis. Certainly, the pressure to terminate the appointment was initiated by Waterfield himself'. By the end of May he was safely back at his room in the Treasury, his brief absence accounted for as 'unpaid leave'.

Again according to Chapman, 'the staff at Peter Jones and the world at large were informed by Spedan Lewis that the "Treasury Authorities"' had asked the company 'as a matter of patriotism, to release Waterfield' to serve as PA to Sir John Anderson, the wartime Under-Secretary for Ireland. Waterfield got married that autumn, and subsequently rose and rose within the civil service and was awarded a knighthood. It is a tribute to both of them that he and Spedan remained friends for life. They wrote to each other regularly, saw each other irregularly, and as time passed shared their passions for gardening and for chess, which they played by post.

'The particular pressures of working with Spedan Lewis' –
considerable at any time, especially for a quiet desk-man – were
made worse because Spedan was in bad shape that spring of
1920, quite apart from the unsettling fiasco with Whiteleys. His
general health was compromised by advanced pyorrhoea –
infected and inflamed gums. He was advised to have all his teeth
taken out and replaced by dentures. The extraction and replace-
ment of all teeth, or what remained of them, whether as a health
measure or for cosmetic reasons, even for young people, was
unremarkable at that time. Oral hygiene had a way to go. The
extractions caused Spedan some pain and he retreated to
Balcombe to recover until his false teeth could be fitted. He was
delighted with the final result. Even his golf, he said, had
improved, and he advised Oswald, who also suffered from pyorrhoea, to have all his teeth taken out too. But Oswald had other
things on his mind.

★

In May 1920 the workforce at John Lewis & Co. came out on
strike. This was shattering. Spedan, had he not been preoccupied
by the Waterfield experiment, Whiteleys, his sore mouth, and his
golf, might have expressed justifiable *Schadenfreude*, and said to his
father, 'I told you so.' If he did, it is not recorded.

Discontent had been building throughout the industry for
decades. Apart from low wages, the dismal conditions provided
for unmarried employees 'living in' was a main focus, exposed by
the *Daily Chronicle* back in 1898. P.C. Hoffman was the author of
They Also Serve: The Story of the Shop Worker, a trenchant and
entertaining workplace memoir. He had served his apprenticeship
with a wholesaler in the Holborn Silk Market, and then was a
'Whiteleys man', before becoming a career trade unionist official
and the representative of the National Union of Shop Assistants,

Warehousemen and Clerks. Trade unions, though legal, were anathema to most employers. Trade papers such as *The Drapery Times* expressed shock horror at demands for a minimum hourly rate. According to Hoffman, employers looked upon trade union- ists 'as Brahmins looked upon Untouchables'.

The expansion of department stores meant an increase in the number of employees. Conditions, as a result, were even worse and more congested than they had been in John Lewis's young days. Even more graphically than H.G. Wells in *Kipps*, Hoffman in his book described his 'shock', back in the 1890s, on finding himself sleeping with six other young men in a filthy attic room so small that they had to stand on their beds to get dressed. Bedbugs lurked in the walls waiting for the compulsory lights-out. For this accommodation, and for inadequate food, money was docked from their meagre wages, and there were fines for petty acts of non-compliance.

The building that John Lewis converted into a staff hostel in Weymouth Street was unlikely, by 1920, to have been quite as bad as that. But remembering the grim accommodation that Spedan found at Peter Jones, only five years earlier, perhaps not so very different; and bad as it was, the late Mr Peter Jones had had the reputation for caring for the welfare of his employees. Mr John Lewis had no such reputation.

The strike at John Lewis & Co. was not unprecedented. The 'needle trade' – the dressmakers – had come out in 1918. In 1919, shop workers at the Army & Navy Stores in Victoria went on strike. Wages had perforce inched up throughout the industry, though opposed by such groups as the West End Drapers Employers. The strike at John Lewis & Co. came as a shock to these 'rich and selfish retailers', as Hoffman called them. Hoffman hardly knew John Lewis, but he knew a great deal about him, devoting a chapter of his book to the strike which erupted in May

1920. Naturally, and not unreasonably, it is the heroism of the strikers and the vital part played by his union which inform his account. Nevertheless, his word portrait of Lewis is unique in the literature.

'The old man had his points,' he wrote. John Lewis & Co. was 'a fine store and it did a remarkable trade'. He appreciated Lewis's trading policies, respecting him for taking less profit on sales than most of his competitors, so that 'the public should get the advantage of a good purchase by his buyers'. He described how Lewis got the benefit of every available discount from his wholesalers because he never bought on credit; and because he had few credit customers himself he saved on clerical costs, as he saved on overheads because he did not advertise.

Lewis was a 'character', a 'card'. He could be both generous and mean. If he did a generous thing that cost him something, he tended to go back on it, according to Hoffman, who told how Lewis had, during the war, volunteered to make up the difference between wages and army pay for conscripted employees, and then retracted the offer. 'It is this mean streak in him which counts for much.' Another example Hoffman gives is Lewis's treatment of the boys who drove the vans delivering goods to be paid for 'cash on delivery'. Sometimes customers made out their cheques omitting fractions of a penny – a farthing, a halfpenny, or three-halfpence. This was common practice, to simplify accounting. Lewis would deduct these paltry sums from the wages of the hapless delivery boys.

It is curious to encounter in Hoffman's pages the man we know all too well by now as husband and father. The perspectives do not really conflict. 'He was,' wrote Hoffman, 'a tyrant as well as a fearless, obstinate man. ... Like a gnarled old oak, representing much of the worst type of employer in the rugged, rather shameless, individualist past of the Victorian and Edwardian period. His store was his domain, his world ... he brooked no opposition from anyone, not even from those of his own household.' That sounds as if the family rows were common knowledge in the trade, as were Lewis's hard beginnings: 'He had had to fight for his rights – so overlooked the fact that anyone else had any. If only he could have had respect for this in others, one could have had respect for him.'

Trouble had first flared with a dispute about an unfairly sacked assistant in the Silk Department, between John Lewis and Mr Yearsley – his chief Silks Buyer of many years' standing (apart from his brief interlude at Whiteleys) and 'probably the best in the country' according to Hoffman. Spedan would not have agreed with that – 'He started in Cottons and he should have remained in Cottons' – though he did think Father had treated Yearsley badly. Yearsley was dismissed. Hoffman, as the union representative, went round to the shop and 'saw all the assistants in that very long Silk Room standing with folded arms refusing to serve customers' unless both Yearsley and the sacked assistant were invited to return.

On this occasion Lewis gave in. The next crisis was over the signing of an agreement between shop owners and shop workers, which included rates of pay and commission on sales. 'Living in' was to be optional, and charges for accommodation and food controlled. John Lewis signed, as he always did sign agreements, never having any intention of observing them.

He walked headlong into trouble by tightening the screws. He began sacking staff wilfully, and hiring new and hopefully more compliant people. He issued a notice stating that 'premiums' – the contentious commissions on sales – were to be discontinued. Staff were forbidden to leave the premises during their meal breaks, or to elect a house committee, and were required to sign an undertaking not to belong to a trade union.

The result was the 'almost strike' which Oswald claimed to
have 'averted' during his first weeks working again for his father.
The matter went before the Ministry of Labour's Court of
Arbitration. Oswald represented his father. Requiring Mr John
Lewis to observe the agreement and retract the strictures that he
was foisting on his workforce, the chairman of the court said to
Oswald: 'You know, Mr Lewis, these things are not done these
days.'

Oswald put up no defence and merely stated that he would
convey the opinion of the court to his father, who ignored it.
Lewis did agree to receive a deputation of three – a buyer, a shop
worker and a (female) sales assistant. They asked him to recon-
sider. He sent them away, saying he 'feared neither God nor the
Devil', as the three reported to a meeting organised by their union
that Saturday evening.

The decision to cease work was unanimous. At six o'clock on
the Monday morning, the pickets were in place outside the shop.

Lewis responded the same day, issuing an illogical, ill-judged
communication addressed to 'Our Young Men and Maidens',
dismissing their grievances: 'I have just learned to my amazement
that it has been said that I am disposed to make changes in the staff
for trivial causes. Nothing can be further from the truth. Take the
ladies first. No small number have lived on here from girlhood to
advanced age. What is it, that has caused this unhealthy atmosphere? It is the vapourings of the accursed Trade Unionists.'

He made no attempt, because he saw no need, to justify his
breaches of the agreement, nor his disregard for the Court of
Arbitration, nor his denial of the staff's legal 'Right of Association'.
In this situation Lewis was no longer the brave, downtrodden,
'little man' demanding justice. The boot was on the other foot –
and he was blind both to the determination and to the calibre of
his selling staff, especially the young women.

Oswald, with his manager Mr Moss, went over to the hostel in Weymouth Street to reason with them. Bobbie Stirling, a vivacious woman from the north of Ireland who worked in the Juvenile Department, told the *Chronicle*'s reporter about their conversation. 'Mr Oswald' asked her if her parents knew what she was doing. She said they did, and they understood. He told her she was 'very silly – a young girl like you with no friends in London'. What if he closed the hostel? What if she lost her job? Miss Stirling remained cheerfully defiant and, like her companions, was not intimidated by Mr Oswald. How long, he asked, was the strike likely to last? 'I told him that it would last so long as he refused to recognise the Union.'

These were poorly educated, working-class young women, bright and independent-minded by definition, leaving home and family as they did, coming to London where they knew no one, bringing with them from far corners of the British Isles their home values and home voices. They were the British equivalent of the Parisian *grisettes*, 'shop girls', poor but honest – well, mostly – and ready for some fun when off duty. They were more numerous than any other category of females in paid employment apart from domestic servants.

'Shop girls' were an identifiable demographic, making their weightless mark on life in the capital and on the culture. A musical comedy, *The Shop Girl*, played at the Gaiety Theatre in 1894, and in 1909 another musical, also at the Gaiety Theatre, *Our Miss Gibbs*, had a successful run of 636 performances, plus a run in New York. Miss Gibbs, played by 'Gaiety girl' Gertie Millar, serves behind the sweets and candy counter at 'Garrods', a department store, where infatuated young gentlemen compete for her favours.

It's a safe bet that Spedan and Oswald Lewis, constant theatregoers, as were their parents, went to see *Our Miss Gibbs*. Did they also see John Galsworthy's powerful play *Strife*, in that same year of 1909, at the Duke of York's Theatre? *Strife* dramatises, over one icy February day, a confrontation between labour and capital during a long-drawn-out strike at a fictional tin-plate works. The strikers and their families, with no wages coming in, are freezing and starving, but their leader is adamant that the fight must go on, whatever the hardship. The owner of the works, a man with an 'iron hand', is equally adamant and will not budge an inch. The play is an argument against extremism. Galsworthy offers a nuanced version of industrial relations in that the union representative, so far from battling blindly for the workers against their harsh employer, speaks with the voice of reason. He withdraws union support from the strikers on account of their excessive, unrealistic demands for which they will sacrifice their families, and argues for compromise on both sides.

Oswald compiled a large-format scrapbook of the press coverage of the strike at John Lewis & Co., which was so copious that his cuttings fill every page in overlapping layers. The press was overwhelmingly supportive of the strikers, as was the public. The prevailing attitude may be summed up by the *Daily Herald*: 'John Lewis is a very old man – in ideas as well as in years. Not all "character" is good character, not all "strong" views are right views.' Even *The Times* opined: 'It is probable that Mr John Lewis and his fellow directors will find cause to change their minds. The shopping public has no sympathy nowadays with obsolete ideas about Trade Unionism and the right of workers to fair treatment.' The popular press homed in on the leading personalities – not only Bobbie Stirling but 'little Hilda Canham', 'the girl in the brown dress', who had been one of the trio who met with Lewis the day before they came out on strike.

The press was unanimous that Mr John Lewis was out of date, out of touch. There were cartoons – the most remarkable of them by the illustrator and designer Edmund Dulac in *The Outlook*, a moderately highbrow and less moderately Conservative political weekly. Dulac depicted a recognisable John Lewis with the body of a gigantic serpent-like creature towering over Cavendish Square, Holles Street and Oxford Street. The caption: 'Pre-Historic'. It accompanied a long article by E.C. Raymond on 'Mr John Lewis of Oxford Street'. An extract:

> He started from nothing or very little; he has got to the magnificence of – to quote Lord Randolph Churchill – a 'lord of suburban pineries and vineries'; he can look round his glove and ribbon departments and indulge a certain Nebuchadnezzar pride of creation. One of those Welshmen who find the natural expression of their genius in the drapery trade – the other normal outlet of the Cymric genius is the milk-walk – he set up his shop far away in the dark Victorian ages. ... Mr Lewis appears to desire to realise an impossible ideal – that of being an absolute patriarch.

He was 'an eccentric Brontosaurus or Dinosaur, who staggers by sheer dimension'. Hence the cartoon.

The writer ended his piece with a reference to the 'hell' of industrial strife, and a plea for 'co-operation, in the spirit and dignity of free men, with the other elements that make up a civilised society'. Those unimpeachable sentiments do not detract from the supercilious malice of the whole, nor from the grains of truth within the malice. Reading this article cannot have been pleasant for the Lewis family.

Every day the 400-odd strikers, of whom a quarter were not even union members, marched round the block comprising John Lewis & Co., escorted by police. They carried placards, made a lot of noise, held up the traffic, and blocked the doors into the shop. It was a spectacle that the public stood on the pavements to watch. The selling staff of other department stores had whip-rounds and sent money – more than £300 from Harrods alone. Wholesale houses and former employees of the firm chipped in. Music halls held benefit performances. The strikers had the active support of dynamic, Somerset-born Margaret Bondfield, a member of the male-dominated Trades Union Council, who was both exceptional and exceptionally prominent. The novelist Arnold Bennett sent money. Queen Mary, consort of King George V, dispatched someone to Oxford Street to drop coins in the buckets rattled by the picketers outside the shop.

The strikers were always smiling, at least for the photographers. It was exhilarating, but after Lewis closed the Weymouth Street hostel, it became harder for them, even though sympathisers and members of the public offered beds and meals. Some of the strikers, with no wages and no roof over their heads, unable to manage, went back to work. Hoffman was heading the negotiating team, and wheeled in John Burns, Lewis's old friend from LCC days. Burns, who had lost his parliamentary seat in 1918, was 'a bit bumptious' in Hoffman's opinion. But it had been he, when John Lewis was in Brixton Prison for contempt of court, who had been credited in the public eye with persuading Lewis to back down and apologise.

So Hoffman and Burns took a walk around the cloisters of Westminster Abbey and talked: 'Difficult man, John Lewis, very difficult. Like Aberdeen granite. ... Look here, I'll see Mrs Lewis up in Hampstead first, and then see him. See what I can do.' At Spedan Tower, Burns saw both Ellie and John Lewis, who wrote in his diary that Burns offered his services as peacemaker: 'I thanked him, but declined lest he should burst himself with egotism.' The Bishop of Birmingham – a former Mayor of Marylebone – came to see him too, and was assured by Lewis that he himself was perfectly competent to resist the union's 'impertinent interference in the management of my business'.

What Hoffman called 'the heroic struggle for freedom' could not just go on and on. Lewis, ever more granite-like, was never going to retract or come to the table. The strikers asked him once more to receive a deputation, through a buyer who had remained 'inside' as a go-between. Back came the answer: 'If they came to me on their hands and knees I would not receive them.'

There was no fanatical leader to bully the strikers into staying out at all costs, as there was in Galsworthy's *Strife*. After six weeks the strike was called off, amid cheers and tears and the singing of hymns and of 'Auld Lang Syne': 'We retire in the belief of the justice of our cause and decide that no one shall return to work with John Lewis.' He wouldn't have them back anyway. Many of them, with the help of the union, found places in other major department stores without difficulty. These were, by most standards, quality selling staff. The manager of Ponting's in Kensington told Hoffman that he would take as many as would come. 'Mr John Lewis lost something precious when he lost that staff.'

John Lewis, who had never shied away from personal publicity, received at the age of eighty-four more press attention than ever before. Not in a good way. The strike damaged John Lewis & Co. 'It had been a disappointing year,' Oswald wrote in his summary of 1920, 'as a result of the strike, and partly of bad slump in the trade ... but our victory in the strike was a great triumph, though to have avoided the strike would have been more intelligent.' Indeed.

John Lewis, one may presume, had little time for women's issues or women's suffrage. But when in July 1921 Emily Davies, dedicated suffragist and mistress of Girton College in Cambridge during Ellie's time there, died in Hampstead, aged ninety-one, he accompanied Ellie to the funeral. Reporting this to Oswald, he added: 'I often reprove Mum for not making more of her faculties. But now I venture to hope that she will avail herself of the opportunity for exposure of the malpractices of the Prudential Insurance Co. She has a strong case, the publication of which would redound to her honour.' He himself was 'under the weather' and unable to deal with something wrong at Peter Jones. 'Mum said, "Leave it to me", went down to Peter Jones and sorted out the problem. What a Draper she would have made!'

This is in its way touching. It is also stomach-churning. Whatever about the Prudential Insurance matter, his appreciation of Ellie's capacities is turned to reproof, as if it were she who had fallen short, as if he and his needs and demands had absolutely nothing to do with her inactivity beyond the domestic sphere. Her capability in sorting out the Peter Jones problem is valued only in terms of his hermetic world view: 'What a Draper she would have made!' Being as he was, that may have been the highest compliment he could have paid her. It is like his remarking that Spedan's problems were all due to his failure to respond to paternal affection as a child.

It takes some mental agility to turn everything round so that whatever happens, it is always someone else's fault. John Lewis could only rarely penetrate his own protective crust, which made life difficult for everyone else, and ultimately for himself. Unfortunately Spedan was to inherit the same mind-set.

★

John Lewis's crust cracked, temporarily, when in that year he lost the last of his five sisters: Eliza, aged eighty-three, the only one younger than himself. When she was failing, he and Ellie went to Weston-super-Mare to be with her. They did not stay at Oswaldene but at the Grand Atlantic Hotel. On 11 February Lewis wrote to Oswald: 'Dear Aunt Eliza passed away easily at 6 a.m. this morning.'

Cousin Mabel was with them. Spedan was soon to 'drop' her beloved elder brother Murray Lewis, in his forties, from his position as general manager of Peter Jones Ltd. In 1949, when Murray's son in his turn was seeking employment in the firm, Spedan wrote to his director of personnel, in a memo marked 'SECRET', that Murray Lewis had been 'well-meaning and in some ways quite a likeable person' who 'got into grave financial trouble through living beyond his means chiefly in the way of maintaining two establishments'. He and Oswald had cleared Murray's debts, but there were always more debts behind the debts. He received a small pension, and 'sponged pretty ruthlessly' on his sister Mabel. It was probably at her suggestion that Murray was summoned to Weston to supervise Eliza's funeral arrangements. Lewis himself, as he said, was not up to it.

'Dad is taking it very hard,' wrote Ellie. Lewis would tell Oswald, when the latter was compiling his 'Notes About My Father', that when Eliza died, 'I went into another room and cried as I had never cried before.' Eliza, childless and unmarried like her sisters, was his last link with their long-ago world of Shepton Mallet. There was no one left now who shared those hard, loving, early memories.

Oswald, always a little worried about his own health, left the Bickenhall Mansions flat in Marylebone in 1921, 'in accordance with Dr Drake's suggestion', and moved to Mayfair – cleaner and quieter, as well as more fashionable. The Manor, a five-storey block of mansion flats with shops on the ground floor, is on Davies Street, adjacent to Berkeley Square. Oswald bought Number 4 – 'a more luxurious affair in every way though approximately the same size', and installed 'a man and wife' to run it for him. The following year at the Motor Show at Olympia, he bought a 20 hp six-cylinder Wolseley, which he kept in the former stables of John Lewis & Co., now converted into garages, and took on a new part-time chauffeur: 'I have not driven myself since I sold my first car, the Vulcan.'

The Oxford Street shop survived the strike and the resulting downturn and ticked along comfortably with Oswald at the helm, not inordinately preoccupied by the job. Meanwhile Spedan was on his uppers again. Though he talked up his better trading figures, if they were 'better' it was from a baseline of nothing at all. No dividends were paid to shareholders, and no more bonuses to Partners. He was still sinking his own money into the project, and borrowing money until there was no one left to borrow from. Oswald's diary: 'Peter Jones Ltd continues to go from bad to worse under Spedan's management ... I do not think he will ever make a success of the business.' In early 1922 Spedan was at his lowest ebb. But that was also the year when the tide turned.

The old man, who still held some preference shares in Peter Jones Ltd, had the books examined by his accountants, and paid his first visit to Sloane Square for seven years. He decided to rescue Spedan once again, whether because he was impressed by what he found – as he should have been, and as Spedan preferred to think – or, as before, because he did not want humiliating failure to rebound badly on the family and the firm.

Lewis made a complicated arrangement, spelt out by Oswald, who liked to keep track of the figures, in his diary: 'Father gave Spedan £20,000 in exchange for a block of his Peter Jones shares, at 5/- a share and a further £28,000 as a personal loan to Spedan, and arranged to supply Peter Jones Ltd with goods [i.e. selling stock] at 6 months credit at 6%.' The package as a whole amounted to about £60,000. It was understood in the family that Spedan would always need to be protected from himself and looked after. Oswald played his generous part: 'I offered Spedan a renewal of the old arrangement we had before I left the business in 1909. Namely that we would divide equally whatever came to either of us by means of Father's death and he accepted very gladly.'

Somehow the brothers kept business and pleasure apart. Spedan, with Eleanor, still shared in Oswald's dinner and theatre parties. Oswald still went down for weekends to Balcombe and played golf. The ease in each other's company was unforced. That summer of 1921 the two spent a whole month away together, fly-fishing for salmon and trout in Norway. Their father wrote to 'Dear Oddie': 'Be sure you give good advice on leaving Spedan, he really needs it, dear boy.'

Their futures and the firm's future both united and divided them. Spedan and Oswald each had an agenda. Oswald back-tracked on what he had agreed with Spedan about sharing equally the ultimate inheritance. He wanted to buy Spedan out altogether right now – in a way, he reasoned, that would benefit them both. He consulted his worldly friend Stanley Holmes about how much to offer. The sum they agreed on, after passing it by the firm's auditor, was £200,000, the amount that Whiteleys had been expected to come up with and did not. Holmes acted as Oswald's representative in discussions with Spedan. The arrangement would permanently solve all of Spedan's financial problems, while securing for Oswald sole ownership of the family business after the death of their father.

No, said Spedan.

He was afloat again, thanks to the intervention of their father, and had no longer any intention of abandoning the Partnership project. He was already working on a new idea. In parallel with his plan to recruit highly educated men into Peter Jones Ltd, he was now setting about recruiting highly educated young women. He approached the women's colleges at Oxford and Cambridge, writing to the principal of Somerville College, Oxford, outlining his profit-sharing enterprise and enquiring if she could recommend any of her former students who might be interested in the post of stock controller at Peter Jones Ltd. The principal, Emily Penrose, sent copies of Spedan's letter to several possibles, one of them being a Miss Beatrice Hunter.

Spedan always said that Oswald had 'all the luck'. Rich, good-looking, and more cultivated than most rich and good-looking young men around town, Oswald in his thirties had plenty of girlfriends. He took photographs of them, in poses demure or seductive. Marriage had to be on the cards, but not yet. His father declared an interest: 'Please bear in mind that I should prefer a fair Swiss to a dark Française for a daughter-in-law.' And it was well known that John Lewis could not stand redheads.

On 30 December 1922, Lewis wrote to Oswald: 'Spedan and his Charmante dined here last night. ... Give my love to dear Mum I think I never felt so lonely.' (He hated being home alone, in spite of servants to look after him.) Who was Spedan's 'Charmante'? Lewis was making ironic reference, not altogether unaffectionate, to Eleanor McElroy.

Beatrice Hunter, by the date of that dinner, had been working for just two months at Peter Jones Ltd.

9

GETTING MARRIED

Less than a year later, on 4 November 1923, the front page of the *Gazette* was taken up by an article by the chairman headed: 'The Place of Mrs Spedan Lewis in the Affairs of the Partnership.'

Partners were informed that Mrs Spedan Lewis was now a member of the board, and of various other committees, including the Senior Appointments Committee. She would be editing the *Gazette* and helping with 'the coding of the Rules'. The chairman stressed the value to the Partnership of the practical female mind as he understood it, and since the majority of the staff were female, it was advantageous to them to have a woman on the board.

Mrs Spedan Lewis was Sarah Beatrice Mary Hunter, known as Beatrice, one of a large family living at 51 Hampton Road, Teddington – an outer suburb of south-west London on the

Thames. Her father, Percy Hunter, of Scottish extraction, was a retired local authority architect. There was not a lot of spare money.

She was five years younger than Spedan, and she was bright. At Somerville Beatrice attained a second-class honours in English language and literature, for which she received a 'Certificate', university degrees still not being awarded to women. After Oxford she lived at home and taught part-time, without much enthusiasm.

The Great War, paradoxically, had been a good time for many British women. They were needed to fill manual and administrative jobs vacated by men away in the armed services, they flew aeroplanes (though not in combat) and served as nurses and ambulance drivers in the field. The suffragists suspended their campaigning for the duration of the conflict in order to do their bit for their country. In 1914 Beatrice was working as the 'organising secretary' for committees fund-raising for British military hospitals in France and in Serbia, before moving on to civil service jobs, shuttled between government departments. A year before the war ended, according to her journal, she was sacked from her post 'in the Welfare Section' because of a dispute with a senior female colleague, and did not get another job.

Because her journal from 1917 to 1922 survives, even though typed out and obviously edited, there is more to be known about Beatrice's views and values at this time than ever again. She was unhappy living at home, feeling that 'life is not worth living', and decided to return to Oxford to work for a Certificate in 'Pass Mods' – the first undergraduate examination towards an honours degree in 'Greats', i.e. classics, though women were only eligible for this first part. To get accepted for Pass Mods, she had to take a preliminary examination.

As well as working on her Latin, Beatrice embarked on a programme of reading which included Balzac, Flaubert, Henry

James, and centred increasingly on Jane Austen. She was exercised by Austen's assumption that domestic happiness is the ideal for a woman, while she herself was finding family life 'intolerable'.

'Today's women', she wrote in her journal, 'are divided into those who marry and those who work.' Those who work 'establish for the most part little houses together' in order to escape 'the particular difficulties of those who work and still live at home'. It was worst of all for those who neither worked nor married and remained at home enduring 'the merciless intimacy of family life'. Their lives were 'modern tragedies'. There were 'fathers who for purely sentimental and affectionate reasons cannot bear a daughter nearly thirty to possess money of her own. To many victims of this loving but intolerable tyranny, the war which has changed this kind of sentiment has been a godsend, bringing independence at last.' She looks forward to a time when 'the young woman is free to leave home as a grown-up like a young man', and to escape a family life in which 'the name of home has not become a synonym for prison'.

But she had been sacked from her job; and in any case, after the war ended in 1918 women were expected to go back into their boxes. The men who returned wanted their jobs back, and the general public was on their side. So after the end of the war, Beatrice was struggling on her own at home with the *Iliad* and the *Odyssey*, school-teaching part-time, playing tennis and golf, and feeling isolated, 'in a fog', lost in 'an internal silence'.

On a November Sunday in 1919 she caught a glimpse of a family life which did not disgust her: 'Dazzled by seeing in church an attractive family – handsome, well-behaved children, a pleasant mother, a youngish, serious, be-glassed father – I should be immensely proud if I produced four such beautiful creatures and brought them up so well and admirably behaved. ... Impressed all day by the health and beauty of the children seen. ... Children grow on me.' There was little likelihood, she thought, of achieving anything similar. In the spring of 1921 she was making notes towards something she might write for publication:

> What I want to do is to give a picture of our generation ... the young women who have worked hard through the war – suffered losses – caught in anti-feminist reaction – blocked careers – little chance of marriage. The young men who have come home mostly married – the loss of chances in civilian life – physical and mental suffering – the deep desire for normal life and marriage. ... General sense of young and damaged lives. Note scene at tea the other day – the women all healthy, vigorous, physically untouched – the men lame, enfeebled, blind – affects their relations.

She told her sister Marion Job, married with children and living in Cairo, that she was a 'temperamental spinster' and would marry 'a millionaire or nothing'.

When in June 1922, out of the blue, she received Miss Penrose's letter, enclosing Spedan's, she responded with alacrity: 'I beg to apply for the post of Stock-Controller.' Beatrice enclosed academic references from her former Oxford tutors, and flagged up her wartime work experience – 'drafting a Blue Book and Statistical Report for the Agricultural Wages Board, reporting in detail on certain trades for the Ministry of Labour. ... Perhaps I may add that as Trade Board Investigator – an official whose main function is to ask questions without giving offence – my relations with both employers and workers were friendly and I was keenly interested in the question of industrial self-government.' A spirited, well-judged letter. Spedan interviewed her but, having already given the stock control position to another university woman, he could only offer to keep her 'on his list', with the possibility of a buyership.

Beatrice kept the ball in play. She was happy, she wrote, to consider a buyership, but needed to know more about the work and its prospects. 'If you have anything of the kind in view you could, presumably, give me another interview!'

The perky exclamation mark did not hurt. The result of the second interview was the appointment of Beatrice Hunter as Boot Buyer. (Boots included shoes, for both men and women.) An agreement was drawn up. She would be employed by Peter Jones Ltd for three years from 18 September 1922 at a starting salary of £250 8s. p.a. rising to £350 2s. 8d., plus 'Buyer's Bonus under New Scheme'. She left home and found lodgings at 86 Oakley Street, down the King's Road. Her first month was spent in training and familiarisation.

Spedan's letter to 'Dear Miss Hunter', written from Balcombe a few days after her employment officially commenced, covers three close-written sheets of foolscap-size paper and goes well beyond what the chairman of a company might normally write to a new 'Rank and File' employee. The applications he had received, he wrote, showed him that 'there is a much greater readiness, than I supposed, on the part of educated women of more than ordinary abilities to enter trade. ...' He expatiated in detail on the importance of buyership and the potential of women, as opposed to men: 'An ordinary Buyer is commonly careless about making sure that there is not already in stock the same thing or something sufficiently like it before he makes a purchase. He is commonly very careless about buying at one time a greater quantity than is necessary. He commonly fails to avoid slipping into too narrow a groove of his sources of supply ... and commonly fails in general diligence "all round push and go". ...' The 'great star' has a 'real gift for spotting good sellers in the stream of things offered by the wholesalers'. A buyer with flair could hope to earn £1,000 or more within a few years. Another of the female applicants '(Newnham, Cambridge – Honours Maths)' had given up a good teaching post and was starting work as a buyer that very week.

And so on and on, for paragraph after paragraph of pure Spedan – the over-verbalisation, the nervous energy, the anatomising of the drama of trade, the age-old tale of the souk and the bazaar – in the context of his Partnership crusade.

Beatrice replied immediately, explaining how, as part of her training, she was attending 'Foot Measurement classes' at the Cordwainers College; she would go to another class, at a wholesaler warehouse in Soho, where 'they teach you to discern between different kinds of hides and leathers'. Privately, she had some reservations. The shop itself did not impress her, as she wrote to her sister Marion: 'I'm going into trade. … It is a cheapish draper's and ladies' outfitters – kind of Bourne & Hollingsworth type but not at present on such a big scale.'

The last surviving entry in Beatrice's journal is for 9 October 1922, her first day on the shop floor: 'Fear the girls in my department have already spotted my inexperience – the things I don't know. … However the other university women are friendly. I learn that L[ewis]'s temper is dreaded – expected as much but it is not cheering. The showroom is untidy and the stock is pretty dud – that however is in my favour. More to make a show on. … So far L has treated me well and I must take him as I find him.'

By mid-November she was describing her employer to Marion as 'a great joke – a real idealist, a wild enthusiast. But also a rather sharp businessman, in other words a typical Welshman.' And in January 1923, feeling insecure in the job because 'he changes like the maddest weathercock', she described Peter Jones Ltd as 'more like a musical comedy than real life'. The chairman was everywhere, 'pouring out 10-page memos from morning to night', and no one able to get on with their work because 'he is always butt-ing in with a new and better idea. I have never met so much restless energy in all my life.'

Beatrice sees Spedan clearly enough and remains fascinated, covering pages and pages to her sister about him and the things he said to her: '"The *dream*, the *aim*, the *ambition* of my life is to secure for everyone in this place *absolute* freedom to do everything exactly as I think it ought to be done" – and then we both *howled*. I'd never credited him with so much detachment.'

She transcribed for Marion, as if it were a play, a dialogue in Spedan's office about how she divided up her stock. After some nervous fencing, she replies that she does it according to skins: glacés, calf, and then the fancy skins, lizard and crocodile. This somehow leads to her quoting from the poet Robert Browning, and Spedan counters by spouting Greek. (She told Marion he was 'an Oxford man', which he was not.) They were stimulating and amusing and impressing one another. Beatrice was not meek. Their courtship, before being acknowledged as a courtship, and once he clocked that she had 'a tongue', as she put it, was conducted through argument, banter and repartee.

In early 1923 Spedan sent 'his admirable Rolls-Royce or what-ever it is' to pick her up from Oakley Street one Saturday and bring her to play tennis at Roehampton Club, in a four 'with his brother and another lady'. They played seven sets and dined after-wards and 'it was a very jolly party'. Tennis at Roehampton became a fixture: 'he has a passion for tennis'.

'I have grown pretty friendly with him lately,' she told Marion, but 'I don't think it will last because I don't think he is the lasting kind.' Beatrice had few illusions, having experienced Spedan's quick temper and his displeasure at any criticism, as when she made a joke about his over-communicativeness – 'he talks all the time' – and he did not like it (Spedan never liked to be teased). He told her he would have to be careful in future as he was 'always cutting his fingers' on her sharpness.

Yet quite apart from sexual attraction, without which nothing would have happened, it was a good match — made, if not in heaven, then in Peter Jones. Beatrice engaged fully in Spedan's plans, and had ideas of her own. He would be gaining a partner in every sense, supportive of himself and of the Partnership. As for Beatrice — she would have a dynamic husband, not one of the damaged survivors of war ('lame, enfeebled, blind') and one who was, seemingly, as near to a millionaire as she was likely to get; and providing her not only with security but a career.

There was a last party weekend, without Beatrice, at Balcombe: 'Dear Buffles,' Spedan wrote to Oswald, 'Bill [Eleanor] and I will be very glad if your friends can come down here for Easter.'

'Bill and I ...' They had surely discussed, off and on, the inevitability of his marrying. Eleanor McElroy was not, at the critical moment, put aside, nor did she distance herself. She was included, and her support and practical help were needed, in all arrangements. She never put a foot wrong.

It was some time in the late spring of 1923 that Beatrice wrote an undated letter to 'Dearest Mother':

Spedan has asked me to marry him and I have said I will but of course I want your and Daddy's consent. He has his people's. I wish he weren't so rich but no doubt I shall get used to it! Of course it's a risk – considering that we've both got tempers but he does care very much, and I wouldn't have him if I didn't think I could make him happy. We're awfully good companions. ... He has been under great strain recently and he has behaved so awfully well that I feel I can trust him. I never meant to marry and feel I'd have been very happy unmarried but that's no reason why I shouldn't be happy married. It does look silly to marry one's employer but it can't be helped.

I am no good at saying the proper sentimental things, but I do hope to make him happy – so do like him. Luckily he has a more sensible name than Spedan, namely John.

Calling Spedan 'John' did not stick. Her next try was to call him 'Dan'. That did not work for long either. She wrote across the top of the letter-paper that this was 'a dry kind of letter', which it was. Also, defensive. Her excuse was that she was 'exhausted'. Her letter is all about how much Spedan 'cared' and how she thought she could make him happy. She said nothing about how she felt about him. Was she in love with him? Sufficiently, probably, and she meant to make it work. As for Spedan, he was very, very lucky.

The new couple were to live in London, and in June Spedan secured the lease of a four-bedroom flat, 37 Harley House in Brunswick Place, between Regent's Park and Marylebone Road, 'and Bill at last is pleased', he told his brother – Bill/Eleanor being heavily involved in flat-hunting and in packing up the house at Balcombe. She set up the Brunswick Place flat, and trained two young girls from Balcombe village, called Hatt and Bonnett, as live-in maids.

In July Spedan made his will, 'leaving a comfortable sufficiency to Eleanor and everything else to Beatrice'. In August he moved by himself into the new flat; and Beatrice's parents were invited to Spedan Tower. Oswald was required by Ellie to source some 'reliable chickens' for the lunch. 'Wish me luck! Festivities which include Dad are never very easy undertakings.'

A week before the wedding, Ellie collapsed. Dr Horder told Spedan that Mother's trouble was 'largely hysterical'. Spedan and Beatrice had been at Spedan Tower 'cheering up Dad'. Fortunately

Dad was very taken by his future daughter-in-law: 'It was astonishing to see how he lit up at Beatrice being there.'

They were to be married in the church of St Peter and St Paul in Teddington on 8 October at 11.30 in the morning, followed by lunch given by the Hunters at 51 Hampton Road. Oswald was best man, and just before the wedding Spedan wrote to him: 'Please don't fail to be at the lunch and to make Father and Mother come too. I'm just a bit afraid of Father's jibbing at the last moment and of the Hunters being rather badly hurt.' There was to be a short honeymoon at the Crown Hotel in Lyndhurst, walking in the New Forest and playing golf. Oswald, as a wedding present, commissioned a portrait of Beatrice by John St Helier Lander, who in that same year painted the young Prince of Wales (the future Edward VIII) in polo kit. Beatrice thought Lander made her look like Nelson's mistress Lady Hamilton and was not displeased.

'We are keeping it as quiet as we can,' Beatrice wrote to Marion in Cairo, 'but being quietly married is almost more strenuous than doing it with a loudspeaker. I shall wear deep cream – almost yellow – lace,' and her accessories were all 'from the shop'. The bridegroom would be wearing 'Gent's Morning Dress' in which he looked 'like the proud Darcy, most impressive' – suggesting that, the close reader of Jane Austen that she was, she liked to fancy a parallel between herself and Spedan with Elizabeth Bennet and Mr Darcy in *Pride and Prejudice*:

After a long struggle I have yielded to bridesmaids. They will be the two Perreur-Lloyds – Marcelle and Odette. Aged 19 and 21. They are the nieces of Miss McElroy, Dan's nurse-housekeeper-secretary of 12 years' standing and they are both in the shop – one as a Buyer, the other running a workroom. They have red, red hair and creamy skins and are as pretty as can be and have charming soft voices with a pretty French accent … and they will wear sort of deep café au lait and will make me look like a piece of string.

Beatrice would never look like a piece of string. She was healthy, vigorous, ripe and ready. It would never occur to her to be uneasy about Spedan's domestic connection with his 'nurse-housekeeper-secretary', the dumpy, post-menopausal workhorse Miss McElroy, though the pressure to which she 'yielded' in the matter of her nieces being bridesmaids can only have come from Spedan.

The week before the wedding Beatrice and Spedan went shopping, with 'disastrous' results: a 'heavenly' tweed walking suit, a grey velour town coat, a green evening frock, silk shirts, 'a cyclamen velvet tea-gown for home evenings – a lovely background for the amethyst pendant he gave me, and Madam, you should see my sapphires. …' There was more, much more. Spedan was making free with the big personal loan from his father. Compared with the Hunters, he really was rich. But Oswald, in his summing-up of 1923, wrote that Peter Jones Ltd continued to lose money. 'Father speaks from time to time of Spedan coming back to Oxford Street but I do not encourage the idea and so far nothing has come of it.'

Oswald's role in the family melodrama was shifting. Spedan and Beatrice, in confident combination and spotlit, took centre stage. The lease of the house at Balcombe being terminated, Oswald solved his weekend problem by sharing with married friends a house called The Arches in Wargrave, a village in the Thames Valley near his favoured riverside weekend place, Maidenhead. The arrangement was that he would pay percentages of all expenses, with the right to invite his own friends there, 'and bring the Wolseley down'. He joined the Old Westminster Lodge (Freemasons) in order to reconnect with former schoolfriends.

December 1923: Beatrice writing to Marion from Harley
House, which she was redecorating fashionably with 'light colours
and pale carpets', though she much preferred 'playing with the
shop than playing with the flat'. Once a week she and Spedan
went to dinner with his parents at Spedan Tower,

> rather an alarming function in some ways, old Mr Lewis is very
> much a 'character' and set in his ways, which at 87 is certainly
> natural – to begin with you must dress [i.e. wear formal evening
> clothes, with dinner jacket and black tie for Spedan]. ... I have a
> long green evening dress with Peter Pan collar and long sleeves
> which fits the bill. Neither man nor woman is allowed to smoke,
> and no drink but water. ... It is a little difficult to be convivial over
> a good solid dinner – always game, fruit and cream, and coffee –
> and no drinks.

Politics, sports, theatres and dancing were 'not popular' as subjects
for conversation, 'but you may take a proper interest in natural
history and beautiful scenery'. It was, she thought, a typical
Victorian household. 'Mr Lewis was a free-thinker in his day and
still hopes to startle me by saying that he doesn't believe everything
in the Bible is true.'

And her mother-in-law? 'Mrs Lewis is interested in anything
and although Victorian in her outlook has genuine sympathy.'
Fortunately she herself was 'extremely popular' with both of them.
She was acquiring 'habits of ease' – taking taxis everywhere, an
unheard-of luxury, though a taxi now seemed 'so uncomfy'
compared with Spedan's Rolls. And they would have to get a
country house. 'I don't think he'll ever be happy without a garden',
although she preferred London and being 'in the middle of things'.

Beatrice spent two days a week in Peter Jones, and Spedan
when he came home talked shop all the time. That was fine by

her, feeling as she did appalled by the boring and 'old-fashioned' lives of young married women she met, who aimed to do nothing at all except move to the country and 'vegetate for forty years'.

Spedan was more anxious than she knew, writing in the same month to beg Oswald to head Father off from interfering at Peter Jones. 'If only he leaves me alone for another twelve months we can, if necessary, start paying off the loan. ... At present we are making very little profit.' He even thought, again, of selling Peter Jones, which would provide him and Beatrice with enough money for the rest of their lives, and enable him to devote himself to collecting birds, animals and insects, and playing golf.

That was not Beatrice's plan at all. She, meanwhile, was talking up the Partnership to Marion with maximum enthusiasm: 'It is really an Anti-Capitalist scheme – the interesting thing being it was evolved by the capitalist himself, and it is simply limiting the earnings of the capitalist to a fair share of the dibs instead of a grossly large one.' She then segued into a detailed, informed account of profit-sharing in theory and in practice.

Had it not been for Beatrice, the embryonic Partnership might never have come to fruition. She did not want to 'vegetate for forty years' in the country with nothing to do, while Spedan collected birds and insects. She believed in the Partnership as a morally worthwhile adventure for both of them, something they would achieve together, while acknowledging the irony of their position: 'Actually we do stand to inherit in all likelihood a ludicrous amount of money from his father which was made by jolly well nailing on to every penny that came his way.'

Then she discovered she was pregnant. This was unplanned and Beatrice was not pleased. The old couple at Spedan Tower, however, were overjoyed. There would be an heir to the throne. The succession of the family business was assured and, even

more importantly for John Lewis, the succession of the family
fortune.

Spedan was taken back into partnership in John Lewis & Co.,
which Oswald had not wanted, though he too benefited from the
general bonhomie. According to his 'Review of Progress' for
1924, in order to avoid death duties, 'Father made over to each of
us £150,000 of his capital in John Lewis & Co. and all his shares
in Peter Jones Ltd', plus other stocks and shares. The brothers
made some adjustments between themselves, Oswald swapping his
share of the Peter Jones Ltd shares for 'a block of Spedan's War
Loans'. He took some more foreign holidays, and bought some
paintings at Christie's.

'We are extremely gilded,' Beatrice wrote to her sister.

10

FREE AT LAST

Although her pregnancy transformed their fortunes because of her in-laws' delight, Beatrice was not too happy. She told Marion she was getting someone else to buy the baby clothes, 'the thought of which bores me stiff. Dan is awfully pleased really for which I am extremely glad. It would be the limit to go through all this and have nobody pleased.'

The baby, a boy, was duly born in July 1924, referred to as 'the Winkie', and named John Hunter Lewis. He was baptised, that being the right and normal thing to do in Beatrice's family. Ellie would have been pleased too, though maybe she was not present at the christening on account of Father's views. She 'seems to think that it will not be possible for her to come', as Spedan reported to Oswald, and 'Father will be all the happier if the superstitious rite is not obtruded on his notice.' But even he was beguiled by the baby: 'It was very funny yesterday to see Father and the Winkie both almost equally thrilled with a toy donkey that nods its head.'

★

Ellie Lewis died quietly four months after her grandson's birth. She was seventy.

She had found some happiness – principally in her sons – and had lived in material comfort, but marriage to John Lewis had, over the long years, worn her down. It takes two to forge the rusty chains of a long relationship, and it might be that in their co-dependency his tyrannical nature was answered by her willingness to play the role of martyr. Her sons' comments on losing her were tacit judgements on their father. Spedan put a notice in the *Gazette*: 'If everyone were like her there would be no sorrow in human life except for accident or illness.' Oswald wrote in his diary, the day she died, that she was 'one of the sweetest, most unselfish women who ever lived', and that this was 'the saddest day of my life'.

John Lewis continued to be driven down to Oxford Street and to assert his authority. In January 1925 Spedan told Oswald how Father was pressing for a total rebuild of Peter Jones. Spedan was against the idea, not only on cost grounds, but because he and Father would never agree on the 'type of building'. He felt that Father 'no longer has the vitality to override opposition'.

He spoke too soon. A month later: 'Father came over [to Peter Jones] this morning and said it must be understood that in everything here his wishes must prevail.' A 'hot quarrel' ensued, as so often in the past, but with a difference: 'I told him he is not to bully me as he bullied Mother all her life. He let that pass. I think it was a shock to him. He threatened repeatedly to strike me. I folded my arms and said, *Do* it.'

This was their last row. Spedan wrote to his father that night, probably after discussion with Beatrice, and apologised for losing his temper. 'I sympathise, more than I can say, with your feelings and I am anxious that your remaining years should be as happy as possible.' It was a long letter, ending: 'Let us live in peace together. Your affectionate son, Spedan.'

The old man, 'poor me' as he wrote, became plaintive, seeking to restore a closeness to his sons that sadly never was. Unable to raise Oswald on the telephone to wish him a happy birthday, he wrote: 'Why is it that my house is shunned by my boys? Your dear Mother would have loved to see more of you both' – implying that they had neglected her too. That was unfair. It was also pitiful.

He complained, fairly or not, that he hardly saw Spedan that first summer after Ellie died. Spedan was busy, and not only with the business. The Brunswick Place flat being unsuitable for family life, with a live-in nanny, he and Beatrice acquired North Hall, a large detached Victorian house (long demolished) set back from Mortimer Crescent, close to noisy Kilburn High Road to the west, and on the fringes of salubrious St John's Wood to the east. They bought the house opposite too, for staff quarters.

Spedan turned part of the big garden into an aviary, commissioning collectors to source exotic specimens for him. In the four years that they were at North Hall, he established an owlery and a pheasantry and enclosures for other rare species, including hummingbirds. He had cages in which he kept lynxes, placed against the netting at one end of the tennis court. This could be disconcerting for friends and Partners invited over to play.

Obviously Spedan could not care for all these creatures himself on a daily basis, nor did he want to. A Mr Gander managed everything for him. Writing in the *Gazette*, Spedan informed the Partners that they were welcome to visit and bring their children and friends, by appointment. The collection of birds and animals could be seen without going through the house, 'so visitors need not have any fear of causing inconvenience'.

It had always been understood by all that Spedan and Oswald could not, temperamentally, work together, sharing the business, after the death of their father. For two more years they negotiated, and the deed formalising their 'divorce' was finally signed on 30 March 1926. Oswald had done the sums. He now calculated that his half-share in John Lewis & Co. amounted to £426,000 and that his ultimate half-share in their father's private wealth would be in the region of £100,000. He told Spedan he would accept just £400,000 – in cash – if Spedan undertook to pay whatever tax became payable on Father's estate. Spedan persuaded his bank manager to lend him £400,000 for buying Oswald out. It was a tough call for the bank manager. Spedan's eloquence and self-belief, and the reassuringly hefty sums of money swilling around in the Lewis family, did the trick.

Both of them got what they wanted. Spedan would have total control of the whole family 'biz'. Oswald, rising forty, had ready money, and thus the freedom to get back into political life, which was what he decided he wanted. But first, he disengaged himself from the house-share in Wargrave, and then took a long expedition by sea, rail and motor car.

Oswald had already seen much of Europe and Africa. This time he covered most of the rest of the world, and was away for four-teen months, until Christmas 1927: India, Thailand, China, Japan, and the countries that now comprise Indonesia. He sailed across the Pacific, through the Panama Canal, and back across the Atlantic via Vancouver and San Francisco. As a confident, well-off bachelor travelling alone, he picked up acquaintances of both sexes along the way as he always had – not from among the popu-lations of all those countries, but following up introductions to representatives of the British establishment abroad. He found a welcome, passed from hand to well-bred hand, in high commissions, embassies, governors' residences, officers' messes. He 'ran across' Old Westminsters and Oxford contemporaries, and hired guides and bearers 'to look after my clothes and see to my luggage and so forth'. He sailed home from New Zealand, and by the time he was back had drafted a book, illustrated with his own photographs, entitled *Because I've Never Been There Before*, which George Duckworth, Virginia Woolf's half-brother, published for him in 1929. It is a period piece from the last unquestioning years before the beginning of serial decolonisation and the end of Empire. As such, it is not without interest. It cannot be said, however, that travel broadened Oswald's mind.

About fifty of the dozens of letters and postcards he wrote from abroad were to a Miss Frances Cooper. Their romance began in 1925 on the tennis court of North Hall, when Beatrice invited Frances to make up a four. The two women were childhood neighbours. Frances was the eldest of the eight children of Dr Harold Cooper, the Hunters' family doctor. Oswald wooed her with determination, but she remained elusive and unsure.

Frances Cooper, familiarly always called 'Coopie', was decidedly pretty. She was a good dancer, and Oswald loved dancing. She played bridge, and so did he. She was intelligent, studying for the equivalent of a London University degree in English at Bedford College for women. She spent holiday time in Egypt (administered and, with the Suez Canal, controlled by Britain), staying with married schoolfriends from her teenage years at Cheltenham Ladies' College. Chief among these friends were Gascoigne Hogg and his wife. He was with the British Army, and a cultivated and interesting man. Frances took off again to Egypt for three months the summer before Oswald left on his great tour. Disgruntlement at her departure may have had a bearing on his own. While in Egypt she received several proposals of marriage from young British officers and, after her return, Gascoigne Hogg appeared in London, also asking her to marry him. It is not recorded in family memory what happened to Mrs Hogg.

Oswald and Frances's son Peter suspected that his mother's heart may have been with Gascoigne Hogg, but her head told her to marry Oswald. Back home, he disentangled himself from a couple of back-up relationships, and asked Frances to tea. Beatrice wrote to him in February 1928, when the engagement was announced (with a notice in *The Times*): 'So that's the kind of thing you do when my eye is off you ... I am delighted with your news and wish you every happiness ... I have known the lady all her life more or less, and she is a most welcome sister-in-law.'

Beatrice and Frances – who abandoned her course at Bedford College on her engagement – were not, then or later, intimates. Though both were keen on sports and games – Frances was a better tennis player than Oswald – Frances was younger than Beatrice, and the two were very different. For a start, Beatrice was deeply involved in her husband's work life, as Frances never would be in Oswald's. Spedan and Beatrice's second child, a girl, was born in May 1927. She was christened Elizabeth Marion, though was never called anything but Jill. But, unlike Frances, Beatrice would never be wholeheartedly embedded in nursery life, taking off for a golf-coaching holiday, for example, while Eleanor McElroy moved into North Hall to hold the fort. Spedan accepted Beatrice's independence as a matter of course (and took Eleanor to the theatre).

Oswald was laying the ground for his re-entry into national politics. While still abroad he wrote to J.C.C. (Colin) Davidson, a Westminster contemporary and current chairman of the Conservative Party, seeking advice about standing once more for

Parliament. On his return he cultivated Conservative MPs, and again badgered Colin Davidson. An MP since 1910, Davidson was a presence at the very heart of Conservative politics not only as party chairman, but as the long-time PPS (personal private secretary) and confidant of both Bonar Law and the incumbent prime minister, Stanley Baldwin.

A decade previously, Oswald was a Liberal. This did not worry the Tories, keen on rebranding their image by recruiting 'progressives' and refugees from the Liberals. Oswald lost in two selection bids, and then was adopted as the Conservative parliamentary candidate for the constituency of Colchester, in Essex. He transcribed for Spedan a conversation one morning when he visited his father, in bed at Spedan Tower:

Self: Well Dad how are you?

F: What do you want?

Self: Oh! I just came to see how you were.

F: What do you plan to do?

Self: Go into Parliament.

F: Lot of good you'd be in Parliament!

Self: I'm sorry to hear you slept badly.

F: I haven't slept badly.

And so on ad infinitum.

From April 1928 Spedan engaged nurses to look after Father, to complement Miss Rhoda Bakewell and her sister Adele, in residence at Spedan Tower as housekeeper-companions. Miss Bakewell was an old friend of Oswald's, who had helped out when Mother was ill. Spedan and Oswald held joint Power of Attorney for their father, and Spedan instructed Miss Bakewell that the old man might no longer draw cheques without reference to one of them, nor was he to wander off out of the garden. Miss Bakewell was much affronted by the loss of her authority over the household, so Spedan sacked her (and her sister), telling the family solicitor Charles Russell that she was 'ill-educated, stupid, conceited and irritable'. But he gave her a pension.

John Lewis died at 3 p.m. on 8 June 1928. He was ninety-two. There was an obituary in *The Times*. His funeral was a quiet affair, though attended as a mark of respect by Harry Gordon Selfridge. He was buried beside Ellie in the churchyard of St John's, Hampstead. The inscription on his gravestone apparently occasioned difficulty for his sons. John Lewis was an atheist, so nothing about 'everlasting life'; he had made their mother's life a misery, so nothing about 'beloved husband of. ...' Whatever they decided upon, they replaced both gravestones in the 1950s, recording only dates of birth and death.

Oswald's son Peter summed up his grandfather's achievement without making extravagant claims:

> His triumph was a personal one, over his own adversity. He made no great discovery or invention. He was not original in his trade. He was far from a William Whiteley, and the opposite of a Gordon Selfridge. He was not the first or the only one to develop a department store, far from it. He was not alone in trading on honesty and low prices. Competition was rife, he was one of those who succeeded. ... But as Spedan pointed out, as soon as the physical size of the business grew beyond a certain point, his father's limitations were exposed. His temperament would not allow him to make sufficient use of other people's talent. He never lost the fortune he had made and never endangered the business he had so far developed, but he was incapable of exploiting the bridgehead.

This is fair enough. John Lewis was caught up and carried forward – as far as he could go – on the great tide of prosperity (for some), and of the rapid expansion of the aspirational middle class, at a time when Britain was *the* world power and London's Oxford Street the epicentre of the retail revolution.

Any objective assessment bleaches out John Lewis's intense lived experience. The business was his universe. He thought of little else. His 'excited brain' was the repository of a culture – the minutiae of special knowledge peculiar to his trade – which was the trade of his home town Shepton Mallet, writ large. He was irascible, irrational, obstinate, and a bully. He had loved some of his aunts (the mysterious Ann Speed?), and his dear sisters, and Nelly Breeks, and he loved his Silks. Ellie was his wife and he did not look elsewhere. His carapace grew so hard over time that not even he himself had much access to his soft centre. Having lived for the business he created, maybe in the eternal moment just before life was extinguished, he was at peace in knowing that the most important thing to him, his fortune, was safely handed on, and in the belief that his business and his name would be perpetuated by his son and grandson.

Spedan and Oswald, liberated at long, long last, wasted no time in restructuring their lives. Oswald's marriage took place, as previously arranged, sixteen days after the funeral. Oswald's diary, 28 June 1928: 'My wedding day. Frances and I were married at St Mary's Church, Hampton-on-Thames ... Frances looked absolutely lovely.' Beatrice's brother, Cecil Hunter, was Oswald's best man. There was a slew of little Cooper bridesmaids; Spedan's son John was one of the two pages, 'and proved very fractious'. At the reception, the bride's uncle proposed the health of the new couple 'and I responded with a very successful little speech'.

For Frances's mother it must have been a difficult day. All was not well in the Cooper household. Frances's father, Dr Harold Cooper, gave his daughter away at the altar, wearing an ordinary suit and tie and not the statutory 'full morning dress' in which Oswald, Spedan, and Cecil Hunter were properly resplendent.

Perhaps he had a train to catch. Immediately afterwards he left wife, home and children, and his GP practice, to live with a married woman, one of his patients, who was by all accounts a well-liked person.

Frances was Dr Cooper's favourite child and he did not want to lose her, or by extension Oswald – to whom he wrote from Cheltenham, where he and his new partner were perching, arranging to play an active part in supporting Oswald's official campaign at the upcoming general election. And then, on 21 May 1929, nine days before polling day, a notice appeared in the 'Personal' column on the front page of *The Times*:

> I, Harold Merriman Cooper, of Denton Lodge, Oxford Street, Cheltenham, hereby give notice that I expressly withdraw all and every authority which my wife A. M. A. COOPER may have at any time, expressly or by implication or otherwise acquired, to contract for me or in my name or as my agent, or is in any way to pledge my credit and that she is sufficiently supplied with all suitable necessities, and that I will NOT be RESPONSIBLE for her DEBTS wherever or however incurred.

Oswald was appalled, for Coopie's sake and even more so for his own, by this public display of the Coopers' acrimonious separation. A pencilled draft survives of a letter to his father-in-law:

> I was very grieved to see your notice in The Times this morning. Under the circumstances, I fear that I cannot accept your help in my election campaign, and have accordingly cancelled the form I had arranged for you to sign. You will I am sure understand that I want Coopie to be kept as far as possible from these unhappy quarrels and that it is all most undesirable from my own point of view that any whiff of this should [*illegible*] about her.

In the event, Oswald scraped in on 30 May with a majority of just 600, in an election overshadowed by unemployment and economic instability – and notable as the first British general election with universal suffrage. The result was a hung parliament. Oswald was to hold on to his seat at Colchester for the next sixteen years.

As for Dr Harold Cooper, he and his partner went to the United States, where he obtained an American divorce; and when her husband died they were married in Reno. Coopie's mother would not give him a divorce, so his new marriage was not legal in England and they remained in exile. He kept in touch with Coopie, always wanting to hear from her. Occasionally, as time passed, she got her children to write notes to him, though they did not know him. He died in 1946. It is hard not to suspect that the pain of the family rupture and the local scandal at the precise time of her wedding might have contributed to the low-level depression from which Coopie was to suffer.

★

Spedan Tower, including all its contents, was left to Spedan, and he and Beatrice moved in briefly with their little family to see if they wanted to live there. They decided against, and in April 1929 Spedan gave first refusal to Oswald who, after talking it over with Frances, declined: 'we feel it would not really suit us as a permanent home and therefore I have abandoned the idea of buying it'. Beatrice decluttered the house, cataloguing books and gramophone records, and packed up silver and glass to be stored temporarily in the strongroom at Peter Jones.

Spedan Tower was let furnished. Spedan had pressed Oswald to take some of the furniture, but all he wanted was 'the small table with folding top at present in the dining-room between the sideboard and the service door', 'the round rosewood table in the drawing-room', and there was 'a painted biscuit-box which I rather covet'. Spedan was surprised, even saddened, that Oswald did not even take the furniture he had bought for the bedroom he used when staying overnight at Spedan Tower, and that he wanted 'so little from the household goods among which you were brought up'.

Oswald was moving along and away from the world of Spedan Tower as fast as he could. What he bought that summer, though geographically close, was more than just a family house, it was almost a 'stately home'. The grounds of Beechwood House abut those of an incontrovertibly stately home, Kenwood House. Both lie back from Hampstead Lane, Highgate, on the northern edge of Hampstead Heath. Kenwood had been left to the nation by the Guinness family and was open to the public. Oswald increased Beechwood's eleven acres by buying a few more from the Kenwood estate.

Oswald's house was – is – a spreading two-storey edifice with a Georgian-style façade, built in 1840. The last time it had been up for sale, in 1921, it was described as having thirteen bedrooms and dressing rooms, and three bathrooms. The reception rooms were large and high-ceilinged, designed for grand entertaining. It went then for only £16,000, because land from both Beechwood and Kenwood was being targeted by property developers. This threat having evaporated, Oswald paid £30,000, and Beechwood remained the family home for the rest of his life.

His and Frances's first child was born there soon after they moved in. A month before the birth, Spedan wrote to Oswald that Beatrice had told him 'certain things that I feel very strongly you ought to hear', and that she would be happy to speak to Oswald herself. 'I hope you will see her as soon as you can. She merely wants to make some suggestions from her own experience,' but 'I feel strongly that you should have them quickly.' Oswald, in

his note about the rosewood table, said that he would see Beatrice
soon about 'the other matter' – whatever that was. Whether the
issue 'from her own experience' was about childbirth in general,
or about Frances in particular, whether physical or psychological,
and why Beatrice could not speak directly to Frances, remains a
total mystery. It could be that Beatrice had only just heard the
scandal surrounding Frances's father, which Oswald of course
knew about all too well already.

When Frances went into labour, on 26 September 1929 – just
after the collapse of the London Stock Exchange, and a month
before the Wall Street Crash – Oswald fulfilled an engagement in
his constituency followed by a lunch given by the Lord Mayor of
Colchester. His diary leaves little doubt as to his current priorities.
After the lunch, 'I rang up home to enquire how Frances was
progressing, and was thankful to be informed that she had given
birth to a boy and that both mother and son were doing well …
Captain Gribble dined with me and we discussed local matters.
Returned to town after dinner.'

The baby was named Peter Tyndale, the first name in commem-
oration of the boy's grandmother's private name for his father.
Oswald had him christened in St Stephen's Chapel in the House
of Commons, inviting Colin Davidson to be a godfather. Davidson
duly attended the baptism but maintained little godfatherly contact
thereafter.

Frances had no interest in politics, and much disliked going
down to Colchester to visit the constituency. She was an attentive
and loving mother, venting whatever were her tensions on the
domestic staff, finding fault, losing her temper and making scenes;
after which she either sacked them or they walked out. She had
seen off three nannies by the time her daughter, Diana, was born,
eighteen months after Peter. 'I am afraid Coopie is terribly tactless
with servants,' noted Oswald. This was never going to change, and

his diary is punctuated with allusions – regretful, not judgemental – to this problem, though even she recognised the fourth nanny, who stayed until the children went to boarding school, as 'an angel'.

Oswald was deeply pleased to be a Member of Parliament. He liked the job itself, and the status and privileged access it gave him. He liked the House of Commons, with its traditions, rituals and ceremonies, and its perquisites. He was never to hold government office, but asked a lot of questions in the House. His first contribution, a month after the election, was to ask what action the government proposed to take on the report of the Standing Committee on Tomatoes. (Not so odd as it sounds: his Essex constituency was a centre of commercial tomato production.) He also had a large private income, an impressive house, and a wife and family. He was, as it were, settled for life.

Whereas, as the Great Depression began to bite, Spedan was proceeding – finally, extravagantly, at top speed, and with un-impeded realisation – across the whole business of the John Lewis Partnership. The dreams of both brothers were coming true.

11

LONG DIVISIONS

Spedan and Beatrice were indeed 'gilded'. Spedan, his financial prospects assured, had made substantial changes in his
life even before Father died. By early 1928 he and Beatrice
were running three motor cars – his green and black Rolls-Royce,
a green Lanchester and a green Humber. He stuck to this dark
'racing green' for all his future cars, and dark green (on white)
became the signature colour of the Partnership's designs and logos
for labelling, packaging and all forms of graphics.

Spedan began developing the 'community' aspect of Partnership
with an equal lavishness. He never forgot Grove Farm, nor his
vision of what it might have become. In 1926/27 he bought an
eighteenth-century house at Odney, with its land, then further
and adjacent properties. Odney, on the south bank of the Thames,
is an outpost of the village of Cookham, a couple of miles

downstream from Maidenhead. Here, close to the river, he established the Odney Club. It became and remained a success, central to the experience of many people working for the Partnership. The staff were Partners, and all Partners – with their families, from the lowest paid of the 'Rank and File' to senior management – could from the beginning visit or stay there at reasonable cost, with free use of the sporting and other recreational facilities.

Like Oswald and Frances, Spedan and Beatrice moved house in 1929 in time for a new baby. Spedan bought from his own capital as the family home a 1,800-acre tranche of Hampshire with a long frontage on the Test, a prime trout-fishing river. The house, Leckford Abbas, was solid and capacious, built around 1900, and the Leckford Estate included several farms as well as houses and cottages in Leckford village.

Their third child and second son was named Edward Grosvenor. He himself would have no idea where the name 'Grosvenor' came from. Beatrice gave him that name in memory of her first and lost love, George Herbert (Bertie) Grosvenor. Spedan knew about him, telling his actress friend Sybil Thorndike forty years later how, at Oxford, Beatrice had been in love with a cousin, and he with her. Their families objected to cousins marrying and, while she was hesitating, he was drowned off the coast of Cornwall.

Grosvenor was ten years older than Beatrice, with a first in natural science from New College, Oxford, and the records confirm that he drowned in 1912, off Polzeath, trying to rescue his brother-in-law, who also died. He was a practical naturalist as well as an academic, teaching entomology and marine biology. His father was a partner in a carpet manufacturing business in Kidderminster. Thus, both his background and his interests were strikingly similar to Spedan's. In her will, Beatrice would leave

£1,500 to New College for a zoology prize, to be known as the Grosvenor Award.

With a family and a complex household to supervise, Beatrice's practical involvement in Spedan's business diminished, but not her commitment and input. In the early days, not all their pooled ideas – originating with her, to judge from their nature – had been good ones. The first issue of the *Gazette* for 1925 had opened with a humorous dialogue between the chairman and Mrs Lewis about the economics of the Blouse Department. It showcased their collaboration and coupledom, and was somewhat laboured.

In the same year Beatrice had enthused Spedan about a Somerville friend, Florence Lorimer, who had an interest in Eastern textiles and artefacts, with the idea of sending her out to India to buy stock for the shop. Liberty's of Regent Street, with its 'Eastern Bazaar' in the basement, had been making a good thing of 'exotic' merchandise for years. The Partnership's Committee for the Economy turned the proposal down, so Spedan financed Miss Lorimer himself, briefing her with a spate of memos – and would she please also send back some owls for his collection?

An area on the ground floor of Peter Jones was cleared to display the merchandise Miss Lorimer had acquired, but customers did not buy it, so Spedan instructed her to sell the stuff on to museums. She remained on the strength for a few years as Buyer of Foreign Carpets, and Peter Jones continued to stock not only 'foreign carpets' but modest displays on the ground floor of Indian and East Asian ornaments and art objects.

By 1929 Beatrice was no longer editing the *Gazette* but was deputy chairman and 'Goodwill Partner', which meant customer relations. The year 1929 also saw the first performance of a Partnership Revue – songs and sketches about shop-floor life and the comical quirks of senior managers, who took part. The Revue became a popular annual event, with which Beatrice was keenly involved. Partnership societies and clubs proliferated mainly under her auspices, including the Music Society, the Drama Society, the Opera Club, and an arts club called the Sabeema – the name formed from S.B.M., the initials of Beatrice's first names.

There were other changes. The nineteenth-century façades of Oxford Street had had their day. D.H. Evans Ltd, a department store founded by a Welshman and trading since 1879, merged its business with Harrods in 1928, with the latter as the senior partner. In the course of remodelling the premises, the company sold off to Spedan for £848,500 an unwanted block adjoining John Lewis & Co. to the west.

Around the same time, T.J. Harries & Co. Ltd, a large drapery and dressmaking shop on the corner of Oxford Street and opposite John Lewis & Co. on Holles Street, became available. Thomas Harries, yet another Welshman, and a good acquaintance of John Lewis himself, died in 1901; and although John Lewis had always hankered after the premises, the shop was bought by a newly formed company. In 1928 Spedan bought T.J. Harries. In order to raise the capital to pay for these acquisitions, and to pay off the duty on his father's estate, he floated John Lewis & Co. on the Stock Exchange. T.J. Harries provided him, over the road, with about the same amount of floor space again, potentially doubling the turnover. It was known as the East House, the original John Lewis & Co. becoming, informally, the West House.

Spedan sent out a circular in the form of a letter to all long-time regular customers on his father's books, touching on Partnership as an experiment in the reform of the retail industry in terms designed to allay middle-class suspicions: such experiments were 'indispensable' in order 'to remove the causes of the present general social unrest that is so grievously injurious to the prosperity of our country', he wrote. He described his plans for the amalgamation of the shops with zeal, however notional the plans (and however likely to be overturned the moment he had a new idea). The East House 'will be used entirely for what are commonly called Show-Room Departments, such as Gowns, Mantles, Millinery, Blouses, Knitwear, Lingerie, Shoes and others which are accessory to these, such as Gloves, Stockings, Handkerchiefs, Umbrellas and Handbags'.

Departments that sold goods by the yard – 'the Silks, Woollen and Cotton Dress Materials, Ribbons, Lace, Trimmings' – would remain where they always had been, on the ground floor of the original John Lewis. Furs would not be moved either. The basement and upper floors vacated by the removal of departments to the East House would accommodate the House-Furnishing Departments. 'The policy of all the Departments will be exactly the same as in my Father's day. We shall continue to try to offer a very complete choice of colours, sizes and so on. We shall continue to avoid most carefully the extravagant methods that have been adopted so generally by the big London shops, and we shall continue never to let ourselves be undersold if we know it.'

This is an early iteration of the John Lewis Partnership defining slogan, soon refined as: 'Never Knowingly Undersold'.

The aim of the letter was to reassure his existing customer base that everything would remain essentially the same and that all changes were for the better, only towards the end of the circular returning to his experiment in industrial democracy, in rather more detail than the recipients perhaps needed: 'I am giving up to the Staff the whole of the profit on condition that they use it to become shareholders and pay off to me by yearly instalments the amount that I am told by very eminent advisers that I could get in cash today if I would sell out to financiers. [This sum, which he did not spell out, was £1 million on 'instant valuation'.] When the payments have been completed, my controlling shares will pass to Trustees.' He enclosed with each letter two printed sheets headed: 'A Brief Description of the John Lewis Partnership', with sixteen numbered paragraphs, and he signed off in traditional tradesman fashion: 'I remain, dear Sir, your obedient Servant'. In his draft, 'Madam' is crossed out and 'Sir' substituted. Although women shopped, their husbands paid the bills.

According to the Partnership's 'First Constitution', while giving away the income from his shares, Spedan took from the business £25,000 a year as return on his capital – untaxed, which upset the Inland Revenue exceedingly, but he was effectively advised by specialist lawyers and accountants who found perfectly legal ways through. Spedan, like his father, was honest. He did not lie or deceive. He treated his money as if it were a river to be channelled, diverted, deployed, and sometimes dammed up. It was a game that he played by the rules as seriously as he played chess, which was very seriously.

Though the Percy Waterfield experiment had failed, Spedan pursued his recruitment drive with young Oxbridge high-flyers, resulting in the formation of a core group of early converts – his 'main men' as Peter Cox called them in *Spedan's Partnership* – who, as time passed, made the Partnership what it successfully became. They all started as 'graduate learners', serving customers on the shop floor, and were fast-tracked to serial senior management posts. One of Spedan's criticisms of his father was that he never used or appreciated other people's talents. He was not going to make that mistake himself. He needed other people's talents to keep the show on the road, and he exploited them. The advantages worked both ways. In the Depression years, well-paid, interesting jobs were thin on the ground, and Spedan Lewis was no ordinary shopkeeper.

Bernard Miller, from Jesus College, Oxford, with a first in history, who was to make his Partnership career on the financial side, joined in 1927, became Spedan's PA, and was company secretary by 1932; his new wife Jessica was appointed Sportswear Buyer at Peter Jones. Paul May, an Old Westminster, was scooped up by Spedan while still an undergraduate at Christ Church, Oxford, where he took a first in 'Greats'. He broke his agreement with Spedan, which had involved some financial subsidy, by going off after graduation to work for Lever Brothers in West Africa, but returned to the fold in 1932 and was soon Buyer of Fancy Silks, on his way to the higher reaches of finance and research.

Michael Watkins, with a first in mathematics from Cambridge, had served in the Great War and was teaching maths at Westminster when Spedan invited him to join the Partnership in 1927. Watkins took over from Beatrice on the *Gazette* and worked in finance and merchandising before becoming Director of Trading, a post he held for many years. He was an exceptional person – Bernard Miller thought he was the cleverest of all of them – and he was the one whom Spedan listened to and valued the most.

Sebastian Earl, Eton and Magdalen College Oxford, joined the Partnership in 1932, following Watkins as editor of the *Gazette*. 'Seb' was enormously tall, conspicuously good-looking, socially well connected – and a champion rower, a member of the Leander eight that won a silver medal in the 1920 Olympics. Spedan loved structure, and endlessly tinkered with the structure of the company; a list of Seb Earl's constantly changing job titles, starting with the chairmanship of the Committee for Petty Sanctions and culminating in the position of General Inspector, evokes a kind of Gilbert and Sullivan improvisation, as if his next promotion might be Lord High Executioner. His father in-law Lord Maugham was, after all, the Lord High Chancellor of England.

And then there was Max Baker, older than the others, and coming to the Partnership from a different angle. He was state-educated, and then a Senior Scholar at Corpus Christi,

Cambridge, with a first in maths and natural sciences and several university prizes. He had already been working for ten years in the textile trade, and had supplied Mr Yearsley, John Lewis's legendary Silks Buyer. He read an article Spedan had written for the trade press about profit-sharing and the Partnership. The ideas appealed to him. He wrote to Spedan, was interviewed, immediately hired, put in charge of the West House of John Lewis, and by 1937 was Director of Buying. Max Baker was completely in sympathy with the idea of Partnership. He was also shrewd, and not uncritical.

The majority of the selling staff were women, and Spedan appointed graduate women as buyers, a key role previously dominated by men. Apart from Beatrice, the only crucial woman at a higher level and at the heart of the Partnership was a lawyer, Enid Rosser. After St Hugh's College, Oxford and the London School of Economics, at the age of twenty-two she was Secretary to the Advisory Committee to the Lord Chancellor, and was one of the first women in England to be called to the Bar. In chambers in Lincoln's Inn, she practised in the Central Criminal Court.

Beatrice met Miss Rosser when they were fellow members of the London Committee of the Oxford Society, and told her about her husband's experiment in industrial democracy. Miss Rosser was intrigued, and Beatrice invited her to lunch at the Langham Hotel, just round the corner from Cavendish Square, where she and Spedan retained a suite for overnights in London.

After lunch, Spedan walked Enid Rosser round and round Cavendish Square, in his frock coat and striped trousers and an old red scarf that had belonged to his father. Writing in old age, her clear memories of how he talked give a vivid idea of the way he inspired his recruits: 'He talked as only he could talk, with enthusiasm, of the Periclean state he was building in his drapers shop in Oxford Street. He talked of the biological basis of his ideas and his dreams of finding the answer to economic problems by common ownership in all business between workers and management.'

He asked her that very afternoon to join the Partnership and to help him to revise its constitution. After discussion with highly sceptical friends, she accepted, becoming in 1933, at the age of thirty-one, the Partnership's first legal adviser, a position she held until Spedan's retirement. 'The next few years,' she wrote, 'laid the foundation of the most significant and rewarding part of my working life.' As time passed, she became his personal adviser and confidante. He would discuss problems with her and bounce ideas off her, and she did him great service by firmly vetoing his wilder flights of fantasy.

'He loved the sound of his own voice,' wrote Enid, 'and a beautiful voice it was.' It is impossible not to wonder whether there was an erotic element in this and other of Spedan's relationships with women. Sexuality cannot be put down like a parcel, it is built in. But this is unlikely, since many men try to get off with women because they cannot get on with them. Spedan did get on with women very well, enjoying, as he described it, the challenges posed by the different way in which their minds worked. Confident women could laugh at and with him and argue, and he dearly loved an argument, provided he felt he had won. Nothing has been found, in either the printed record or in orally conveyed evidence, which suggests the slightest whiff of a rumour that Spedan was sexually predatory.

There were many other clever young men and women recruited over a period of about ten years, and most were both overqualified and underqualified for whatever was to be required of them, which could be unnervingly vague. Enid Rosser had no set hours and worked 'with compete independence of authority'. In 1985, to celebrate the centenary of Spedan Lewis's birth, the Partnership published an anthology of long interviews with many of those still surviving who had worked for and with him from these early years until their retirement. They nearly all recounted how they barely thought twice before accepting a job offer from Spedan Lewis, largely – as with Enid Rosser – on account of the over-whelmingly powerful impact he made upon them at their first meeting: his forceful physical presence, his high energy, and his inspiring belief in the importance and viability of the Partnership project.

Not everyone found him so charismatic. There were former military and naval men needing the work who did not care for what they would have called the cut of his jib. They thought he was something of a 'cad'. If they did not become converts to Partnership, and some did not, they left.

Spedan saw his core group almost as his extended family. There was skiing in Switzerland and weekends at Leckford, playing tennis and fishing, for the main men and their wives. Spedan was rarely alone – which, as his secretary Constance Lynne commented, 'must have been a great worry for Mrs Lewis', though Beatrice was an accomplished hostess. Entertaining his core group and their wives at Leckford was not, or not only, for the pleasure of having company. It gave him the opportunity for sharing and airing his plans and fostering informal and open-ended discussions.

Social life unconnected with the Partnership interested Spedan hardly at all. The gentry around Leckford left their calling cards, thinking to establish normal neighbourly acquaintanceship. Spedan had a card printed, announcing that he found his friend-ships within his business and was not available for social visiting. But were they really 'friendships'? Enid Rosser, who married and became Mrs Locket, wrote that she was, right up to Spedan's death, 'perhaps his closest friend and colleague', and she may have been right. Several contributors to the centenary memorial volume volunteered opinions on a shortfall in his relationship skills. He lacked emotional intelligence.

Paul May said that although Spedan could be incredibly kind, 'he was curiously blind at times to what he was doing to individuals'; none of them were his friends 'in the true sense of the word'. Bernard Miller thought his concern for people in the mass was 'genuine and evident', but, in regard to individuals, 'the human factor was sometimes ignored'. C.M. Jones, who worked with Spedan for thirty years as managing director of the Leckford Estate, transforming it into a prosperous commercial enterprise, recognised Spedan's positive qualities but was forthright on his shortcomings: 'His personal relationships I always thought were pathetic.' And Max Baker: 'It was a vision that inspired him, and he sacrificed a lot for it, not least his own family. ... He should not have sacrificed his family to such an extent.'

★

Neither Spedan nor Beatrice was an instinctively natural parent. To employ staff to look after children was standard for people in their income bracket. They took delegation to extremes. Lucy Worrall, the Norland-trained nanny they engaged for their first-born, John, was in 1925 paid a mere £120 a year with six weeks' holiday. According to the agreement, she had 'entire responsibility for the care of the child, to have entire charge of him until he is old enough to go to school'. She was soon to have entire charge of Jill and Edward too.

It was Lucy Worrall who was responsible for knowing when the children needed new shoes and clothes, and for ordering them. It was she who accompanied them on summer holidays in rented houses by the sea. The children were lucky to have her, and so were their parents. After she left, with a pension, Spedan wrote appreciatively to her about 'the atmosphere you gave to their nursery years. ... Whenever I hear the children refer to you, I always feel what a very good influence it must be for the rest of their lives.' Beatrice always kept in friendly touch with her, sending news of the children.

Spedan lived and breathed the Partnership, which included the development of Leckford, necessitating an increasing number of managers, experts and garden designers and naturalists; the aviary there was managed by the already elderly Miss Ethel Chawton, passed on to him by the Avicultural Society. With so many irons in the fire, it just would not have occurred to Spedan to give children much of his time.

Beatrice, as we know from her journal, had her own strong views on the 'tyranny' of family life as she had experienced it as a young woman, and was maybe determined not to impose the same on her children; and she had been appalled by the narrow domestic existences of women she met when she was first married. The first claim on her time and energies was Spedan himself, and the Partnership. She found her own pleasure and respite in amateur dramatics, in organisations connected with the training and employment of women, and took time away to pursue these interests, and also for adult holidays with her own family and friends. When Constance Lynne described Christmases at Leckford, 'with all the trimmings, enormous Christmas trees, presents in the hall, and so on', she did not mention the children – usually the focus of a family Christmas.

Both Beatrice and Spedan would surely have said that they loved their children. From the evidence, they regarded them as necessary and desirable adjuncts to their lives who, having every advantage, would grow up to succeed in life and to do their parents credit. Beatrice was a true believer in industrial democracy, but seemingly not in many other kinds of democracy. The children's education, and education in general, may have been under discussion when she wrote a memo to Spedan dated January 1932. She was, she said, against 'expensively over-educating the working-class and people of a low culture and mediocre abilities', because 'their earning power could never meet their acquired aspirations', resulting in their becoming 'unhappy, ill-tempered and bad citizens; through no fault of their own'.

Six months later, in the summer of 1932, John, aged eight, their eldest son and heir presumptive to the family business, was delivered to a boarding preparatory school in his new uniform of grey shorts, navy blue blazer and jersey, and pale blue cap and tie – his first step on the educational ladder climbed by his parents and by nearly all the sons, and sometimes the daughters, of the British middle and upper classes.

The chosen prep school was not, however, altogether conventional. Spyway School was in the village of Langton Matravers, a couple of miles from the resort of Swanage on the Dorset coast. It was opened five years previously by Hester Chapman, a daughter of T.P. Pellatt, owner and headmaster of Durnford House, a traditionally tough and spartan prep school in the same village. Pellatt built this much smaller, more familial and less challenging prep school on the Durnford estate for Hester, with her husband, Nigel Chapman, as the titular headmaster. She ran the show and was in her early thirties when young John Hunter Lewis arrived at Spyway.

In his first term he did not settle well, and caught chickenpox. Beatrice was away, and Eleanor McElroy was named as the responsible person if there were any complications. Beatrice, reporting this to Nanny Worrall at Leckford, said she heard from Mrs Chapman that John had become 'much more quiet and sensible and was getting on better with the others'.

Towards the end of his second term, John developed meningitis. The next day he lost consciousness, his parents were alerted, and within three days, on 16 December 1932, he died.

His death was unforeseeable and unpreventable. According to Beatrice, it was 'influenzal meningitis'.

Pregnant with a fourth child, Beatrice miscarried. She wrote from Leckford a painful letter to her sister Marion a month after the loss of John, stressing that doctors with whom she discussed the case all said that it had been a matter of 'pure chance':

> The fact that John happened to have an excitable brain did not affect it – a dull brain would have stood no better chance though it *may* have made the illness shorter in John's case … John was delicate in some ways and I hate anyone to think that he was unsound. He was not. His was a first-class life with a first-class brain and we have not to add to our grief the idea that it would have been better if he had never been born. He was a child we had every right to be proud of. … It is such a relief to both of us to *know* that it was not a matter of John's constitution. We could not bear the thought that this fate had been perhaps hanging over him all his life. It is as if he had been run over by a car.

There it is again, the 'excitable brain' – like his grandfather, like his father, the now-familiar phrase implying the now-familiar cluster of characteristics: a propensity for uncontrollable rages, the channelled, obsessional mind-set, and a limited ability to empathise with others. This sounds like a description of autism from someone who has not heard of autism. Spedan harnessed his excitable brain, in most ways, very creatively. Beatrice learned to live with it by being away a lot.

Implicit in Beatrice's letter is a fear, albeit negated, that there just might have been something 'unsound', as she put it, about

John. It is surely correct that the meningitis was 'pure chance'. Yet the choice of Spyway School, with a hands-on female at its head and a family atmosphere, might suggest its attraction for parents of little boys who did not 'fit in', and some tacit anxiety about John's development.

The evidence suggests that the brains of John Lewis and of Spedan Lewis were wired differently from most people's. Neurodiversity – including autism and Asperger syndrome – is now recognised and better understood. There is a relationship between autism spectrum disorders and epilepsy – autistic people are more likely to develop epilepsy than those who are neuro-typical. Epilepsy was given as the cause of death of old John Lewis in the Shepton Mallet workhouse. Some autistic people have communication, learning or behavioural problems; others, differ-ently affected, may have extraordinary abilities in a single and particular sphere – music, mathematics, chess, art, entrepreneurial drive – and are justifiably spoken of as having 'genius'. Several people, starting with his first fiancée Nettie Griffith-Jones, felt that Spedan was a genius.

Retrospective diagnoses are unsafe. Yet there can be little doubt that the expression 'excitable brain' was the Lewis family's way of describing something for which there was as yet no description or name or diagnosis. It is more than likely that both father and son, John Lewis and Spedan Lewis, were, in different ways, 'on the spectrum'.

And young John Hunter Lewis too? There is a cruel sequel.

The marriage of Hester and Nigel Chapman broke down. Hester Chapman left Spyway and reinvented herself successfully as an author, making her name with popular historical biographies. Before she struck that vein, she wrote a number of novels. Her third, published in 1943, was *Long Division*, the first-person story of a young woman in an unhappy marriage, running a failing seaside preparatory school. The narrative voice is waspishly psychologically perceptive.

The plot turns on the death of a pupil from 'influenzal meningitis'. The boy's father, Graham Sheldrake, a hugely wealthy manufacturer of bathroom fittings, is shamelessly modelled on Spedan Lewis. The narrator, Mrs Pirrington, half-mocking of him and half-dazzled by him, knows him by repute as 'a revolutionary in many ways, inheriting his father's business qualities … and swallowing up nearly all his rivals'. When he comes to look over the school, his appearance is 'a shock'. He was 'the handsomest man I had ever seen'. His expression was 'remote and high, again that of a fictional idealist and leader of men'.

She dwells on his long, beautiful hands, his 'noble Roman profile', while 'from those sculptured lips there poured a ceaseless flow of measured, Gibbonian eloquence', samples of which sprinkle her pages.

Neatly, twenty years passed between Hester Chapman's contact with Spedan and the publication of *Long Division*. She could have written it earlier, or taken notes at the time. Peter Lewis, although too young to appreciate Spedan at that particular time, has said that Chapman was 'pitch-perfect' in reproducing his uncle's conversational style and manner.

There is in the novel a return visit from the Pirringtons to Graham Sheldrake's country house in order to meet Sheldrake's son Sebastian, 'a miniature edition of the father without his blandness'. Sebastian was 'jerky, inconsequential and shrill', in a 'siege-world' of his own, while his father reprimanded him in vain. 'I was not surprised at the apparent permanent withdrawal of the child.' He was 'a difficult child', Mr Sheldrake explained, and 'highly strung'.

At school, Sebastian is found standing alone between goalposts on the football field 'giving out short sharp screams'; he screams during meals and screams uncontrollably when a fellow pupil repeatedly sings a particular song. (The song was 'Frankie and Johnny'.) He is seen as 'unmanageable'. Mrs Pirrington asks Mr Sheldrake what methods they use at home to control him:

'Reasoning … and Reciprocal Violence.'

'"Sebastian's only nine," I said at last.'

At the end of the novel, two years after Sebastian's death, Mrs Pirrington's husband having absconded, Mr Sheldrake proposes marriage, kissing her with a disturbingly 'measured experience', his approach having something 'Juggernautish and sinister' about it.

This is the moment to remind oneself firmly that *Long Division* is a work of fiction. For a start, in order to make possible this final plot twist, Graham Sheldrake is a widower. It was perhaps excusable for Hester Chapman to use Spedan Lewis so obviously as her model for the child's father, and to imagine a sexual encounter with a man who had both fascinated and appalled her. That is the kind of thing that novelists do. What is egregiously callous is Hester Chapman's account of an actual child who died of influenzal meningitis – and making out of it an anecdotal case study of the acute mental distress of an autistic boy.

Autism, in this clinical sense, was first named and described in 1943, the year of the novel's publication, which is cutting it a bit fine. Chapman may not have known there was a name for the syndrome she was describing. Schools not uncommonly had experience of 'difficult' or 'highly strung' children. She wrote about a struggling, misunderstood child who may have been based on little John Lewis, alias Sebastian Sheldrake. Or not.

Beatrice read *Long Division*.

She recognised her husband, and maybe the screaming child too. She kept the book from Spedan, who did not read novels anyway. She consulted lawyers, who strongly advised her not to sue. It was a burden she had to bear alone.

John Hunter Lewis was buried three days after his death in Godlingston Cemetery, newly opened in countryside outside Swanage, and only a couple of miles from Spyway School. It seems a strange decision. Beatrice, in shock, was perhaps not up to having him brought home to be buried in the churchyard of St Nicholas's in Leckford, and face outpourings of sympathy. The Chapmans would have been anxious to avoid all publicity, for commercial reasons. The death of a child at a school is the kind of thing that puts prospective parents off.

To cover the grave Spedan commissioned a slab of granite with, at the four corners, carvings of the emblems of the four evangelists; John's dates of birth and death in Roman numerals, and words from Psalm 124: 'Escaped as a bird out of the snare of the fowlers.'

There is a family photograph in which a smiling John sits cradling on his knees a large toy railway engine. Inset in the slab was a piece of green slate, on which was carved in shallow bas-relief a toy railway engine. So he had that to keep him company, though not for ever. Over time, the slate deteriorated and cracked, and some twenty years later was cleared away, and a witch hazel planted in the space.

The death of John, if not quite a taboo subject, was not much spoken of publicly. For Spedan and Beatrice the loss remained a defining tragedy. As time passed, Spedan idealised John as the lost 'Crown Prince', destined to have become the perfect heir to and future leader of the Partnership. Eleanor McElroy, secure in her Catholic faith, wrote unselfconsciously about the 'little Ambassador up above' keeping watch over Spedan and Beatrice.

12

ONWARDS AND MOSTLY
UPWARDS

After John's death, Spedan intensified his drive both to acquire more shops and to pursue his leisure enthusiasms, though 'leisure' is an inappropriate word for his strenuous activities.

He loved music. He bought an enormous number of gramophone records. He particularly loved opera. John Christie, landowner and entrepreneur, and his wife, the soprano Audrey Mildmay, planned a theatre to be built on to his house on the Glyndebourne Estate in Sussex. The Glyndebourne Festival Opera opened in 1934 with professional performances of Mozart's *Così fan Tutte* and *The Marriage of Figaro*. In the years before World War II temporarily put a stop to it all, the season and the number of performances expanded, the operation financed and managed by Christie himself, and always with a strong emphasis on Mozart.

Spedan was an early supporter and patron, and took other people along as his guests. Terry Jones was the talented, unassuming naturalist and ornithologist (not to be confused with estate manager Maurice Jones) who managed the breeding of Spedan's rare waterfowl at Leckford. The 'least musical of people' by his own account, Terry remembered being invited up to Leckford Abbas with others before going to *The Marriage of Figaro* and listening to it with Spedan and Beatrice on the radiogram in the drawing room, in preparation. They were all provided with musical scores, which Terry could not follow, and they were all handed scores again at the actual performance at Glyndebourne.

Spedan and Beatrice would stay at the Grand Hotel in nearby Eastbourne, or in a rented house in Seaford, with Francis their chauffeur ferrying them and their guests back and forth – eight or ten guests for every performance. Spedan bought fifty or sixty tickets each season and arranged for typed lists of dates and performances to be sent to senior Partners and other friends, to be returned to him with their choices marked. For many, including the unmusical Terry Jones, this was a pleasure and a privilege. Spedan was hurt when people were slow in sending back their marked lists. Some few politely declined.

For there was something off-key about Spedan's plutocratic generosity which could elicit resistance. He misjudged, and overdid it. When, for example, in 1939 his Old Westminster friend Donald Robertson – from 1928 Regius Professor of Greek at Cambridge – fell ill, Spedan consulted Eleanor McElroy as to what foods would best build him up. She suggested turtle soup, liver pâté, Brand's Essence, and a 'tonic'. Spedan added a case of Burgundy, and ordered a 3 oz jar of caviar to be delivered every single day by Fortnum & Mason to 56 Bateman Street, the Robertsons' house in Cambridge. Donald's wife Petica had to ask Spedan to cancel the order: Donald could not eat all that. When opera at Glyndebourne picked up again post-war, Donald himself asked Spedan to stop sending him lists of Glyndebourne performances, confessing that he had never really enjoyed opera. He was fond of his old friend, Spedan, but quite a dry man.

Spedan did not actually write his letters to Donald, nor to anyone else, nor the multi-paragraphed memoranda to Partners, nor anything at all. He dictated, fluently and unselfconsciously.

Three secretaries were necessary to service his requirements, taking everything down in shorthand. They were Constance Lynne, known as Lynne, Muriel Elliott, and Phyllis Kay. Spedan did not self-edit in the interest of confidentiality, even in letters to Beatrice, 'My darling'. The secretaries were, in their own persons, repositories of everything about his business and his personal life.

In London, where Spedan also had a PA, the secretaries worked in the office at John Lewis & Co., often getting the last train back to wherever they were lodging. At Leckford they lived as a family, dining formally in evening dress, and were included in the party of whoever might be visiting. Lynne, the only one of the three who survived to contribute to the centenary memorial volume, was seconded at different times to work for Mike Watkins and Bernard Miller. Nevertheless, she retained vivid memories of what was a relentless seven-day-a-week commitment.

All three secretaries gave over their lives to Spedan. None of them married. They had no definite time off, no set holidays, just the odd grabbed weekend. They worked in relays, taking over from one another and rushing back to the typewriter to transcribe their shorthand notes, while Spedan went on dictating sometimes late into the night − and there would be 'a terrific row' if everything was not typed up and placed in front of him by early next morning. He would dictate in the bath, or while shaving, with one of them sitting outside the bathroom door.

Why ever did they put up with this regime? 'I think it was the pure magic of the man,' said Lynne. 'He was an absolute genius, no doubt about that.' They felt privileged: 'Of course we had many, many perks, which most secretaries don't have, like being taught to ride, taught to drive a car, taken to Switzerland, taken to Glyndebourne. Even when he took people out to dinner he usually had a secretary with him. So life covered a very large field and I shall always be grateful for the education I got with him.'

★

During the 1930s, Oswald, when not in the House of Commons, was still a world traveller (Coopie's second child, Diana, was conceived in Panama). He went on three extended safaris, two in India and one in East Africa, finding no conflict between his active support of the conservation of wild animals and his enjoyment of shooting them dead.

At Beechwood, which he remodelled inside from top to bottom, the oak-panelled hall was hung with heads, stuffed and mounted. His son Peter lists his total collection of trophies as comprising two buffaloes, one bison, two rhinos, two tigers, three lions, a leopard, a cheetah, a hyena, a wild dog, a warthog, many varieties of antelope, a crocodile and a python. His and Coopie's social life included her cheerful, staunchly Conservative and numerous relatives, in warm contrast to Oswald's own sparse family. He was convivial, and still loved dancing. There was of course a full staff, including a butler at Beechwood (as at Leckford). Oswald, in short, became a rather happy grandee.

Spedan too, in his different way. In 1935 he approached the College of Heralds with a view to discovering some illustrious Lewis ancestor through whom he would be eligible to claim a family coat of arms by descent. The Hon. (later Sir) George Bellew, the young Somerset Herald, responded: 'I think we shall probably find that your family is Welsh: but that does not mean that they cannot be traced.' He thought it 'unlikely' that they would be able to establish a right to arms by descent, and reminded Spedan that he could always acquire a coat of arms by letters patent, simply by paying for it.

Spedan was undeterred and filled George Bellew in with what he and Oswald knew of their father's background in Shepton Mallet, including special reference to the mysterious aunt, Ann Speed, 'for whose kindness he had throughout his life a very warm gratitude and in whose memory he coined my own second name'. As already noted, John Lewis's time spent with Ann Speed in childhood was very limited, and Bellew's research did not come up with any information about what became of her.

Bellew's researches – no genealogical websites, no digitalisation of parish records – were extremely slow, and had to be paid for. By 1937 he had discovered that the first relevant Lewises to be established in Shepton, in the eighteenth century, probably arrived from the nearby Somerset village of West Pennard, near Glastonbury. He will also have discovered from the death certificate that John Lewis's father died in the workhouse, but he did not tell Spedan that. When Spedan made an appointment to meet Bellew for a discussion, Bellew became unavailable and Spedan saw his assistant.

Oswald, interested at first, dissociated himself from the project, telling Spedan it was not worth wasting more money on. Bellew's assistant thought it doubtful whether, among the hundreds of Lewises in the West Country, they would find any connection with any 'armigerous' (arms-bearing) family, 'or anyone significant'. As Spedan reported to Oswald: 'At present it is just a catalogue of names.' He still wanted to press on, however.

A weary George Bellew came back to Spedan the following year, requiring top-up payment and explaining that 'the quest would have been greatly simplified if the family had been possessed of any land or inheritance in Shepton Mallet, but from the particulars already ascertained, this would appear not to be the case'. He could provide a 'nice pedigree', or family tree, but could find no connection with anyone armigerous. 'This is regrettable but it is, I suggest, better to know the truth rather than remain in doubt.'

The College of Arms did produce a 'very nice' handwritten pedigree of John Lewis's immediate forebears and, maybe to show that they had not been slacking, garlanded the five pages with numerous generational sequences of other Lewises, none of whom had any discoverable connection with the Lewises of Shepton Mallet, nor with each other – like a game of patience which will never come out. This was signed off by Spedan and by the Windsor Herald in 1941 (by which time George Bellew had been called up for war service with the RAF). In the top left-hand corner of the pedigree is a sketch of the coat of arms of one Barnaby Lewis, gentleman, of Stoke in Dorset, granted way back in 1595. Spedan, describing this to Oswald, said its most prominent feature was 'regrettably, three boars' heads'. (Spedan, though he hosted shoots at Leckford, disliked blood sports as much as Oswald enjoyed them.) 'On the other hand, the crest above the shield is the head of a remarkable fowl. Clearly that is the part that belongs to me.' It did not belong to either of them, as Spedan knew by now perfectly well.

Paul Lewis, grandson of Murray Lewis, living in New York, has at the time of writing a coloured copy of the 1595 Barnaby Lewis coat of arms 'certified' by George Bellew. The present Somerset Herald, David White, surmises without seeing it that this is most probably a painting, commissioned by Spedan, and the authentication simply certifies what it is, implying no right to the arms by John Spedan Lewis. David White confirms from the records that there was never any grant of arms by descent, nor by letters patent, allowed to John Spedan Lewis.

★

In September 1934 Spedan had told Petica Robertson how Macy's in New York 'have a prodigious trade in women's stockings. They sell more than a million pounds worth of stockings a year. They got their Buyer by persuading a lawyer to give up the law. He spent a year in factories learning how stockings are made and the present trade is the result.' Mike Watkins and a colleague were just back from the US, where they had been researching volume sales and volume buying. 'Volume' was now on Spedan's agenda. By 1935 the Partnership owned six department stores – all going concerns – and the Partnership was employing between 2,000 and 3,000 people.

Spedan turned fifty in 1935 and his main men were maturing with him. He enacted a 'trial retirement', to see how they got on without him. His policy of making use of the talents of others proved disturbingly effective. They got on very well indeed without him. His trial retirement was brief.

Nevertheless, as his empire grew, there was no way that he could retain personal control of it all except at the highest level of finance, policy and Partnership ideology. He had no qualms about rapid expansion, equating human organisation with that of other species, where the evolution of big groups of animals results in increased energy and ingenuity.

The fact that other businesses were doing the same acted as a spur. He was very wary of the rise of Marks & Spencer, founded on market stalls in the north of England in 1884, its branches now proliferating, with a similar programme of quality plus value for money. In 1928 Marks & Spencer had introduced its own-brand label, 'St Michael'. The Partnership countered with the brand

name 'Jonell', later 'Jonelle'. This meant dipping a toe into manufacturing; Spedan began to acquire, or to set up, factories for the
production of own-brand merchandise.

The retail revolution was taking another turn. The volume of
stock required to supply numerous stores made central buying an
economic necessity, as well as establishing the Partnership's 'look'.
So, for example, whether in Tyrrell & Green in Southampton or
Jessop & Son in Nottingham, customers would find the same
display of towels, in three sizes, in every colour of the spectrum
and in half a dozen shades of that same colour, at reasonable prices,
and each with the John Lewis label attached. It was 'value and
assortment', his father's creed, from which Spedan never wavered,
taken to a higher level. These economies of scale necessitated
warehouse facilities for storage and distribution of stock, known
as 'Clearings'.

This was invisible infrastructure. Spedan's most conspicuous
achievement, however – and one which did more than anything
else to enhance the image of the Partnership – was the rebuilding
of crumbling old Peter Jones.

Charles (later Sir Charles) Reilly, a decade older than Spedan,
headed up the innovative Liverpool School of Architecture from
1904 to 1933. He first met Spedan Lewis in the late 1920s at a
midsummer house party at Overbury Court in Worcestershire,
home of the Martins of Martins Bank. Reilly found himself sitting
at dinner opposite 'a handsome man of forty with a Byronic cast
of features', and noted his wife, 'looking very lovely in a very
exciting French frock'. After dinner he walked in the garden with
Beatrice; and then, until two o'clock in the morning, with
Spedan. 'He turned out to be full of ideas with a scheme, so it
seems, for altering the whole commercial life of the country. I
went to bed feeling a new world was in process of construction,'
wrote Reilly. Back in Liverpool, he received a letter from Spedan

Mr Waite (left) and Mr Rose (right) in 1908.

Waitrose Ltd. in Acton, 1914. The Partnership acquired the company in the 1930s.

Spedan aged 29, chairman of Peter Jones.

Spedan's wife Beatrice Hunter, aged 23.

Family group with John (and train engine), Jill and Edward.

Spedan with John.

Longstock House, its land combining with Leckford's to form the 4,000-acre Leckford Estate.

Spedan's water garden at Longstock.

Oswald Lewis MP in 1930.

Oswald's wife, Frances Cooper.

Oswald as a young officer in the Westminster Dragoons, 1914.

Oswald and Frances in middle age.

Beechwood on Hampstead Lane, Highgate, home of
Oswald and his family for nearly four decades.

Oswald's impressive swimming pool at Beechwood.

Devastation at John Lewis following a German bombing raid on Oxford Street during a September night in 1940. Three firemen died.

A family business: John
Lewis aged 72. He lived
for another 20 years.

Spedan Lewis, founder
of the Partnership,
in retirement, and
(below, right) Peter
Lewis, chairman of the
Partnership 1972-1993.

Spedan's radical new Peter Jones, now a listed building.

Modern John Lewis building with Barbara Hepworth's *Winged Figure*.

'consisting of a great many paragraphs, the first of which began: "From now on please consider yourself my architect".'

So it began. Their first collaboration was to plan an ambitious development at Odney, planned to house dozens of holidaying Partners, between the clubhouse and the river. Reilly described the concept as like an American university campus; Spedan saw it as a village. In any case, although designs were drawn up, the cost was too high, even for Spedan, and the project was abandoned. When around 1932 plans were afoot for Peter Jones, Reilly declined to take the commission himself, being near retirement, and recommended his former pupil, William Crabtree, still in his late twenties. Crabtree collaborated with a young architectural practice, Slater & Moberly, called in by Spedan, with Reilly retained as a consultant. Reilly had been an enthusiast for Victorian Gothic and the Arts and Crafts movement, and took longer than Crabtree and the younger generation to embrace modernism and to exploit new technologies and new hard materials – concrete, steel and glass.

Remembering how Harry Gordon Selfridge once told him that British architects did not work closely enough with steel engineers, Spedan engaged one. He wanted to break away from the convention of window displays embedded in heavy stone-clad frontages, 'enormous piers of sham masonry, which is not what people have come to see'. He sent Crabtree off with Mike Watkins to Germany, the cradle of European modernism, to look at what was done there. The glass curtain-walling for Peter Jones in Sloane Square was the first recorded use of this technology in England.

The construction was undertaken by a new company set up by Spedan, John Lewis Building Ltd. The iconic inward curve of the façade is said not to have been an original design feature, but the response to Chelsea Borough Council's objection that the building line at that point would impinge too closely on the

pavement. Spedan gave an account in the *Gazette* in 1935 of how
the thinking evolved, reminding readers that shops began as
converted dwelling houses. The design team tried to imagine
what people would want a shop to be like 'if no one had ever
seen a shop before'. Their chief criteria became lightness – the
maximum possible natural light, airiness and ease of moving
around. The footprint of the building was extended, but maximising every inch of floor space for selling was not a priority.
There must be no 'depressing over-crowding', no 'dark depths'.
Since inequalities of spending power and of culture in the population were 'destined to disappear', customers would expect the
'grace and comfort' already manifested in the modern design of
cinemas and tea shops – he was thinking of Lyons Corner Houses
– which would have seemed 'absolutely incredible' to people in
the past.

The result, wrote Spedan, was a building 'extremely different,
so far as I know, from any in London, and, I believe, somewhat
different from any other shop in the world'. That last claim was
only loosely true, and while the 'shell' and ambience of the shop
were startlingly innovative, the Victorian interior was not radically
remodelled, which made circulation, and the positioning of es-
calators, awkward; and the extended site did not allow for the
floors to be all on one plane.

Privately, Spedan was less bullish, writing to Donald Robertson
in the year before the reopening: 'I feel it could have been easily
a better building but it is not too bad.' Unsurprisingly, he had not
always seen eye to eye with William Crabtree, who was not, he
thought, a real 'team-player', and he did not work successfully
with him again.

Nothing in Crabtree's later career transcended this commission,
and Peter Jones was, and remains, a transformative piece of British
architecture and is listed Grade II★ by Historic England.

Enter, stage left, Mr Waite and Mr Rose.

The new Peter Jones opened in 1937, and in that pivotal year Spedan added to his portfolio a chain of ten grocery shops trading as Waitrose Ltd. Marks & Spencer had begun selling food at their new flagship store at the other end of Oxford Street. The Partnership had to keep up, and Spedan saw trading in food as yet another experiment, and as a safeguard against worsening sales in department stores if war with Germany should break out again, which seemed increasingly likely. People would always need food. On the high streets no one was spending, and in 1938 all Partners, except for the lowest paid, had to accept a pay cut.

Whether Spedan knew it or not, Wallace Wyndham Waite was brought up in Shepton Mallet, and briefly attended the grammar school there before becoming a grocer's apprentice in Pontypool, south Wales. Waite's wife was also from Shepton. He was the third of the twelve children of a peripatetic Welsh agricultural engineer. His mother was 'a cut above', from a farming family connected, at many removes, to the earls of Pembroke.

At the age of sixteen Waite, like so many, took the train to London allegedly with a £1 note in his pocket, and picked up work in one grocery after another, before making friends with two fellow shop assistants, Arthur Rose and David Taylor. In 1904, the three of them – lean, keen and dapper, all in their early twenties, and with splendid moustaches – quit their jobs to start their own business. Trading as Waite, Rose & Taylor, they set up shop in Acton at 263 High Street, part of a new shopping parade in this developing west London suburb. (There is now a plaque near the building in honour of 'the first Waitrose' and its three founders.) Wallace Waite was the moving spirit, and did the buying. Arthur Rose, who married one of Waite's sisters, was company secretary and accountant. David Taylor, the shop manager, left after two years to go back to his old job.

Waite and Rose formed a company and put their names together to make Waitrose, with Waite as managing director. They expanded into adjacent shops and took on more staff. They were public-spirited, selling food cheap to a local charity to feed the poor at Christmas, and – most unusually – closing their shops for an hour in the middle of the day to give staff time off for lunch.

Between 1913 and the end of the Great War, Waitrose Ltd opened two more outlets in Acton and branches in nearby west London suburbs – and, ambitiously, in Gerrards Cross and Windsor, prosperous communities further out of London, while both less than twenty miles from Acton. Windsor, with its castle, a royal residence, was a different world. Food hygiene, however, was largely unregulated and often questionable. Waitrose's selling point was wholesome food in clean surroundings. Their slogan was 'Seeking to Attain Perfection', and the Windsor Waitrose received the Royal Warrant of King George V.

In 1915 Arthur Rose enlisted in the Army Service Corps, returning from the Great War with his health impaired. He left the business in the early 1920s. In the 1930s, Waite himself was ready to wind down. A chance meeting with Mike Watkins led to negotiations. When the Partnership acquired Waitrose in October 1937, combined sales over ten shops amounted to £167,000 in the year. All the Waitrose staff immediately became Partners. Though no one realised it at the time, Waitrose was the shrewdest investment that Spedan ever made. Mr Waite remained with Waitrose until he finally retired in 1940.

★

The 1930s, depressed and depressing for so many, were a dynamic decade for Spedan, who found the money to pounce on opportunities. The Partnership, growing in size and capacity, was up and running along the lines he envisioned, even though no bonuses were paid to Partners from 1940 until 1952. He had waited so long, with his pent-up energies, to put his ideas about co-ownership into practice, writing in *Partnership for All*: 'If my father had retired, as all members of the Partnership will have to do, not later than seventy-five, the Oxford Street business would have been at my disposal in 1911.' He was forgetting that Oswald and he were joint heirs to all that their father had, and that negotiations to buy Oswald out of the business had been late, tricky and long-drawn-out.

The brothers never fell out, but they drifted apart; Oswald noted in his diary in 1937 that he and Coopie hardly ever saw Spedan now.

Oswald and Coopie were establishing a different kind of family life, taking their children away to big seaside houses in the summer holidays. There were some tensions. Peter left an affectionate, clear-eyed account of his parents. Reading his late father's diaries revealed a constant anxiety about Coopie in the 1930s. Their marriage was unquestioned, and stable – so many of his entries beginning 'Coopie and I ...' – but she was not happy. 'She seems very depressed and is far too thin,' observed Oswald. Top doctors found nothing organically wrong. She was 'irritable', she 'made scenes', and would leave the dinner table in a rage. She did not share Oswald's desire for a more sophisticated social life, nor appreciate his liking for taking enthusiastically to the dance floor with pretty women. All those dancing lessons had paid off. Even his daughter Diana acknowledged that he was a lovely dancer.

Coopie's predicament was surely that of thousands of educated or semi-educated, middle-class women with no definite vocation, who were not expected to work after marriage, had staff to run their households, and did not share in their husbands' professional lives. They found themselves stranded, and were bored. Oswald,

September 1938: 'Coopie made a scene before going to bed. Half
crying with mortification she declared she had nothing to do. The
approaching departure of Peter for boarding school has apparently
got on her nerves.' Both parents took Peter down to Bigshotte
School in Berkshire for the start of his first term at prep school,
Oswald noting that 'Coopie bore up very well.' The children
knew nothing of all this. Peter and Diana never realised their
mother's unhappiness. To Peter, as a child, she always seemed
'easily dominant and socially secure ... I felt until I grew up, that
she was an ever resourceful, protective and optimistic mother.'

Oswald's real interests lay in the outside world. Unconvinced by
Spedan's quest for distinguished ancestry, he sought to enhance his
social credentials in his own right. He commissioned a portrait of
himself from the society painter Simon Elwes, which was hung in
the Royal Academy in 1935, and then one of Coopie by the same
artist. (The two portraits subsequently presided over the dining
room at Beechwood.) And he became a member of a livery
company – the Worshipful Company of Farriers.

These companies are the descendants of medieval trade and
craft guilds, many with headquarters in ancient 'halls' in the City
of London. To be a liveryman confers clout in the eyes of those
to whom it matters, providing Oswald with a convivial base for
networking, and involving the administration of substantial charitable giving. The remit of the Worshipful Company of Farriers
has been to regulate and promote the craft of horseshoe-making,
and by extension 'the welfare of the Horse'. There is precedence
among the livery companies, and the Worshipful Company of
Farriers is not high on the list. The Worshipful Company of
Drapers ranks much higher and, on the face of it, was more
appropriate for Oswald. But he may not have wished to empha-
sise the drapery connection and besides, he had a contact in the
Farriers.

Fortified as ever by the sense of entitlement bequeathed to him by his mother, Oswald then conceived the idea of sitting in the House of Lords as a peer of the realm. In December 1938 he went to see Lord Marchwood, Treasurer of the Conservative Party:

> I discussed with him the possibility of getting some unpaid appointment important enough to justify my transfer from the House of Commons to the House of Lords. I pointed out that I would save so much heavy expense in Colchester [his constituency] and that I would find a capital sum of £2,000 which I could give to party funds. He was very friendly but told me frankly that I had no chance of going to the H[ouse] of L[ords]. Coopie and I went to Bigshotte to see the school play.

What did they talk about that evening in the back of their chauffeur-driven car? Oswald was not the first nor yet the last to try and buy his way into the peerage, and it often worked like a charm. He did not give up. He went on pursuing the matter even during the coming war.

★

While the Partnership expanded and thrived and Spedan seemed to be riding high, home life at Leckford Abbas in the 1930s remained overshadowed by the death of John. As a displacement activity in more senses than one, Beatrice obsessed about the accumulations of unsorted and unread books and papers that piled up, week after week – not only the unshelved books that Spedan ordered every week, but periodicals, pamphlets, reports, transactions, bulletins and catalogues from all the many natural history, horticultural, zoological, literary, cultural and political magazines to which they subscribed, and from the organisations and learned societies to which they belonged. There were duplicate copies of almost everything. Beatrice explained why to John Penoyre of the Society for the Promotion of Hellenic Studies, to which both she and Spedan belonged: 'My husband and I both subscribe to these societies mainly with the idea of supporting their work, and we have not ourselves at present the leisure to benefit from them, either by attending their meetings or reading their publications. Consequently the house becomes littered with unread periodicals and I feel there must be many people to whom they would be both useful and extremely enjoyable.'

Really? It was not so easy. Beatrice sorted and catalogued and made lists. She trawled through random piles, looking for missing issues in order to make up complete runs, so as to make them more attractive to libraries. She sent Spedan typed memos with numbered paragraphs, just like his, headed 'Mrs Lewis to Mr Lewis', about problems he might be able to solve, such as missing numbers of *Avicultural Magazine*.

Spedan played his part. They were extending the bookshelves in the billiard room up to the ceiling, 'which will mean getting rid of the stuffed birds'; would Miss Chawton, his bird lady, like to have them? And some runs of bird magazines too? He put a notice in the *Gazette* in the hope that Partners might be interested in acquiring old magazines and periodicals. Beatrice sent a bundle to Westminster School library and unloaded hefty batches on to University College, Southampton. And there were still all her father-in-law's books from Spedan Tower, still in packing cases, unsorted.

The severe paper shortage occasioned by the war was to provide a partial solution – pulping, and recycling.

Spedan and Beatrice had become accustomed to having other people doing everything for them. Whoever was Spedan's PA, for example, sometimes a graduate trainee destined for senior management, was charged with booking theatre, restaurant and travel tickets, sending flowers, and buying and wrapping birthday and Christmas presents for friends, colleagues, relatives, tenants, domestic employees and dependants. The daily lives of their children, Jill and Edward, were similarly delegated.

In September 1937 Jill, ten years old, having a race with Edward in the garden, crashed into the guinea pigs' house, breaking through a window with her hand. She severed the artery in her wrist, 'tore off a large piece of skin and damaged some tendons', as Beatrice reported to Nanny Worrall, who had left them three years before. Beatrice was not at home but the staff did all the right things and Jill was taken to hospital in Winchester. She had surgery, then convalesced in a nursing home, her arm in plaster for weeks. Beatrice stayed with her in the nursing home while a Miss Dereham-Reid was 'coping with Teddy [Edward]'. Beatrice, not for the first or last time, asked Nanny Worrall to come back. She did not.

Both children were found to have problems with their eyesight, each with a 'lazy eye', and were prescribed corrective spectacles – 'a rather serious disappointment for B and me' was how Spedan chose to put it to Petica Robertson. Edward's hearing was not good. Both children had their tonsils out. Beatrice had been 'dazzled' as a young woman by the handsome family she saw in church, and especially by their 'healthy, well-behaved' children. Her surviving children were neither particularly healthy nor particularly well behaved. Jill was a fierce little girl. Her cousin Peter saw how she bullied her younger brother Edward, whom he liked better. As for John, their lost elder brother, Jill told Peter: 'I hated his guts.'

★

At the beginning of September 1939 Britain and France declared war on Germany; the lights began to go out all over Europe, and everything changed. But even after war was declared, Spedan went on acquiring – borrowing from the bank in order to do so.

The great Mr Selfridge had come a cropper. For twenty years after his wife died in the flu epidemic of 1918, the year in which he published his book *The Romance of Commerce*, he had spent much more money than he made. Sales at Selfridges, as every-where else, dropped during the slump. He lived flamboyantly, conducting expensive liaisons with 'showgirls' and society women, and entertaining celebrities in grand properties rented from the aristocracy – Lansdowne House off Berkeley Square in London, and Highcliffe Castle in Dorset. Naturally, he had a yacht.

By the beginning of the war Mr Selfridge was in debt to the tune of six figures each to his firm, and to the Inland Revenue, and to his bank. He was a totally different character from John Lewis, but they had in common a resistance to retiring from the businesses they had created. In 1941, when his board finally forced him out, he was eighty-three years old.

Spedan, in the fallout, scooped up Selfridge Provincial Stores Ltd (SPL), a batch of no less than fifteen department stores in significant towns and cities, as well as in London. For a controlling interest in this ailing but potentially profitable company he paid a knockdown price of £30,000. The addition of SPL to the Partnership's portfolio increased the employees by another 4,000 and contributed to a JLP turnover of £3.3 million. (A few of the fifteen were sold off in subsequent years.)

The original structure of the Partnership was like a Christmas tree with the council as the star at the top supported by a descend-ing hierarchy of interlocking committees. With such expansion, this could not be sustained. The spreading 'branches' were chang-ing the shape of the tree. Within three years branch councils were

set up, each with their own chairman, and some branches producing their own *Gazette*.

Spedan assured Oswald that the acquisition of SLP was 'brilliant'. So it was. But then something happened so damaging as to
stymie all his calculations.

13

THE WAR

This war was not going to be like the Great War. It would be waged at home as well as in foreign fields, and death and destruction would come from the sky. Preparations had already been made – air-raid shelters, gas masks, and the blacking-out of all lights at night. Oswald was an ARP (Air Raid Precautions) warden for his area of London. John Lewis shops sold 'shelter suits' and blackout curtain material.

The air raids of the Luftwaffe caused far more damage and destruction, and took many more Londoners' lives, in the East End and the docks than in central London and the West End, but these parts were not spared either. During the first onslaught of the Blitz in 1940, just after midnight on 17/18 September, and continuing over several hours, German bombers blasted Oxford Street from one end to the other and back again.

Fires raged down the whole street, which became a horror of broken glass and burning debris. Nearly every shop was damaged or destroyed. John Lewis's West House, on the original site, on the corner with Holles Street, an Oxford Street landmark since 1897, received direct hits from both incendiary (burning oil and petrol) and high-explosive bombs. The flames were blown across Holles Street and the East House too caught fire.

The interior of the West House became a fireball. Three firemen lost their lives that night. Pictures of the ruins were on the front pages of the national newspapers. The 200 live-in Partners who were using the basements as an air-raid shelter escaped unhurt. George Orwell, then working for the BBC, walked past the burnt-out shell and noted in his diary for 24 September how unclothed mannequins from the window displays, piled up outside, looked unnervingly like corpses.

The very next day after the catastrophe a rousing four-page letter was circulated to the firm's chief suppliers and shareholders. It began dramatically by describing the events of that terrible night and the extent of the destruction. It addressed the losses to be faced, and the steps to be taken for the welfare of employees, and culminated in a declaration of confidence in an Allied victory and the Partnership's future prosperity.

The length of the letter, the speed with which it was produced, and its peculiar vitality, strongly suggests that it emanated from Spedan himself. But there is no first-person reflection, and it was signed by the company secretary 'on behalf of the Board'. The directness and simplicity of the presentation suggests equally strongly that Spedan, for once in his life, submitted to being edited, and for the better.

Staff carried still usable merchandise out, and sold it on the pavement. Incredibly, the charred East House was cleaned up and open for business within three weeks. A shorter letter went out to regular customers asking for their support at this difficult time, this one signed by the general manager. The Accounts Department had escaped, so invoices were being sent out as usual. Little could be salvaged from the skeleton of the West House, although the rear section, rebuilt with an entrance on Cavendish Square itself, escaped serious damage. The rest was to remain derelict, a bomb site, until work started on rebuilding in 1954. When the new building opened in 1958, Spedan had been retired for three years.

★

In June 1940 Oswald asked a question in the House of Commons of Ernest Bevin, the Labour trade unionist and Minister of Labour and National Service in Churchill's wartime coalition government. He directed the minister's attention to the 'large number of employees of Fulham Borough Council registering as Conscientious Objectors, and would he make enquiries to see what subversive influence is at work in that district?'

The background to this intriguing question is maybe impossible now to discover, though it sheds light on Oswald's stalwart patriotism and his opinion of conscientious objectors. In the foreground was his continuing safari to bag a peerage. He made three approaches to the Conservative chief whip. He put in for the chairmanship of the Assistance Board: the previous incumbent having been awarded a peerage. He offered to give up his seat in the Commons in favour of a candidate who needed one in exchange for a seat for himself in the House of Lords. In 1943 he approached Bevin, offering to chair, without salary, a commission concerned with the Catering Wages Bill, in exchange for a seat in the House of Lords. He put forward further proposals, all of which elicited either courteous and perhaps embarrassed rebuffs, or silence. He himself was not embarrassed at all, and not discouraged.

'Why did he do it?' wondered his son Peter, and found some answers. Oswald was accustomed to getting what he wanted, and it had become an obsession. Perhaps he wanted to leave to his family 'an heirloom that could not be taken away', and 'of course he wanted, and wanted passionately, a trophy, something to hang on the wall between buffalo and bison, something to justify his choices in life and dangle before Spedan'.

Oswald and Spedan, with their wives, saw more of one another immediately after the outbreak of war, Spedan commenting on how his brother and Frances – he never called her Coopie – had aged; while Oswald remarked on how tired and strained his elder brother looked. Spedan had started 'skipping dinner', having just 'soup and a couple of biscuits' in the evenings.

But when, less than a fortnight after the bombing, they all lunched together, Oswald was amazed by how unperturbed Spedan and Beatrice seemed to be: 'I would have thought the losses incurred would have ruined Spedan but he speaks as if it all amounted to no more than a nasty set-back to business.' This was maybe little more than the protective euphoria of crisis, and a proud intention not to appear downhearted.

Spedan let down his defences with the Robertsons, to whom he dictated a long, introspective letter. He had half expected to be bombed, he wrote, and 'to lose my life's work'. He sometimes wished he had sold out ten years ago 'and gone in for writing or running a newspaper'. Before the war, there was a payroll of 6,000. Now the Partnership needed to cut back on selling staff because of poor trading. Michael Watkins, to whom Spedan always listened, felt this was the right move; but they received 'a rather spiteful attack from the National Association of Shop Assistants, an attack of such a kind that I cannot help thinking that they are influenced by hostility to us because of the disastrous failure of the strike that occurred in my Father's business soon after the last war'.

Spedan introduced a non-contributory pension scheme, and made up the pay of Partners called up for war service to what it would have been had they remained in their jobs – something his father had resiled from in the previous war. While never directly condemning trade unions, his line always was that in a business run on fair and equitable principles they were just not necessary. When Petica Robertson surmised that Hitler 'might go Marxist', Spedan replied that his own notion of Marxism was 'too vague' to allow his forming any opinion. But he did worry that 'the Left Wing' in Britain was producing 'so deplorably little real ability and so high a proportion of selfish adventurers'. His analysis of national or international politics was never highly evolved.

Petica Robertson was killed on the street in a bombing raid on Cambridge in March 1941, while working as an ARP warden, guiding people to shelters.

Rural Leckford Abbas was thought to be safe, in spite of its proximity to Southampton, where the docks and town centre were targeted, and the Partnership's store, Tyrrell & Green, took a bad hit. Beatrice wrote to Oswald offering his family a home at the Abbas, to escape the attacks on London. Beechwood, even though up near Highgate and Hampstead, was not safe. There was a battery of anti-aircraft guns on Hampstead Heath, protected by a barrage balloon. This was shot down, and landed in flames in the garden of Spedan Tower, requisitioned for the duration of the war by the ATS (Auxiliary Territorial Service) – the female branch of the British Army; during air raids the young women took shelter in the basement billiard room.

Oswald did not take up Beatrice's offer. Coopie had found a house to rent not far away – Gaddeshill, in the village of Eversley in north Hampshire. The family went up and down to Beechwood, maintained by a staff of just two, taking refuge when necessary in the well-furnished air-raid shelter dug under the vegetable garden.

Bombs did fall in the grounds, mercifully missing the splendid swimming pool in which Oswald was addicted to swimming lengths. They were at Gaddeshill in the school holidays. Although a spacious house, on twelve acres, it was not a mansion on the scale of Beechwood, where adults, children and staff all had their own ample quarters and the children might spend much of the day apart from their parents.

At Gaddeshill the family lived and ate together, and played cards and board games round the same fire in the evenings. Oswald acquired a bicycle. The children got to know and to appreciate their previously often absent father. Coopie was no happier, nor better-tempered with Oswald or with the servants, as Oswald's diaries sadly record. But as Peter wrote, for him and Diana, 'home was paradise' during the war, 'our parents seemed in rock-like support of each other, and none of the disgruntlement disclosed in the diaries was ever apparent on the surface'.

Oswald was not without his own worries. He was not given any parliamentary job during the war, and it was difficult to get to his Essex constituency from Gaddeshill: all but essential travel was discouraged, petrol was rationed and Everest, his chauffeur, had been called up for war service. As a result his popularity in the constituency fell away. He attended debates in the House of Commons when he could and was present on 26 June 1942 to ask the Minister of Information, Harold Nicolson, 'to discourage the over-frequent publication in the Press' of photos of bomb damage, as the repetition was calculated to exaggerate German success 'and cause despondency and alarm among the population'.

Oswald had two houses – Beechwood and Gaddeshill – to maintain, and school fees, and his investments were doing even worse than usual, chiefly as a result of the war. In autumn 1943 Spedan wrote asking him whether, if he were to lose his seat at the next general election, he 'would care to give to the JLP [the John

Lewis Partnership] whatever time and energy you would have available?' It was tactfully phrased. Oswald was not quite ready to envisage such an eventuality.

When Beatrice at last got round to opening the packing cases of books from Spedan Tower, Spedan offered Oswald 'the small edition of Scott that used to be in the middle of the big book case in the drawing-room'; this letter morphed into what would be a bitter refrain for the rest of his life: 'Father by not retiring when he was seventy-five paralysed fifteen of the best years of my life and now I have lost by this war another five years.' Oswald wrote half-reassuringly: 'I have always thought the knowledge that you have brought prosperity to many people is a very complete justification of your profit-sharing experiments. Whatever the ultimate future of the organisation may be.' Conditioned to see Spedan as unpredictable and vulnerable, and to be sceptical about his chances of success, Oswald could not withhold that final pull-back.

Spedan always encouraged senior staff to add to their commitments by accepting public service appointments outside the firm; such marks of distinction reflected well on the Partnership and on his own shrewd recruitment. Michael Watkins, while holding serial influential positions within JLP, was in 1940 appointed to the Industrial and Export Department at the Board of Trade. This was the body which, at that time of shortages and rationing not only of food but clothing, furniture and raw materials, devised the 'Utility Clothing Scheme' – simple clothes manufactured to high standards and sold at low prices. Top designers lent their services free, and the scheme was extended to include furniture. To prevent the rich from scooping up more than their fair share of what was available when there was not enough of anything, every man, woman and child was issued a ration book. The coupons in the book were exchanged, along with the purchase price, for meagre weekly rations of food, clothes and other essentials. No coupons left, then no purchase possible. (There was, of course, a flourishing black market.) Very few commodities were 'off the ration'. In this context the low-price, reliable and often attractive Utility products, bearing the familiar 'Utility' label, became popular.

Michael Watkins jump-started the scheme at the Board of Trade as director general of Civilian Clothing, though he did not remain long. According to the response to a question in the House of Commons in November 1941, 'Mr Metford Watkins' had resigned 'for private reasons' – probably ill-health. (He was Michael or Mike in the firm, but 'Metford' in official capacities elsewhere.) But his contribution led, after the war, to his appointment as chair of the Council of the Royal College of Art, and to a knighthood: Sir Metford Watkins. He was also instrumental in setting up another wartime enterprise, this time for the Partnership: the Odney Pottery.

Before the war Watkins, as Director of Trading, introduced one of JLP's China and Glass Buyers to the much admired studio potter John Bew in the Rhondda Valley in Wales, where he was working with a Quaker settlement providing occupations and craft training for out-of-work miners during the Depression. Bew's values seemed to be a good fit with the Partnership's. In 1943 Odney Pottery Ltd, headed up by Bew, with Partners and other trainees working with him, was established in buildings on land belonging to Grove Farm – another Grove Farm, a few hundred yards from the Odney Club. (The site is now occupied by the JLP's Heritage Centre.) The wares produced here, in the style and idiom of Bew's great near-contemporary Bernard Leach, were sold in the Partnership's shops.

John Bew was an artist. He did not appreciate being required to turn out what the Buyers of China and Glass thought their customers would want. When the war ended, and imports of exciting new ceramics began arriving from Europe and Scandinavia, sales of Odney Pottery declined.

Bew did receive public recognition. His work was prominent in the studio pottery section at the Festival of Britain in 1951. But he was a troubled man. In 1954 his abandoned bike was found by the Thames at Taplow, and his body washed up two years later at Windsor. The Odney Pottery was closed down.

War service claimed many of the 'Rank and File' and some of Spedan's senior managers, among them Max Baker who served with the RAF. Paul May, a particularly able man with a sure touch for human relations in the workplace, joined the Ministry of Aircraft Production. T.G.M. Snagge, then editing the *Gazette* and in charge of the Sailing Club, served with the Royal Navy and was awarded the Distinguished Service Cross. Spedan himself was asked to contribute to a series of talks on post-war economic solutions at the Royal Society of Arts, and spoke about the idea of Partnership as the way forward, as he had so often done. 'I am like one of those electrical machines of which it is the nature to emit a series of sparks not a continuous current,' he said.

The exodus to armed and public services solved some of the problems of too many Partners during the years of low trading, but Spedan had to make some more than normally unusual appointments to fill gaps. Rudolf Bing, rising forty, was the Austrian-born opera impresario who worked with John Christie at the Glyndebourne Festival Opera, which closed down during the war. In his memoir, *5000 Nights at the Opera* (1972), Sir Rudolf, as he became, told how Spedan Lewis wrote offering him work and he accepted, 'much to my own surprise'.

Bing was put to work at a desk on the ground floor of Peter Jones, helping customers work out what they could buy with their precious clothing coupons, since the regulations changed constantly – was a pair of stockings four coupons or six coupons this week? He was promoted to assistant to the Director of Selling, at that time Sebastian Earl, 'a dominating presence, six and a half feet tall, handsome, always well dressed'. Earl, like Spedan, had been a generous Glyndebourne patron before the war, and so 'we had a strange relationship, both of us ill at ease in our respective roles ... I was very unhappy in this job and Earl no doubt was very unhappy with me'. Bing was reassigned to Peter Jones, whose general manager was another of Spedan's maverick appointments, a retired admiral 'who knew as little about retail as I did'. As one of three division managers, Bing was in charge of Ladies' Hairdressing, which he enjoyed a lot because 'everyone was hysterical, and it reminded me of the theatre'. He also inaugurated a Books Department.

Spedan tried to pin Bing down by offering him a high salary in exchange for a binding long-term contract with JLP. 'Department stores were still definitely what I did not want to do with the rest of my life. I could not tell Mr Lewis that.' He struck a deal with Mr Lewis that if Glyndebourne were to start up again after the war, he would be released from the agreement, which Spedan honoured.

Bing was co-founder and first director of the Edinburgh International Festival in 1947, and in 1951 embarked on his twenty-two-year career as general manager of the Metropolitan Opera in New York. His story is one of many examples of people distin-guished in other fields who, at a strange juncture, worked for Spedan and the JLP. Spedan's own commitment to Glyndebourne was substantiated in 1950 by the Partnership's underwriting of the first full post-war season – his contribution, according to Sir Rudolf Bing, being 'up to twice as much as that of John Christie himself'.

★

After a bad bout of pneumonia in 1940, and after the bombing of John Lewis, Spedan, rising sixty, began to lose his panache and his appetite for business. He went even less often to the office, withdrawing from his earlier compulsive hands-on day-by-day involvement in the firm, while continuing to send out memos on policy and governance to the management. The Letters pages of the *Gazette*, and his own responses and contributions, were now his main way of keeping in touch. Rather few Partners actually knew him. He was slowing down. As he told Eleanor McElroy, his articles were taking six or eight hours of his time to write, 'and Heaven knows how much of Phyllis's and Muriel's'. Once a week he had 'a long, leisurely talk with the holders of the more important posts in the management'.

Spedan's confidential correspondence with Eleanor has survived from the war years onwards. She, in retirement, had been boarding, and helping out, at the Notre Dame convent and school in Clapham, south-west London, where she was happy. It closed in the war, and she found another perch in the less congenial Convent of the Holy Ghost in Basingstoke. When this too closed, she went as a paying guest to St Joseph's Convent in far-away Stafford. These moves were dispiriting. Spedan told her that Sally (Beatrice) said, 'there would be room for you here if you would care to make your home with us now'. (Eleanor was the only person to whom he referred to Beatrice by his private name for her, and Eleanor too called her Sally.) Eleanor deflected the offer gracefully.

Spedan paid for Eleanor's bits of furniture to be shifted from convent to convent, sending a car with Phyllis to settle her in. He ordered flowers, wine, eggs and fruit to be delivered to her regularly – much too much of everything of course, and she begged him to send less. He paid her an allowance or pension – tax-free, since it was presented to the Inland Revenue as a series of one-off money gifts.

Thanking him for being 'generosity itself', she added: 'Had you decided, on parting, that all was to be at an end, I should naturally have said Amen. But I am afraid I should have regretted more than ever giving up my Royal National Pension Fund for Nurses, for Peter Jones Ltd, in 1915 – a very sore point with me.' That suggests her ambivalence about her dependence on him and on his good-will. She meant that if, when he married, he had made a clean break with her, she would have been fine; but he had bound her to dependence on him way back in 1915 by persuading her to stop paying into her professional pension scheme because he would always look after her, and that this remained 'a very sore point' with her, although due to his generosity she was infinitely better off as a result.

Spedan dictated a letter to Eleanor once a week, as he presum-ably had for the past eighteen-odd years, unburdening himself of his anxieties, and she was, as ever, his health adviser. Beatrice thought he was a bit of a hypochondriac. He kept Eleanor apprised of his every ache and pain. She told him to try and get two hours' sleep before midnight each night, as being most beneficial, and to eat charcoal biscuits.

Jill and Edward (normally now called Ted) went to boarding prep schools in Winchester. Spedan was thinking rather more about the children, writing to the Robertsons just after the outbreak of war: 'Though I have never given them nearly as much time as I could have, I miss the children a good deal.' Both chil-dren were intelligent and in good health and spirits. Beatrice, as Spedan told Oswald, thought the trouble was that they had just 'too many attractive occupations open to them' compared to his own childhood, when 'moths were really the only source of colourful excitement'.

Jill, for her secondary schooling, went to Moira House in Eastbourne, a family-run boarding school for girls, its ethos modelled on that of King Arthur's Round Table. With the coming of the Blitz, the school relocated for safety to the Lake District, taking over a hotel in Windermere. Spedan told Eleanor in the summer of 1941 that 'Jill is undoubtedly getting stronger and growing fast'. He had given her a fox cub to look after and feed at school – Moira House was indeed progressive – 'and I am told that after some weeks she still does it'.

Spedan himself was not much good with animals, unless caged. He was a bit afraid of dogs. Winged creatures – birds, butterflies and moths – were his loves. His commitment to the Royal Zoological Society (RZS), of which he was a fellow and a member of the council, was of long standing. But this became less pleasurable to him. In 1935 Julian Huxley, who among his many distinctions was an evolutionary biologist, was appointed the secretary – which in effect meant the director – of the RZS, responsible for running the society, London Zoo and Whipsnade, the latter founded by his predecessor, zoologist Peter Chalmers Mitchell, with a guarantee against loss by Spedan. Chalmers Mitchell had been in post for thirty-two years. His predecessor held the post for forty.

Huxley was a prickly new broom. Among other innovations, he made London Zoo child-friendly for the first time and ended the practice of closing the zoo to the public on Sundays so that fellows and their guests might have privileged, private access. He antagonised most of the council, used to the conservative, uncontentious directorship of Chalmers Mitchell. In *Memories* (1970), he described the RZS Council as 'a curious assemblage ... of wealthy amateurs, self-perpetuating and autocratic'. It must be said that John Spedan Lewis, who in 1939 was elected a vice-president of the society, fitted this profile pretty well. In 1942 he was complaining to Eleanor about his disagreements with Huxley, and how he tried to resign but was persuaded by fellow traditionalists to stay on. There was so much faction-fighting in the council that he thought the zoo 'should be brought under public management, like the [British] Museum'. By this time, however, Huxley was on his way out anyway, ousted on a technicality.

A year after the fox cub experiment, Spedan was less optimistic about Jill: 'I am rather worried by what kind of mind and nature Jill is going to have … of Ted, I am beginning to think very well indeed.' He was thinking aloud about the succession, dynastically: 'If the Partnership wins his heart he may I think, make an excellent second Chairman and I have no serious fears that if I do not last long enough to give him a full chance to make up his mind, his mother will make an excellent job of that, and in the meanwhile hold the fort perfectly well.'

This was to Eleanor. For Eleanor's seventieth birthday in April 1942, he sent her a money present 'with a grateful affection that for thirty-two years has been growing stronger'.

14

DISAPPOINTMENTS

I n 1942 the cousins Peter and Ted, much of an age, were due to move on to their public schools. Ted went to Winchester College, a top school among the handful of ancient foundations which included their fathers' old school, Westminster.

Peter got into Eton, the top school of all, with a long waiting list, by means of Oswald's unabashed persistence – aided by the arcane fact that the wife of Peter's eventual housemaster, John Butterwick, was the sister-in-law of Viscount Davidson, Peter's ennobled godfather, a relationship of which both parties were until now barely aware. Nevertheless, as Oswald recorded, it 'oiled the wheels very much'. Peter's younger sister Diana inherited from Oswald a childhood tendency to asthma and bronchitis, and had changed prep schools half a dozen times. She went to a small, undemanding girls' school close to Gaddeshill.

Spedan, since his earliest days, claimed that Oswald had 'all the luck', and told Eleanor that Oswald had 'all the luck' yet again when it came to children: 'At fourteen, his boy is six feet tall' and 'extraordinarily good at cricket, and has brains'. Peter was head of the lower school at Eton and picked up a scholarship. As for Diana, 'as a small girl she was one of the most charming children I have ever seen'.

Ensconced at Leckford in the war years, Spedan observed his own children with a dispassionate objectivity more apposite for zoological specimens. 'Whatever Jill may lack in equipment for life in the wider world, she is tolerably provided with verbal memory.' Beatrice shared Jill's facility and the two of them would recite together whole tranches from Shakespeare's plays at mealtimes. Spedan read Greek with Jill while critically scrutinising her appearance – her facial features, the way she carried herself – and relayed his observations to Eleanor. He played chess with Ted, who was his house's chess champion at Winchester. Spedan himself played tournament chess by correspondence for the County Chess Association for Hampshire, of which he was president. 'Although Ted shambles and hangs his head as if he were pretending to be a scarecrow,' he seemed 'in excellent spirits', did well in his School Certificate (the equivalent of GCSE), and was 'monstrously easy on the eye'. He thought, much later, that if he had known that Winchester would 'provide so poorly for boys not good at moving-ball games', he would have sent him to Westminster, or to Gordonstoun in Scotland – 'I think he might have been far happier.'

In May 1944 Beatrice had 'some sort of heart attack', though probably some sort of panic attack. 'I had said goodnight to her at 11.45 but by luck went back at midnight to find her with palpitations and obviously rather badly frightened,' Spedan wrote. They woke Phyllis, who called in the district nurse. All was well, 'but it made for the fourth or fifth broken night'. He thought Beatrice's troubles were 'to a large extent nervous', like his mother's. If so it could have been for some of the same reasons, though he did not make the connection.

A contributing factor to Beatrice's nervous condition may have been her reading around this time Hester Chapman's *Long Division*, an ordeal she did not share with Spedan. As for him: 'My own heart is very apt to beat violently upon some kinds [unspecified] of excitement,' due to his 'highly geared nervous system'. He discussed Beatrice with Eleanor and with Donald Robertson as dispassionately as he did the children: Beatrice works very hard 'but her flow of nervous energy is not too good and she rather often shows signs that look like a tendency to crack'. She was good at 'dealing in a leisurely way with a limited number of really big things. She is not able to take trouble over trifles without letting them worry her excessively. They get under her skin in the way in which losing at a game has always been terribly apt to get under mine, making her terribly bad-tempered.'

Spedan was writing, or rather dictating, a book. He had been at it, off and on, since 1941. It was to be the story of the Partnership, and his manifesto. 'I thought it would be a quick, easy job,' he told Eleanor three years later, 'since in effect I have already written it many times over' – in his thousands of memos to management, in speeches, in articles in the columns of the *Gazette* and elsewhere. The difficulty was ordering the material. The book progressed by means of drafts, redrafts, revisions, insertions, and it all piled up. The secretaries had a hard time. 'Muriel asked me yesterday whether we were going to scrap several acres of paper, mostly typed up around midnight on Sundays,' he noted. 'When I said yes she replied, "My God". A nice child, but spineless.'

In September 1945, again to Eleanor: 'The finishing of this awful book that I have been struggling with these past four years is complete.' But it wasn't. Months later it was still being cut and edited. A whole two more years elapsed before he finally called in 'a journalist' (unnamed) to pull it together. In 1948 *Partnership for All* by John Spedan Lewis, 'Founder of the John Lewis Partnership, a thirty-four-year-old Experiment in Industrial Democracy', was published for the John Lewis Partnership by the Kerr–Cross Publishing Company.

Spedan expressed himself as satisfied with the scanty reviews, especially those in the *Economist* and in the weekly tabloid *Everybody's*, thus covering both the establishment and the popular market. He said that it sold 'about 2,000 copies', which probably meant it sold something over a thousand.

The book deserved, and deserves, better. It is in its way phenomenal. If Spedan Lewis had been born a century earlier, and if evangelical Christianity not industrial democracy had become his religion, he would have been one of those charismatic popular preachers, celebrities of their time, attracting huge crowds held transfixed by sermons which went on for several hours. The book is partly a compilation. Articles and letters written for the *Gazette*, and significant memos, are incorporated. It is personal, quite unlike any other 'business book', or the academic books on political economy – from his mother's Cambridge days, to the library at Spedan Tower. *Partnership for All* does not betray the pain and grief that went into its composition, powered as it was by his proselytising vigour.

If he had been more selective, if he had been able to desist from anatomising in minute detail the responsibilities of every committee and of his role as chairman, if he were not addicted to piled-up subordinate clauses and showers of Capital Letters ... but then it would not have been a book by John Spedan Lewis. The elaborate index, by the way, does not work, probably because it was compiled before a final revision changed the page-numbering.

Moving ever further down the path of delegation, Spedan was 'trying to develop an executive management as separate as possible from the controlling Board and the Chairmanship', i.e. let management manage. His intention now was to work on JLP business only four days a week, and only till lunchtime. No more micromanaging.

Democratisation was coming from below: the workforce, including management, well schooled in Spedan's theories, and feeling – to paraphrase *Animal Farm* – that while all Partners were equal, some Partners were more equal than others. From 1946, no less than five elected 'Rank and File' Partners sat on the Central Council.

As chairman, Spedan still came up with new ideas – for example to open a 'Medical and Surgical Department' in John Lewis. Eleanor, from her convent in Staffordshire, increasingly frail but sharp as a tack, advised against. Such an enterprise, she said, could never compete with John Bell & Croyden, the large, comprehensive and long-established pharmacy in nearby Wigmore Street; and Spedan duly desisted. Another project, post-war, when he and Beatrice were taking winter holidays in South Africa, was to open branches selling just fabrics, in Cape Town, Port Elizabeth and Johannesburg, under a single managing director. This did not work out well and the three shops were closed in 1954. JLP was a big, solid organisation with an impressive turnover, but actual profits did not allow for any bonuses for Partners until well after the war.

In 1944 Enid Rosser, JLP's legal adviser and Spedan's personal counsellor, married George Locket, a master at Harrow School, who met Spedan for the first time when the new couple were invited for a weekend at Leckford Abbas. The Lewises still changed into evening clothes for dinner during the war, even though there were only themselves and the secretaries at the table.

George Locket was impressed: 'Never had I met a human being with such vitality,' he wrote. 'I remember still seeing the set of his jaw, and the intense direct look, and his eyes. ... The atmosphere was heavily paternal and the conversation not general but directed from the chair, which is not to say that Mrs Lewis was anything other than the wonderful hostess she always was. Somehow the occasion was not gloomy and suppressed, in spite of the paternalism.' Later over brandy and a cigar: 'I lost my game of chess without dishonour, and he told me things about himself and his family which surprised and delighted me.' One can only wonder what those things were. Uniquely, so far as the record goes, Locket noted Spedan's 'impish sense of humour', and how 'gloriously wicked' he could be in conversation when in the mood.

Locket, an arachnologist, recognised Spedan as 'a naturalist of his time' – with an aesthetic appreciation, and a remarkable memory for identifying and naming obscure species, but not in any sense 'a scientific naturalist'. He confided to Locket that first evening how his bird collecting began: he had complained to Alfred Ezra of the Zoological Society of London, a wealthy breeder of exotic birds, that he had no time for bird-watching, and Ezra suggested he keep some in captivity. So he did, and he never did anything by halves.

That was many years ago. Now he was letting some of his exotic birds go. In 1945 he sold to London Zoo 'for a satisfactory price' the 'most delicate and expensive' – among them some tragopan pheasants, natives of the Far East and bred at Leckford. Other birds went to France, to Jean Delacour, a distinguished French collector connected with the Avicultural Society, whose precious birds were casualties of the war. Spedan contributed to a new collection, providing Delacour with a pair of black swans, some rare geese, South African sheldrakes and red-crested pochards.

Spedan made one new and impetuous foray into collecting, not birds but apes. He borrowed a bunch of gibbons from London Zoo with the idea of 'homing' them down by the river at Leckford. Gibbons have loud voices and their songs, usually duets, can carry for over half a mile. He received complaints about the sound and sight of the gibbons from the lady living at Longstock Park on the other side of the river – only what you could expect, she told him, from 'a jumped-up draper'.

Revenge is sweet? In June 1945 he told Eleanor that 'the big house across the valley from here, Longstock Park, is coming on the market. I hope to buy it and move.'

★

In February that year, Oswald addressed a question in the House of Commons to the President of the Board of Trade, Hugh Dalton, about 'Children's Rubber Footwear' (there was a shortage of Wellington boots). In June he attended a debate for what he knew might be the last time.

When the war in Europe came to an end in spring 1945, the general election in July resulted in an overwhelming Labour majority. Oswald to his diary: 'I have lost my seat by 246 (my majority last time was 578) … I did not bargain for the enormous swing to the Left all over the country. The Labour Party have swept all before them.'

It was a bad blow for Oswald. He lost his foothold in public life and politics, and all the contacts and ceremonial occasions that he so much valued. He bore the loss stoically. His constituency agent strongly advised him not to think of standing again. 'It would be unpopular with the rank and file,' he noted. 'Apparently there is widespread resentment at my having visited the division so seldom during the war and a general idea that a younger candidate would stand a better chance of regaining the

seat.' He was fifty-eight. His further prospects for public service
and a platform were remote.

Although by normal standards he was still a wealthy man, he
had no outside sources of income. He had never made economies.
His capital base was continually eroded, his dividends went down
and only taxation was up. He sold the gold watch and chain that
his father had given him for his twenty-first birthday, for just the
value of the gold. He and Coopie decided to sell Beechwood and
live more cheaply in the country, only to discover that the kind of
house they envisaged, specifically Ovington Park not far from
Leckford, described by Spedan as coming with '40 acres, a farm
and 18 cottages', cost more than Beechwood was currently worth.
After much havering, they stayed where they were.

Oswald put together a second book from his travel diaries and
photographs, mostly about big-game hunting, and called it *I'd
Like To Go Again*. This time he was less lucky with a publisher and
had to carry the costs himself. He had a few more shots at becoming Lord Lewis, even offering to take the new government's whip
if they would give him a peerage. He canvassed William Wakeley,
who was Labour's chief whip, with the supporting offer to set up
a housing fund. 'W.W. made no comment on the question of a
peerage but seems friendlily disposed towards my proposal', which
came to nothing. Even with the best will in the world, there was
no earthly reason why Oswald Lewis, one conscientious former
Tory backbencher among many, should be elevated to the peerage.

Spedan had his own disappointments. Some valued Partners, to
his chagrin, never came back to the company, or left, after the
war. One such was the mathematician Hugh O'Donel Alexander,
whom Spedan had recruited back in 1938 as Head of Research.
During the war Alexander had served as a cryptanalyst at Bletchley
Park, the secret and now legendary intellectual hothouse which

broke the German Enigma code. Afterwards he joined GCHQ –
Government Communications Headquarters, the epicentre of
intelligence and security services – and remained in post until his
retirement.

JLP's chief accountant, Tom Robinson, left the Partnership
after the war on grounds of ill-health; as did Sebastian Earl,
exhausted to near breakdown by his wartime workload as Director
of Expansion, responsible for the development and control of the
swollen portfolio of branches. Spedan could not but accept his
resignation, but was outraged when, after a barely decent interval,
Earl took on a top job at the newly constituted Selfridges. 'Moving
on' is normal in professional lives. But where his main men were
concerned, Spedan saw moving on from the Partnership as a dere-
liction.

Another disappointment concerned the Partnership College, a
project dear to Spedan and especially to Beatrice. It was set up
early in the war, finding a home in a capacious house, Dial Close,
to the west of Cookham. The library was largely stocked by the
overflow from Leckford Abbas. The idea was to provide further
education for Partners who had left school early and wished to
continue learning and improve their minds and their prospects.
There were two residential courses a year of six weeks each, for up
to twenty Partners, with resident tutors. The curriculum favoured
the humanities. In the afternoons there were outdoor sports and
games and sailing, and boxing for the men. Some evenings,
outside speakers from the world of books came in to give talks and
readings. The students paid a nominal sum for bed, board and
tuition, and had their travel paid. The warden was R.L. (Reggie)
James, formerly a lecturer at Bristol University, aided by his wife
Charity.

An early student, Joyce Smith, left an account of a visit to the
college by Spedan and Beatrice. Spedan was becoming a mythical

figure, known only through old-timers' colourful anecdotes: 'We were all trembling in our shoes until Reggie James said to Spedan: "The students have requested that you tell them how you founded the Partnership."' Spedan proceeded to talk non-stop for at least an hour. 'Mrs Lewis dropped off.' Afterwards Spedan 'was smiling as he shook my hand!'

For Joyce Smith, it was like meeting royalty. It was a not unusual reaction. When Spedan and Beatrice rolled up in the Rolls to have lunch in Berkhamsted with Paul May (then financial adviser) and his family, he seemed 'an awesome figure' to the teenage Stephen May, who later made his own successful career in the Partnership. Spedan was wearing spats – short cloth gaiters to protect shoes and socks from mud – which the boy had never seen before. Hardly surprising, since they had been out of fashion since the 1920s.

The Partnership was paying for the college. In 1948 Reggie James sent in his resignation to JLP's Education Committee, the responsible body. Because of the cost, it was decided to close the college temporarily. It never reopened. It was a fine idea, but a bad time for such a venture, and maybe the JLP management was never fully behind it.

In the post-war period, Spedan thought that the Labour government was 'on the whole the best thing for the country'. On the title page of *Partnership for All* is a quotation from Churchill: 'England is moving towards a classless society.' Yes and no. But just for a start, girls and women who during the war had worked in munitions factories, on the land, or with the armed forces, were no longer interested in domestic service. Beatrice had 'very bad luck' with cooks, and at Beechwood, Coopie moved into the kitchen herself, a fact recorded by Oswald with admiration.

Building restrictions, shortages and rationing continued into the 1950s and male conscription, in the form of two years'

National Service, did not come to an end either. Ted and Peter when they left school did their National Service with the army – Peter commissioned into the Coldstream Guards as a Second Lieutenant. Ted, remaining in the ranks, went to Egypt with the Middle East Land Forces. 'Two people could hardly be more different in general make-up,' Spedan wrote about Ted and himself at this time, 'but we get on very well and I think always shall.' In other moods he revealed his doubts, agonising over Ted's 'slowness' and lack of drive, though he had 'a good brain' and 'could be one of the most important people in the country'.

Poor Ted – and poor Jill. In 1946 she was accepted by Somerville, her mother's old Oxford college, to read Greats (Classics). Whatever Spedan had implied by her 'lack of equip-ment for the wider world', he was right. She failed 'Mods', the first-year exams. Beatrice wrote to their former nanny, Lucy Worrall, who remained in her confidence, that Jill had 'had some kind of breakdown' (as had her grandmother Ellie, at Cambridge). 'She is quite confident that she wrote all the time but the invigi-lator says that she scarcely wrote anything at all,' though the little that she did write was 'of the expected quality'.

Beatrice went to see the principal of Somerville, Janet Vaughan: 'They think the strain is too great for her and she should give it up.' Jill started working at John Barnes, the big department store on Finchley Road, one of the Selfridges group acquired by JLP in 1940. Spedan and Beatrice took a flat in St John's Court, above John Barnes, to stay in when they were in London, and another in the same block for Jill. But she did not settle at John Barnes, nor anywhere.

Spedan did buy Longstock Park, and moved his household across the river in autumn 1945. The basic house itself was very old and had been altered and enlarged in the nineteenth century.

It was more attractive than Leckford Abbas, with more and better proportioned rooms. Beatrice liked it.

Spedan sold Leckford to the Partnership, and lent back the money straight away to refund what he had apparently borrowed from the firm to buy it. The arrangements were typical of the byzantine way in which Spedan, always legally, shuffled his personal money and JLP's. The Partnership bought Longstock for £45,000, and leased it to Spedan, with the Partnership paying for maintenance; a special committee was formed, to which Spedan and Beatrice submitted estimates of expenses for each coming year. Longstock was integrated into Leckford Estate Ltd, creating a 4,000-acre holding. The estate had its own council, and everyone working there, in whatever capacity, was a Partner. It already had its own monthly *Leckford Gazette*, produced by Muriel Elliot.

Bernard Miller and his young family stayed at Leckford Abbas for the last Christmas in that house. There were, according to the Millers' son Peter, bell-ringers in the hall and, as every year, the now aged Ethel Chawton, the bird lady, was invited up for the day. The three Miller children saw little of their hosts, who were 'moving on different rails'. In 1946, for the first Christmas at Longstock, Oswald and his family came. Peter recalled how unlike it all was to their own easy-going Christmases. At Longstock, no one might open any presents until after tea, and then only after two general knowledge questions had been answered correctly. Some years later, again at Longstock, in the hall, Muriel said to Peter: 'I wish we could import some of your family's happiness here.'

Nineteen fifty was another pivotal year. In June, Anthony Devas came to Longstock and painted a powerful portrait of Spedan at sixty-five: crisp white hair receding from a domed forehead; large, compelling dark eyes challenging those of the viewer; a powerful cleft chin. Spedan always cared about how he looked. When

Donald Robertson, 'the great friend of my boyhood', came to stay that summer, he, Donald, 'gave the impression of being quite a lot older than I suppose myself to be'.

In July Ted 'came of age', on becoming twenty-one. Spedan had inscribed a copy of *Partnership for All* to 'my son, and I hope my successor'. Beatrice outlined to Oswald the programme of celebration parties – 'one for the Partnership, one at Longstock, and the dinner party' – this sequence merging with parties for the first post-war opera season at Glyndebourne, underwritten by Spedan.

Ted was the Crown Prince. But no announcement was made about the succession. Spedan wrote to Oswald in October: 'Strictly between ourselves I'm considering very carefully whether I ought to give Ted the refusal of the chairmanship.' The loss of John, he wrote, had been 'a tremendous stroke of bad luck'. Young though he was when he died, 'there was not the slightest doubt he would have been a first rate choice'. He believed that because he needed to believe it. Enid Locket, in her unpublished memoir, wrote that Jill and Ted felt they could never live up to the 'cherished memory' of John.

Everyone liked Ted. He was good-natured and good-humoured, and in his first year at Oxford, reading law without much enthusiasm. He was vague, short-sighted, and still a bit deaf. He had grown up knowing his father's great expectations for him and lived under that gilded burden. He was a loner, and eccentric, not quite like other people. He was high-achieving autistic, not that such a diagnosis was ever thought of, until he made it for himself many years later. With his friends he could be high-spirited and very funny, 'someone who made you laugh', said Bernard Miller's son Peter, who remembered swimming with a teenaged Ted below the weir at Odney, both of them laughing all the time; as again, some years later, laughing while Ted drove them back to the flat above John Barnes in his open-topped sports car after some evening escapade.

Spedan, having decided that his son was not after all capable of being his successor, called him in for a formal talk. Enid Locket was present. She told Peter Lewis long afterwards how unbearable the interview was 'to listen to and to watch'. Spedan 'ensnared' Ted into thinking that he had a choice. (That may have seemed the kindest thing to do?) He lectured Ted about the importance of 'proper modesty', and the heavy duties and responsibilities of chairing the Partnership; and told him to go away and sleep on it. In the morning Ted 'put his father out of his misery'. Ted's feelings were his own, and unfathomable.

But if not Ted, then whom? Spedan had already decided. It must of course be Michael Watkins, Sir Metford – even though his adviser Enid Locket was not keen on him because he had 'a strong dislike' for working with women, which he made no effort to hide, and the majority of shop-floor Partners were women. The women buyers, 'a tough breed, fought him mercilessly and generally mistrusted him, not without reason'.

Yet of all his main men, Watkins was the one whom Spedan most liked, trusted, respected – and used. Watkins had been worked to the bone. He said (not to Spedan) that he had been squeezed like a sucked orange. He told Spedan he was just not up to it. He was ill. He had been working part-time for quite a while. He was in fact dying, and died very shortly afterwards, aged fifty.

Beatrice as always dealt with worry and stress by going away. She went abroad, and also attended courses run by the British Drama League, founded to support amateur and professional theatre; she was still directing plays and the Revue for the Partnership. She went more than once to the College of Education housed in Alnwick Castle in Northumberland, a post-war teacher-training establishment for women. In another life, she might have made a career in women's education, in theatre, or in drama teaching.

When Beatrice was away, Spedan dictated a letter to her every night. One long letter from August 1950 was particularly depressed and introspective. His gradual withdrawal from everyday involvement in JLP, which he called 'my experimental demise', was proving a disappointment. He saw mistakes being made everywhere. He rehearsed for the hundredth time his litany of 'bad luck', starting with the loss of Grove Farm, and 'every day I feel more and more calamitous our loss of J'. He felt, too, 'the weight that has fallen back on me with [the loss of] Tom Robinson, Seb [Earl] and Michael'. Tom Robinson, however, was another of whom Enid Locket had a low opinion. To her, he was 'a feeble ineffectual person who would desert any principles if it suited him'. As for Seb Earl, she had worked with him on the First Constitution, with difficulty, 'because he had no idea of time and a mind I could not fathom, and [was] physically so large as to be repellent'.

The people in the Partnership whom Spedan most liked and valued were the precise ones whom, in her memoir, Enid criticised and debunked. Devoted to Spedan and fiercely protective of her position as his confidante and best friend, it is as if she resented any other power behind the throne. She acknowledged that Spedan liked Seb, but recounted how, during the constitution drafting, 'Spedan goaded beyond endurance shook Seb violently by the shoulders and shouted, "Seb you'll drive me dotty and you are nothing but ivory from the neck up".' Before Seb could retaliate Beatrice came into the room and told them all to go home.

How often did Beatrice have to rescue Spedan from the excesses of his bad tempers? In the same long letter he told her how he made mistakes because of 'lack of poise' caused by overstrain. He had been 'sceptical' when Michael said he was not up to succeeding him; he had spoken 'too energetically' to Oswald, which probably means he shouted. He had maybe spoken 'too energetically' to Michael too. 'If my head were not so tired I would not have such difficulty in keeping letters short.'

He destroyed Beatrice's replies, but she certainly did not answer at the same length nor in the same vein. He referred to the 'cheerful chirruping' of her letters to him.

As a result of these crises, Oswald, at a loose end and glad of a bit of money, came back into the firm, as Director of Financial Operations, at the end of 1950. It was, Spedan told Eleanor, 'a part-time job that he reckons to be equal to a day a week. It is part of what Sir Metford did.' While Spedan's interests lay increasingly elsewhere – landscaping and planting at Longstock on a grand scale – Oswald was back in the family 'biz'. Who would have thought it?

15

BEATRICE

I n early 1950 – before the crunch with Ted and the death of Watkins – Spedan had laid out the ground for the terms of the succession, his own retirement, and the disposition of assets to the Partnership. This 'Second Constitution and Trust Settlement' took a lot of working out with accountants and lawyers, chief among them Enid Locket, and with his senior management colleagues.

Under the first settlement in 1929 Spedan had diverted his income into a trust, to be distributed as profit-sharing among the employees. He retained his controlling shares in the company, leaving them to Beatrice in his will. Now, under the second settlement he gave away those shares too, into a new trust company to be chaired by whoever was the chairman of JLP. The transfer was designed to be irrevocable. Spedan could not change his mind and

reclaim the shares, nor could he wind up his experiment in industrial democracy. The trust settlement guaranteed the continuance,
security and ethos of the Partnership, for the benefit of all
the Partners as owner-employees. It put an end to any further
financial gain for Spedan or any of his family. According to
Enid Locket, Jill and Ted had received 'large settlements' on their
twenty-first birthdays, but there was to be no more.

Spedan signed the documents at Longstock in the presence of
Enid Locket, the other lawyers, and his senior colleagues. It is said
that he murmured, after signing: 'It's funny that none of you ever
advised me not to do this.' A good point. But it was what he
wanted to do. His legacy was to be the Partnership he had created
– a final moral riposte to his father, for whom amassing and safe-
guarding a family fortune was the whole aim of being in business.
The paradox remains that, had it not been for the family fortune,
the Partnership would never have got off the ground, nor survived
the years of little or no profits, nor have expanded as it had.
Spedan was to have no pension, but would still receive regular,
tax-free instalments of the £1 million previously negotiated.

Future chairmen, according to this settlement, would have to
retire by the age of seventy-five, with the right to choose their
successor. Spedan himself undertook to go in 1955, at seventy,
with the provision that he could appoint his son to succeed him if
he wished. The 'choice' he presented to Ted, three months later,
was unrealistic. Ted, even if he had been willing and able, could
not have been ready or able to take on the chairmanship within
such a short period. He would leave Oxford, aged twenty-three,
in 1952, and even if he spent the next three years learning the
business from the bottom up, the idea was a non-starter.

It would have made some sense to build in a plan by which Ted
joined the firm on leaving Oxford as a management trainee, leaving the door open, if it all worked out, for his taking over at some

later date. It seems not to have been mooted, then. But when in 1955 Ted got a job 'as the most junior kind of audit clerk with a respectable firm of accountants', as Spedan put it to Oswald, he was still voicing the hope that Ted might come round to the idea of joining JLP. Ted took some accountancy exams, but never qualified.

Subliminally, Spedan surely knew for some time that his dream of father-to-son continuity could not come true. It was his son who suffered the most – a sense of failure, and of 'soreness and sadness', according to his friend David Culverwell. Ted never broke with his father. (Nor did Jill, though she drifted away.) Home was home. When, on vacation from Oxford in 1951, Ted seemed unwell, probably depressed – Spedan called it 'listlessness' – he was sent to a slew of doctors. Spedan gave him Charity Farm House on the edge of Longstock village. Ted liked it, though later sold it to the Partnership.

In 1950 Bernard 'Sunny' Miller was officially named as Spedan's successor as chairman of JLP and of the John Lewis Partnership Trust Ltd. He was appointed deputy chairman the following year, the office previously held by Beatrice. Everyone called him Sunny, apparently his nickname since boyhood, when he was thought to look like Sunny Jim, the cartoon character on packets of Force Wheat Flakes, with a toothy smile and a receding chin. Enid Locket had a different explanation. The nickname, she believed, arose because he never smiled at all. She found Miller 'completely without charm', with 'no idea of relaxing friendliness'. It's possible that some of Spedan's main men found Enid as difficult as she did them.

Miller was not 'the last man standing', though the phrase has been used. He was a cornerstone. He had been with the firm since he arrived in 1927 as one of Spedan's earliest 'graduate learners', responding to the theory and practice of Partnership:

when reading nineteenth-century history at Oxford he said later, in interview, 'I was very taken with the Owenite experiment and trade union relations … it was something that clicked into place.' Even the caustic Enid acknowledged that he was 'steeped in the Partnership and one of the few people who grasped its intellectual principles', and came to respect his work ethic and, subsequently, his chairmanship.

Miller knew the business backwards and from the bottom upwards, having been in his time PA to both Spedan and Michael Watkins. ('Of course,' said Miller, 'Michael himself was outstanding. There was nobody like him in the Partnership.') Miller subsequently held many of what, in a national government, would be called the great offices of state, sometimes simultaneously. He had seen the company through the war as financial adviser and General Inspector – the latter's function being 'to shine light into dark corners', according to Paul May's son Stephen, who himself held the post in later years.

Miller had performed in the Partnership Revues, was a natural at all sports and games – almost enough in its own to endear him to Spedan – and he was a great skier. He and his wife Jessica, who was also a Partner, joined the Lewises both on family skiing holidays and on group Partnership trips: Spedan was 'a very keen skier but he wasn't any good and would get exasperated'. Miller played billiards and pool with Spedan, and chess, at which they were well matched. Since Spedan hated to lose, sometimes Miller let him win, 'when he had been working hard and was getting a bit uptight'.

So Sunny Miller knew his man. Weekly policy meetings at Longstock continued, as Spedan was still chairman and absolutely required to be informed and consulted over major innovations – and there were indeed innovations. In 1951 Waitrose in Southend was the first branch to become self-service, putting an end to personal counter service, now seen as old-fashioned. The abandonment of the slogan and practice of 'Never Knowingly Undersold' was discussed, and firmly rejected. The Partnership bought two textile manufacturing firms to produce fabrics and designs unique to JLP. Miller was in charge, putting the house in order, and imposing a pay cut in 1952. The following year, Partners' bonuses were paid for the first time since before the war.

It was at Spedan's suggestion that Oswald became even further entrenched in the business, filling a vacancy caused by the death of Watkins as President of the Central Council. In the earliest days when Spedan still chaired the council, he used to open the proceedings by leading the group in a rendition of 'Jerusalem'. The council had now become a large, intractable body. Oswald's son described the president's role as 'Speaker-like', which of course suited Oswald with his parliamentary experience down to the ground; whereas what suited Spedan, literally down to the ground, was the creation of the Water Gardens at Longstock over four acres of the Test Valley. This became his overwhelming preoccupation.

Spedan's ambitious concept was for small lakes with interconnected islands, intersecting waterways and little wooden bridges winding through woodland and massed plantings of flowering shrubs and water plants, incorporating the river itself. The plans, and the revised plans, were pinned up all over the house. New channels were pegged out and dug. The one existing lake, made long ago, was silted up and its surroundings degraded.

Young Jim Saunders was among the first to turn a spade there. He remained for the next twenty years and recorded those early days in the *Gazette* in 1964. The work of digging out, clearing, landscaping and the planting of hundreds of trees was all done with wheelbarrows, pickaxes, spades and shovels, the ground being too boggy to admit mechanical diggers – so, as Jim Saunders made clear, it was very, very labour-intensive, and remained so as the gardens were developed. Spedan told George Locket that a million snowdrops were planted in the woods. Perhaps an exaggeration. But even half a million snowdrops do not plant themselves.

Sweet-natured Terry Jones, in charge of breeding the waterfowl at Longstock, never fell out with Spedan. He remembered estate workers and local people referring to Spedan as 'Father', in a maybe ironic but he thought affectionate way. Maurice Jones, with a degree in agriculture from Cambridge and a distinguished war record, who came in 1945 as general manager and then managing director of the Leckford Estate, saw that his boss was 'brilliant' but did not find him loveable and was critical of his methods. This finds a reflection in a vignette from Maurice – on the river bank, with Ted and 'one of the secretaries', and Spedan talking to Ted about the breeding habits of some water fly. When Ted said he hadn't known that, Spedan turned to the secretary and told her to look out the file of his 'Talks to Children' to check that Ted had been told before (so should have remembered). From anyone else, this would have been a joke. Perhaps Ted took it as such.

Spedan's concern for education, like Beatrice's, was genuine enough, even though sometimes lost in translation. They responded to an appeal for investors in a coeducational boarding school, Stanbridge Earls, which Anthony and Molly Thomas were starting up not far from the Leckford Estate. It developed into a special needs school for children with conditions such as dyslexia and mild Asperger syndrome (and was closed, after the Thomases' time, following a flurry of scandals in 2014). Beatrice invested £200 in debenture stock, which in 1952 paid her a dividend. What was concealed from Mr and Mrs Lewis was that Mr and Mrs Thomas were the son-in-law and daughter of a lady who was at open war with the Partnership.

The conflict came about when, in the early 1950s, the bombed-out West House – the original John Lewis store on Oxford Street – was at last to be rebuilt, incorporating the newer and unharmed section at the back and the shops on Old Cavendish Street to the west, which necessitated the Partnership's acquisition of all their freeholds. Just one shop in Old Cavendish Street refused to sell. Blumer & Bourne was a flourishing manufacturing and wholesale haberdashery business, owned by two intrepid entrepreneurial women – Mrs Barbara Bourne, Molly Thomas's mother, and Mrs Bourne's old schoolfriend Miss Elsie Blumer. Mrs Bourne died in 1952. Elsie Blumer hung on for another year or so, finally selling out and exacting a hefty sum from the Partnership. By that time construction was well under way, with a section of the new store designed to fit tightly around her shop. 'To this day,' says Mrs Bourne's grandson, Richard Thomas, 'there is a kind of cave in the Old Cavendish Street end of the store manufactured by a clever architect, functioning as the goods entrance.'

★

Spedan was envious of Oswald's offspring as compared with his own. Oswald, as he wrote in early 1952 to Donald Robertson, the Cambridge professor, was 'full of sinful pride because, out of 240 contenders, his boy was one of only two to be placed in the first class in a Bar examination on Roman law'. Spedan bemoaned his own children's 'lack of intellectual interests'. They were both 'neurasthenic'. What they both liked best was 'solitary motoring', and they were both 'capable of really serious silliness'. He was still writing to Donald as frequently and as freely as he did to Eleanor, and begging him to write back every week: 'As you may remember, as I once told you before, "I did ever love thee".'

As for Beatrice, 'her housekeeping and so on are extremely efficient but she is a worrier and makes heavy weather of things'.

Spedan was still sending off for about six new books every week and Beatrice, 'a born librarian, groans under the burden placing and categorising them'. She hated getting older, feeling that the war years had robbed her of the fun she would have had 'in travel and private theatricals, in which she delighted exceedingly'. His own life, 'with my temperament and opportunities might have been fantastically happy', had it not been for his 'bad luck' culminating in the 'calamity' of the loss of Watkins. 'In between times, Beatrice and I are very happy.' Examples of the couple's private playfulness are rare. Here is one from December 1952: 'I have long reckoned that in the next world Beatrice will be a Celery Fly and I an Asparagus Beetle.'

★

Beatrice was suffering from pain in her legs in autumn 1952. It was thought to be rheumatism. They went away as usual in the winter to South Africa, and she was well enough on their return to act in a Partnership play. But when she was with Jill in Brighton in the early spring the pain returned, this time in her back. Further investigation was thought necessary. The Westminster Hospital lost her X-rays and test results. Spedan wrote to his MP and to the Minister of Health to complain, and Beatrice went into the Middlesex Hospital for a second lot. He was taking bromides twice a day for the anxiety, he told Eleanor.

Lung cancer was found and had already spread to her bones. Spedan wrote to Oswald on 3 April 1953 that there was talk of alternative treatments, but 'I am very much afraid that it would be little more than a way of avoiding admitting that nothing can be done.' She was in and out of hospital, and then came home.

Beatrice had always been a heavy smoker, with a deep, fruity smoker's voice. During the three days when John was ill at school she had thrown away her cigarettes and sworn that if he recovered she would never smoke again. But he did not recover. She was sixty years old, somewhat overweight, and hitherto healthy enough. Spedan's health had always been the topic, not hers.

Spedan went to ground at Longstock and communicated with almost no one. He read aloud to Beatrice during her spells in hospital, and he wrote to her, mainly about the new book he was writing about Partnership. His aspirations for it were sky-high, and not altogether to be mocked, in spite of the twitch of self-mockery which she would have understood better than anyone. He saw the book, he told her, as a set of essays, 'to include the Nature of Things and the human mind's workings'; it could be 'the Scriptures of more advanced religions'.

He wrote to her too about Jill, with him at Longstock. 'Her mind is not quite as lively as my own but she has plenty of will-power.' He and she had hot arguments: 'Yesterday alone might well have loaded her nerves beyond the point at which it is easy to keep a really good poise' ('poise' is the word they used for 'self-control'). In the very next sentence he is recalling how 'the tremendous stress of living with my father' had taught him 'to use my nervous energy to the last drop'. Maybe he did not himself know whether he was identifying with Jill, or with his father.

It was Ted who, on 27 June 1953, wrote to Oswald and Coopie, who was his godmother: 'Jill and I hope that our affliction will not prove to be a portent, for our Mother has now very few hours to breathe, and the doctors say they can prevent her ever recovering consciousness. I feel sure that she would join me in wishing you better fortune than has been hers, till the end of your days.' This is enigmatic and possibly refers to his Uncle Oswald's pipe-smoking.

Beatrice died at 6.50 a.m. the next morning. It was a Sunday. Oswald and Coopie received the news as they were preparing to welcome guests to a lunch party celebrating their twenty-fifth wedding anniversary.

Oswald went to the cremation. Spedan did not go, nor did Jill. Ted was there and, Oswald recorded, 'bore himself like a man'. At Longstock afterwards, Oswald did not see Spedan at all; he spent the day down in the Water Gardens. 'I understand he is quite broken down by the strain of Beatrice's illness. Jill is a poor thing at the best of times and has taken to her bed.'

At her own request, Beatrice's ashes were scattered at sea in the English Channel. Geoffrey Snagge, commodore of the Partnership's Sailing Club, hired a luxury yacht and a skipper and accompanied Spedan. Unfortunately the weather was dangerously rough. Spedan, a very bad sailor, became distressed and 'it was a pretty hairy experience for him. ... However, he went out [on deck] and dropped the ashes overboard and we came home. The old boy behaved magnificently on that occasion.'

Spedan commissioned a memorial to Beatrice from the sculptor G.N. Norwood, who had carved the stone covering their son John's grave. The upright slab was set up in a railed enclosure across the road from Longstock churchyard, with the inscription: 'I like, she said, little pleasures.' A strange choice of words, seemingly not a quotation, and for Spedan, if not everyone else, expressing the essence of her.

In her will, as well as funds for the Grosvenor Award at New College, Beatrice left money to Somerville College for a John Hunter Lewis Fund, 'commemorating her son who died in childhood, to contribute to the stipend of a Tutorial Fellow in English Literature to be known as the Beatrice Lewis Fellowship'. The fund still exists, used for its original purpose, though Beatrice's name has fallen away. Some years later Spedan responded to an appeal from Somerville for funds to build a graduate centre, with the request that a room be dedicated to Beatrice Lewis, a request that seems not to have been honoured.

One of Spedan's secretaries, Constance Lynne, had been working for Michael Watkins and then Sunny Miller. After Beatrice died she returned to Spedan at Longstock, combining running the house with secretarial work. Phyllis stayed on for a few more years, and Muriel was there for the long haul. The cooking was done by Kate Bonnett, who as a young girl had come to the Lewises as a parlourmaid when they were first married, trained by Eleanor McElroy. There was still a butler. The gong was still banged every evening for dinner at 7.45.

Spedan managed to finish his second book, *Fairer Shares*. The subtitle says it all: 'A possible advance in civilisation and perhaps the only alternative to Communism.' It is a book for the post-war world. The greater speed with which this work was produced suggests that it incorporates surplus matter edited out of *Partnership for All*, but the tone is different. The first book was personal and passionate, with a strong autobiographical quotient and animus against his father showing through, and represented the Partnership as an ongoing experiment in industrial democracy. In *Fairer Shares* Spedan set 'producer-cooperation', his new term, in its historical context – no longer as an experiment but as a pragmatic socio-economic programme, showcasing the Partnership's management strategies, employee representation and corporate structures. 'The Nature of Things and the human mind's workings' may be inferred.

On the dedication page there are four names: 'To My Father', 'To My Mother', then 'To Metford Watkins', with a brief CV, and the statement that when Watkins was dying 'he said that he could not have made of his life a use that would have given him more peace of mind'. Lastly, 'And To My Wife', without any expression of personal loss, but saying that, had he died before her, the controlling interest would have passed to her, and 'I felt quite sure that in her hands the Partnership would be safe'. Her death was 'a 'grievous loss' to the Partnership, 'not least in the difference that she would have made to this book'.

He was certainly right there. He reproduced verbatim in *Fairer Shares* not only a serious, drily critical anonymous review of *Partnership for All*, but his own even longer refutation of the review, written at the time for the letters pages of the paper (which he does not name). His letter was not published. He also reproduced an editor's standard reply to writers of unpublishable letters, saying that his own would be passed on to the reviewer, 'and should he desire to take up your points I am sure he will be in touch with you'. The reviewer did not contact Spedan, who expressed in *Fairer Shares* his 'disappointment' with those who had 'selfish motives for opposing change in the general state of affairs that gives us our unhealthy world of millionaires and slums' – thus reclaiming the moral high ground. Yet one of the reviewer's main pull-backs had been Spedan's 'appalling ignorance' of the principles of trade unionism and its importance to 'lower deck' workers. Spedan always tied himself in knots arguing against trade unions. All he could do in his now-published unpublished letter was to assert that for 'a good many of "lower deck" Partners, the Partnership was a matter of passionate devotion'.

It is indeed most likely that Beatrice would have rescued him from this gratuitous misjudgement, as from the many that were to come.

Fairer Shares was published by Staples Press in 1954, not 'for the John Lewis Partnership', as *Partnership for All* had been, so he probably paid for it himself.

★

The big family event that same year was the marriage of Oswald's daughter, Diana. She had studied medicine at Newnham College, Cambridge, with the intention – unrealised – of becoming a doctor. She was a pretty and popular young woman with a great many admirers.

The family were not thrilled by her choice of husband, Simon Young. On the face of it, he was eminently suitable – the son of a distinguished military man, he had been educated at Eton and Cambridge, where he and Diana met; he was a director of the prestigious publishing firm of John Murray, who had been Lord Byron's publisher.

Diana's brother Peter would later marry the daughter of another well-known publisher. When asked about the problematic Simon Young more than sixty years later, Peter paused, and finally said: 'He was … *artistic.*' This seemed to mean that he was not all that interested in cricket or tennis or fishing or shooting. Sports and games were so central to the Lewises' ideas of the good life and of themselves that this lack made Simon seem almost an outsider.

But they made the best of it, and also the most of it. On 1 May Diana had a white wedding at St Margaret's, Westminster, then still the parish church of the House of Commons and so available to the father of the bride as a former Member. There followed a reception for 320 people at Beechwood.

The house and gardens, a couple of years before, had been the subject of a gratifying four-page spread in *Country Life*, after which Oswald opened the gardens to the public for charity once a year.

Spedan talked and wrote about his gardening projects, and the gardens at Longstock became renowned. The grounds and garden at Beechwood were, in Oswald's prime, extraordinary in a different way. Bounded to the south-west by uninterrupted views of Hampstead Heath, the terrain was wildly varied, with steep slopes and declivities; in a boggy bottom Oswald had a stream dug out, with pools and waterfalls. There were great stands of mature trees and space for a squash court, a hard tennis court, and secluded staff dwellings, greenhouses (vines, peaches, melons), garages, vegetable gardens and chicken runs. There was the old ice house, and the air-raid shelter that Oswald built in the war was furnished with sofas and equipped with all modern conveniences.

The swimming pool where Oswald swam lengths, competing against himself, was said to be one of the largest private pools in the country, set in solidly elegant stonework and shielded by plantings. There was 'a palace of a dovecote' at the edge of the main lawn. He was himself no gardener – never even dead-heading a rose according to his son – and employed four or five gardeners. Indoor staff and part-timers included, at Beechwood's peak there were fourteen people on the payroll.

This was traditional garden-making in the grand style of the Edwardians, to whom Oswald temperamentally belonged. One year at the Chelsea Flower Show he bought up the entire exhibit of azaleas from the winner of the Gold Medal and created a mass display back home. In the 1930s, the rose-growers Cants of Colchester, in his constituency, bred for him the rose 'Mrs Oswald Lewis' – canary yellow with flame-coloured tips to the petals – a vigorous grower with an intense fragrance, according to the official description. It was planted plentifully in the rose garden and around the swimming pool. 'Mrs Oswald Lewis' did not, however, live up to her description or thrive in the soil of Beechwood and was always unimpressively pallid.

For Peter and Diana, to whom Beechwood was home from infancy to adulthood, it was an inexhaustible paradise. Their father had moved out of Spedan Tower as soon as he could. Peter as a young adult and a barrister found no reason to leave home, though he made a few unsuccessful experiments in setting up on his own. His parents felt the same, and were disappointed and baffled when he finally did move out, by which time he was nearly thirty.

16

END GAMES

I t always made Oswald feel happy and fulfilled to be as firmly embedded as he could manage in the national establishment – in consequential public service, with interesting and influential friends. He wanted to belong and to be seen to belong. His aspirations were conventional; he was a converger.

Spedan – the outlier, the diverger – did not give a toss for most social life outside the Partnership, though he liked being president or vice-president of the institutions and organisations he supported. He was never an establishment figure and his self-presentation could be flamboyant and somewhat eccentric. The interior of Longstock House, however, was comfortable but not ostentatious – a background, not a showground, for the life within it. Very Peter Jones in fact, and probably Beatrice's choices.

In 1951 Spedan had written to her that if he were running the country, 'I would reset the whole of industry and trade with an increasing net gain of production and general social vitality.' But – and here was a rare piece of self-knowledge – 'if I had gone for a political career I could not have known enough, not the ideas, but the essential "Know-How" for further transformation into practice'. What he still thought he might achieve was 'a parallel development', through the Partnership. He was the leader of his own pack.

He wrote many hundreds of words, in his two books, in the *Gazette*, and in cascades of memos, about 'Leadership' – very much with a capital L – and the role of the chairman or chief executive. His general point was that while teamwork was central to the success of any undertaking, there had to be a Leader. The role of a Leader was to be a self-starter who inspired others. Just one sample, from a memo of 1943 to a 'Miss M': 'The reason why Leadership is needed at all is that human beings are so apt to be short of engine power and that they cannot make full or nearly full use of their abilities unless their energy is supplemented by that of somebody else. The inertia of their machine is high. ...'

Turning constantly to simile and metaphor, he wrote that the Leader was like the captain of a cricket team. Or the captain of a ship. He was the commodore of a naval flotilla; the general commanding a division of an army. Onwards and upwards: he was in charge of a whole navy or a whole army, with the names Nelson and Napoleon cropping up with increasing frequency. In 1954, the year before Spedan retired, he likened the Partnership to a 'constitutional monarchy'. Such imagery is inflated, but seems less so when planted among thickets of subordinate clauses and spread over thirty-odd years of communications. There remains a poignant residue, as of the daydreams of a schoolboy.

By his own free choice, his Leadership was ebbing. He was already uneasy, telling Eleanor that he saw 'mistakes' being made everywhere in the business. Nineteen fifty-five arrived, and he turned seventy on 22 September. His birthday was properly celebrated. He retired. His new official title was 'the Founder', a term first used under his name on the title page of *Fairer Shares*. His letters and memos from now on were rubber-stamped with the words 'FROM THE FOUNDER'.

Spedan had his last blasts in the gardens at Longstock. Some time in the mid-1950s, Maurice Jones came upon a gardener sitting on an upturned bucket and sandpapering a great pile of horse chestnuts. This was because Spedan had been to the Chelsea Flower Show and ordered 1,500 yellow crocus corms and 1,500 mauve ones. There were a lot of horse chestnuts – conkers – that year, and Spedan instructed Mr Kinch, his head gardener, by memo, to have half the conkers whitewashed, then put with the others in a bag, shaken up, and scattered over the grass in the park. Where white conkers fell, they were to plant yellow crocuses, and mauve ones where the natural-coloured conkers fell.

But the whitewash just slithered off the shiny skins of the conkers. So Kinch had set a gardener to sandpaper them instead. Spedan's memo to him ended with the requirement that if, once scattered, the distribution of conkers looked unnatural, the gardener should collect them all up and scatter them all over again.

In retirement Spedan became an old gentleman, unrecognisable as the man in Anthony Devas's portrait of a decade before. He was very thin, he grew a pointed white beard, and wore large round spectacles. Oswald thought it a pity that he had made no local friends. His and Coopie's social life, as they grew older, centred on the Highgate Bridge Club. When Spedan first retired, Oswald suggested that he should join a gentlemen's club in London to find congenial companionship, and in 1957 he did become a member of the Athenaeum in Pall Mall; but it did not 'take' with him. He had a minor heart attack that year, another in 1960, and hardly ever went to London anyway.

Spedan's paradoxically turbulent inner life in retirement can be traced through surviving letters, equal in confidentiality, to Donald Robertson, Eleanor McElroy and, less so, to Oswald, and occasionally to a good acquaintance, the ageing actress Dame Sybil Thorndike, still in demand on stage and screen, who responded to his confidences briefly and kindly without engaging with any particulars. Donald Robertson could never answer Spedan's letters with anything approximating to their prolix intimacy. He remarried in 1957, and brought his new wife Margaret to Longstock to meet Spedan, who was faintly disapproving.

Soon after Spedan retired, Ted too got married. His wife Mary, 'the pleasant daughter of a professional soldier', was ten years older than he. Spedan was pleased, and for once pulled rank, though on his son's behalf: 'She is a Lubbock, related to Lord Avery.' Ted soon had two little daughters 'which seem to delight him', and then two more.

Ted had a fourth-class honours degree in law from Oxford, a distinction in itself as being within a perilous hair's breadth from failing altogether. It was not a good omen for becoming a barrister like his cousin Peter, 'a choice that his slowness of mind and lack of memory made a hopelessly bad one', as his father put it. Ted 'served his articles' for accountancy, though never fully qualified. The money Spedan had settled on him meant that he and Mary should be 'quite comfortably off, though not so much so as to make some professional earnings quite unnecessary'.

Spedan still referred to Jill and Ted as 'disappointments', as if their problems were misfortunes visited upon himself; yet he was a better and more concerned parent to them. Jill, now over thirty, was in a psychiatric hospital, 'certified' and with a diagnosis of schizophrenia, for nearly the whole of 1959, having checked herself in after making 'a scene' in the office of the family solicitors. Spedan had written to Donald three years earlier about a similarly affected Partner: 'I suppose most people are to some extent schizophrenic.' The same may apply to autism, which has no hard borders. But it would have been unlikely to figure in a differential diagnosis for Jill. The incidence of autism is higher in men and boys and, at that time, was rarely considered in relation to girls and women.

However it was, no one ever understood Jill. Oswald had taken her to the opera at Glyndebourne in the season following Beatrice's death because Spedan himself could not bear to go, and he kept kindly tabs on her through Muriel. She let him know that Spedan dictated a letter to his daughter every single day when she was in hospital and that she wrote back: Spedan said 'her letters have been very cheerful, very intelligent and very amusing but I was horrified to learn very lately for the first time that in her final weeks in London … she was to a serious extent drinking', and had taken off, driving her car. He wished for Beatrice 'several times in every day' but was glad she was not there, as 'this would have broken her heart'.

There was another spell in hospital for Jill, and her vagaries when trying to live independently caused headaches to Enid Locket, who had to sort out some muddles. Oswald continued to take an avuncular interest as time passed, gleaning from Muriel in 1962 that Jill was living in a basement flat in Wharfedale Street, west London, with her dogs – bull terriers. She had a van, and spent time with Ted and Mary and their family.

Jill had a 'strong liking' for Sunny Miller, so maybe, Spedan hoped, a place might still be found for her in the Partnership? That was not to be. Spedan too liked Miller very much, and also his 'shrewd, high-minded' wife Jess; two of their three sons became Partners. The Millers came to Longstock for weekends, when Spedan and Sunny would discuss, according to Miller, 'the pay-sheet, the figures and the way the branches were working out'.

For Miller, this was a matter of courtesy. But he, and his senior management, drew the line at involving the retired Founder in the reorganisation of the executive management structure and the resulting recruitment of some new talent. Spedan was outraged at being left out of the loop. As Miller put it, he 'could not bear not to have his advice taken'. This conflict, and then others, built up into what Miller called 'a festering sore'.

By the autumn of 1960 Spedan was writing to Miller: 'You are breaking my heart.' He had to concede, to Eleanor, that the Partnership had just had a good year – which would have been 'very much better if my advice had not been brushed aside by people seemingly confident they are entirely free from any jealous greed for power but in fact are so anxious to give me not the smallest share of power of which I could have kept the whole of it to the end of my life. I have to look on while they play the fool.' He dictated letters, one consisting of more than two hundred numbered paragraphs, telling Miller exactly where he was going wrong. Consumed by hurt and anger, he became incoherent and irrational. Pity poor Phyllis and poor Muriel.

At the General Council's annual dinner in 1962, the Founder made a rambling, intemperate and generally misjudged speech, received in silence. Earlier in the year, Oswald retired as President of the General Council, where, in a difficult position because of the Founder's behaviour, he conducted himself with propriety and good sense; he was presented with a hefty silver salver at a celebratory retirement dinner at Claridge's.

Spedan's unfortunate speech was printed in the *Gazette*. He had made the *Gazette* his battlefield, trying to force the members of the council – while Oswald was still president – to vote in favour of reserving a quarter of every issue for his own contributions. 'I think by that time he had lost his judgement,' said Sunny Miller in retrospect.

Spedan spun further out of control when Miller ruled that the *Gazette*, 'which I [Spedan] founded 42 years ago', could publish no more of his hectoring letters and articles. 'I should have added a proviso to the Settlement that I had the right to four pages of the *Gazette* in every issue for the rest of my life.' The Partnership's treatment of him since retirement was 'particularly foolish, hideously ungrateful and callously cruel' and two Partners were especially 'ill-bred cads'. (Sunny Miller was 'stupid' and 'caddish', but he did not name the second cad.) Spedan had thought that 'the evening of my life' would be happy, after having 'such terrible luck with the children and Beatrice. The disappointment has been very complete.' Miller and the other senior managers 'have joined in making me very unhappy indeed'. He gave an interview to the *Daily Express*, headed 'I Have Been Sent to Coventry'.

Miller's summing-up was measured: 'It really was a very difficult time for me,' trying to stop the Partnership at large from 'being beastly' about the Founder: 'I kept having to tell them that what they'd got was because of what the Founder had done for them. It was a very unpleasant period.'

There was one painfully obvious comparison to be made, and Oswald made it: 'Father, when he should have retired, could not bear to see you managing the business which he had created. You, when you have retired, cannot bear to see Miller managing the Partnership which you have created. Is there a curse on the concern?' It was, he said, like a Greek tragedy.

That is not quite the last word. Max Baker was one of Spedan's most practical main men, who held key posts in the Partnership from 1934 until his retirement, and compiled, under the title

Retail Trading: The Philosophy and Practice of John Spedan Lewis, an anthology of short, themed extracts from Spedan's letters, articles and memos. He intended it as a 'working handbook' for Partnership. He did not append his own name to the privately published volume. In a clear-eyed introduction he, like Oswald, found mythic significance in what might seem the temper tantrums of an egotistic old man, and made Spedan appear not ridiculous. He likened him to Ulysses, who tied himself to the mast of his ship in order not to be seduced on to land by the irresistible singing of the Sirens – not beautiful treacherous women, in Spedan's case, but the Siren songs of power and control.

'Having created the Partnership,' Baker wrote, 'he had made the kind of sacrifice to which very few of us could rise. It is true that later on he railed against himself for having done this. … But it was not the sacrifice that he regretted – merely some of the incidental consequences of having made the sacrifice … Spedan Lewis, like Ulysses, had by his own act and his own forethought made sure that no weakness he might show could undo what he had caused to happen and what he wished to go on happening. He listened to the Sirens, but he was tied to the mast and could not give in to them.'

Agitation and anger, gradually, turned to sadness. Spedan knew he must get on with 'the really heartbreaking job of trying to cope with that disappointment. Even now I have a real difficulty in believing that I am up against such stupidity and such ingratitude.' Oswald, throughout, seemed unflappable and sought to reassure.

Perhaps Oswald felt their mother had been right when she said, long ago, that he would have to look after Spedan, and that Spedan would always need him more than he needed Spedan, to whom he wrote before Christmas 1961: 'You have given spectacular demonstration that a great business can be conducted effectively for the benefit of the workers and many people have had better lives because of you.' This comforted Spedan and he copied Oswald's words into his own Christmas letter to Donald Robertson.

Spedan's mental turmoil was compounded throughout by sorting through old family letters and reading his father's diaries, in preparation for moving out of Longstock Park. In May 1959 he told Sybil Thorndike how he 'found all the letters I wrote to Beatrice before our wedding day and a great many of hers ... and many of later years. I am profoundly glad to have seen them again. ... It is a wonderful experience to see such letters in the evening of one's life.' The Partnership was establishing an archive, and he was saving some items for it, 'but there is a very great deal that Beatrice and I would want to keep private'.

And so he lit his bonfires. 'I am not leaving behind anything I consider private,' he told Donald Robertson, disliking the way that 'people nowadays published things that to my mind no one can ever really have sufficient reason for wishing to read ... even to break into secrets carefully concealed as has happened lately in the case of Dickens.' Since Donald did not want to have his 'delicious' boyhood letters returned, he burned them too.

Here we touch base with where we came in, and Spedan's agonised outpouring to Oswald. Nothing upset him more than the reading of his father's diaries. Beatrice, had she been there, would have been able to defuse his agitation over the diaries, just as she could have tempered his total 'lack of poise' over the Partnership. Reading the diaries, he was dragged back to old battles from his early days running Peter Jones, when Father sabotaged his every innovation, and he was revolutionising the Millinery Department's floor displays and someone told Mother at a tea party that the department was now 'the best hat shop in London ... I could no more bear it than Nelson could bear at Copenhagen the orders of a stupid, jealous, Commander in

Chief'. He was reminded of things he had long forgotten, like the first time that Father had slapped his face. He learned of the disloyalty of those who kept in with Father by agreeing that he himself was bound to fail.

'It was, as you will realise, a pretty painful shock to find yesterday in the diary a mention that he had heard I was on the point of selling Harrow [Grove Farm] and that he sent for me trying to dissuade me on the argument (this from Father!) that John Lewis and Peter Jones could always use it for playing fields.' Years later, he had been 'deeply shocked by his saying to me, as he lay on the sofa in the dining room, that he was sorry I have parted with it, and that, had I asked him, he would have sent me the money to keep it'. These were perfect examples, Spedan felt, of 'Father's ability to forget what he did not choose to remember and to remember things of the truth of which he wished to persuade himself and other people'.

When Oswald's son Peter left Oxford the idea of his joining the Partnership was discussed, but his father strongly felt, and Spedan concurred, that he would do better for himself by going to the Bar; and Oswald, as was his wont, pulled strings to facilitate his son's smooth progress up the ladder. But a few years later Peter found himself dissatisfied with his own performance, and not at ease either in court or in chambers. A moment came in 1959 when he was being headhunted by several legal entities and the idea of change took root. He abandoned the law altogether and joined the Partnership. He had been impressed by Spedan's ideas – he had read *Partnership for All* – and believed he would feel 'at home' working in that atmosphere, as indeed he did.

The decision process, however, was difficult. His father was 'mystified, horrified, and deeply disappointed'. His wonderful son was abandoning a promising professional career and status to go back into 'trade' – shopkeeping – which he himself had spent much of his life escaping by swimming energetically in the opposite direction. Peter's mother, though also puzzled and disappointed, basically always wanted Peter to have whatever he wanted.

Peter entered as a management trainee, and gained his shop-floor experience in the Stationery Department in Oxford Street; by the end of the first year he was managing the department. Management trainees if they show ability are fast-tracked. Sunny Miller had to be scrupulous about not favouring a family member, with the eyes of the Partners upon him, but Peter Lewis was a natural.

In 1961, two years into his new career, there was another family wedding when Peter married Deborah Collins. Her father, William Collins, was chairman of the Glasgow-based family publishing business of the same name, with a 200-year history. With both their children married, Beechwood became an old persons' house. Domestic staff were hard to get and to keep, but unlike Spedan, Oswald and Coopie never thought again of downsizing.

Spedan was to leave Longstock more or less intact, destined as it was to be a recreational retreat for what Spedan called 'the Partnership's Intelligentsia'. He had burned the letters and diaries, but two years after his death, Ted was still reporting to Enid Locket about having cleared the safe but failed to clear the strong-room, and arranging for Jill's belongings to go into store.

Opposite the gates of Longstock Park a new, smaller home was constructed for Spedan by the Partnership's Building Department. It had three bedrooms, three bathrooms, and was called The Burrow. It took two years to complete, and in March 1961 he moved in with Muriel and Kate Bonnett to look after him. The arrangement was that after his death The Burrow was Muriel's for her lifetime, and would then revert to the Partnership. Spedan hung on to his Rolls-Royce and to the Wolseley, the son-in-law of his old chauffeur Francis acting as his driver. There was a croquet lawn, and he made a pond, telling Eleanor, 'I must get some rudd for it in memory of Grove Farm. I can still remember the sound of tiny but rather energetic kissing they made when sucking eatables.' Grove Farm was still 'a loss I can hardly bear to think about'.

Eleanor had been distressed by Spedan's state of mind and his bitterness about the Partnership, receiving as she did weekly bulletins of his miseries. She wrote to Oswald in September 1961 and, after thanking him for remembering her eighty-ninth birthday: 'I wish you could make Spedan cease to worry … if you could make him see that Winston Churchill does not worry when his followers do stupid things.'

A month later she suffered a stroke and was taken from her care home in Westbourne Grove to the Hospital of St John and St Elizabeth in St John's Wood. Her last letter to Spedan arrived after he heard the news. She did not recover.

Eleanor's death hardly came as a shock, given her age and frailty, but was another blow. She had been a mainstay of Spedan's life and the repository of his hopes and fears since his early manhood. As long as she was able, she had helped the family out in practical ways in times of stress. Over all the years, he had cared for her, keeping her supplied with luxuries and with clothes designed and made for her at Peter Jones. Cars had been sent to waft her on visits to Leckford and then Longstock. In more than half a century there had been no break in their relationship. There is no hard border between devotion and love.

★

It is not surprising that Spedan, in these bad, sad years, welcomed some fresh and flattering attention. Kenneth Hudson was a producer with the BBC West Region, and lived near Shepton Mallet. He recorded a radio talk by Spedan for a series called 'Dear to My Heart', and a TV interview, with Spedan explicating the principles of Partnership, sitting on a bench in the gardens at Longstock. The contact was made before the bonfires, when Spedan was reading his father's diaries. Hudson definitely had a sight of them, since verbatim extracts survive in his handwriting.

In August 1961 Hudson wrote asking Spedan if he might write his biography, 'because you are far and away the most interesting man I have ever met'. Spedan was not displeased, seeing the project as a collaboration. Hudson, alarmed perhaps by Spedan's current obsessions, decided to mix biography with a selection of his writings. After Spedan's death he did produce a manuscript, which does not seem to have been preserved. It was up to Ted to decide whether it should be published, and he decided against it.

On 29 January 1963 Spedan told Sybil Thorndike that he wanted to take her to see Beatrice's memorial ground. 'Her ashes went, as will some day mine too, into one of the Channel's deepest places.'

His third and final heart attack came soon and with no warning. Less than a month after he wrote that letter to Sybil Thorndike, on 21 February 1963, he went upstairs early to watch television. When Muriel looked in to say goodnight, she found the television still on, and Spedan dead in his bed.

The cremation was private. Later, Commander Geoffrey Snagge put out the Partnership's first-ever sailing craft, the *Ann Speed*, and scattered Spedan's ashes into the Solent all by himself. He recorded that 'there is a mark on the chart that marks the spot'.

There was a Partnership memorial service, very well attended, especially by retirees and old-timers, at All Souls, Langham Place. On his retirement, the Partnership had established the John Spedan Lewis Trust to further research into the flora and fauna of the Leckford Estate, and after his death the trust set up a natural history study centre. Years later a functional Partnership Services building in Bracknell was named Spedan House. The Founder has no other physical memorial. The year after he died, JLP celebrated the centenary of the opening of a small drapery shop on Oxford Street in 1864.

Oswald's health now began to fail. He had to have a leg amputated, and his final months were hard – recuperating from the operation, learning to live in a wheelchair, trying to walk with an artificial leg. At Beechwood his bed was brought downstairs to the library. He never complained. Both Peter and Diana had children but he was not greatly interested in them. He was never reconciled to Peter's joining the Partnership. When Peter showed him his letter of appointment as Director of Trading for Department Stores – the highest purely 'shopkeeping' post at that time – he said nothing, looked out of the library window, and handed the letter back. He died on 12 February 1966, and was buried in Highgate Cemetery.

In July 1966 the estate agents Knight Frank & Rutley took a whole page of *Country Life* to advertise the forthcoming auction of Beechwood House with its eight principal bedrooms, three bathrooms, four reception rooms, staff accommodation, entrance lodge, cottage, bungalow, garage block, squash court and heated swimming pool, set in twelve acres of 'magnificent gardens and grounds'.

In the event, prior to the auction date, Beechwood was sold privately for around £165,000. The purchaser was one John Hine. His son, the historian Richard Davenport-Hines, later changed his surname to dissociate himself from his father, whom he has judged, giving full particulars, as 'an inveterate confidence-trickster, liar and impostor'. If so, he was competent in his confected self-presentation. Peter Lewis found him perfectly pleasant and easy to deal with – 'a most engaging man' – and the sale went through.

Richard Hine, as he then was, as a young boy accompanied his father on a visit to Beechwood during the negotiations with Peter Lewis, 'who seemed scrupulously polite, reticent, fastidious and perhaps a bit depressed: all natural reactions to my father's character'. More likely, a natural reaction to losing the family home. 'Frances Lewis with Diana sat in the library looking frail and downcast. ... The house was musty and smelt of invalids.'

John Hine made changes. He whitewashed the unpainted stucco of Beechwood, 'put in bathrooms everywhere', and removed the back staircase and servants' bedrooms in order to create 'a great tall room which was called the Armoury because it had a few swords on one wall, but which was dominated by a ping-pong table'. Eleven years later, in 1977, John Hine needed to sell the house in a hurry, and was convinced that only Arab wealth could come up with what he was asking. The King of Saudi Arabia, through negotiators, made an offer of £1.9 million on condition that he could have immediate possession. Beechwood had to be cleared within a week.

The Saudi royal family sold Beechwood on to the Emir of Qatar. Both these oil-rich owners transformed both house and grounds with opulent extensions and additions, much to the agitation of the Highgate Society. On a single visit at the time of writing, Beechwood looked to be pretty deserted behind its chained gates on Hampstead Lane, the only sign of life emanating from the drone of a lawnmower somewhere in the grounds.

Diana's husband Simon Young died aged 57 in 1984. She had four children with him. In 2000 she made a late second marriage

to John ('Jacky') Shaw-Stewart, also widowed and with four children. He had proposed to her, and then introduced her to Simon
Young, when they were all at Cambridge.

★

Jill, the daughter of Spedan and Beatrice, did not have a long or a
happy life. On 5 April 1968, Edward – Ted – wrote to Enid
Locket from Leckhampstead House, his family home near
Newbury: 'You may know already that my sister died suddenly on
the 2nd.' The cremation was fixed for 3 p.m. on Monday 8 April,
'the very short notice' being 'unavoidable'. The heart attack of
which she died was described as myocardial infarction 'due to
coronary thrombosis caused by atherosclerosis'. Her address at the
time was Flat 11, 102 Maida Vale, London NW9, and the death
certificate, from which Ted transcribed the causes of death, was
issued at Charing Cross Hospital. She was just forty years old.

Ted wrote again on 14 April apologising to Mrs Locket for not
having told her the place of the funeral: 'I rushed it through in
order to keep some appointments next day – but rushed it too
much.'

It was 'the least poignant yet, in my experience, of funerals'.
The mourner 'with chief cause to mourn', wrote Ted, was Hilda
Thomas, a Partner who had kept in contact with Jill over the
years, looking after her affairs. Jill seemed 'to have been utterly
withdrawn into a world of her own which can have given her
little joy'.

She had been detained in psychiatric hospitals at intervals, and
self-medicated with drink and drugs. The enigmatic tone of what
Ted wrote, and his decision to 'rush it through', suggest that the
end of life was a release for her and also for him. Her death was
referred to the coroner, who found no reason not to 'authorise
interment without inquest'. Ted, who arranged for the cremation

within less than a week, would not have wanted an inquest. As he expressed it to Mrs Locket, he felt his sister preferred to 'pass away thus, quickly, without giving anyone at all any opportunity to worry about her in a prolonged final illness with the least disturbance to anyone and without occasioning regrets or mourning'.

Ted lived to a good age but his death was no less bleak. Widowed early, at the end of his restless life he was living with one of his daughters in Loughton, Essex, on the edge of the ancient woodlands of Epping Forest.

On 20 October 2007 *The East London and West Essex Gazette* reported that 'a body believed to be that of a 78-year-old Loughton man has been found in Epping Forest'. Other local papers also carried the story. The body was that of Edward Lewis, 'who suffered with general degenerative health issues, and was partially blind and deaf'. He was last seen at his home, wearing a red roll-neck sweater, a green anorak over a tweed jacket, and blue trousers, at about 8.15 a.m. on 8 October. There were no suspicious circumstances.

Just a tranche of this family has been illuminated. Family history has no beginning and no end. Beyond the grandparents of John Lewis, darkness falls over the irretrievable past. The lives of the children and grandchildren of Peter and Diana Lewis and of Edward Lewis lie outside the spotlight, and extend into an unforeseeable future. There remains a legacy: Spedan's Partnership.

EPILOGUE

A SEQUENCE OF SEALED BROWN ENVELOPES, AND A SEA CHANGE

The Partnership thrived after Spedan's death. His vision of Partnership, which had inspired his early 'main men' – now middle-aged and in senior executive positions – remained untarnished. Bernard Miller – no longer known as 'Sunny' but as 'OBM', his first name, coincidentally, being Oswald – was just over fifty when he became chairman and, released from coping with the Founder's resentment and sadness, was almost as impatient to put his plans into practice as Spedan had been on the death of his father. He presided over further expansion: the acquisition of more shops, a textile printing works, the computerisation of stock control, and all backed by sound financing. In 1950 there were 12,000 Partners and sales of £28 million. By the time Miller retired in 1972 there were 20,000 Partners and sales of £240 million. Staff bonuses were being paid in cash.

During his tenure, Miller was as active outside the firm as within it – a member of the Council of Industrial Design, of the Monopolies Commission, and of the National Economic Council for the Distributive Trades; he was on the governing body of the London Graduate School of Business Studies and was a General Commissioner of Income Tax. When he was knighted in 1967 it was for 'public service'.

Miller commissioned a piece of sculpture to celebrate in 1964 the centenary of the opening of John Lewis's little drapery shop on Oxford Street. The work would embellish the gleaming new John Lewis store which was at long last opened in 1961, rising from the ruins of bomb damage. Barbara Hepworth was the chosen artist. Her brief was testing. The work should 'express the idea of common ownership and common interests in a partnership of thousands of workers'. Hepworth's first design was not accepted. So she took up a small abstract work in wood, dating from 1957, entitled *Winged Figure*, and enlarged and adapted it to be cast in aluminium and stainless steel.

The piece, almost six metres tall and up-soaring, is more 'wings' than 'figure'. Hepworth suggested that the asymmetric wings, linked by radial retaining rods, might represent the union of Capital and Labour. *Winged Figure II* was installed on 21 April 1963, a Sunday, two months to the day after the death of Spedan. High up on the east-facing wall of the building, it is easily missed.

The Partnership also acquired a castle. A sixteenth-century fort built on Brownsea Island in Poole Harbour off the Dorset coast – transformed into a residence, and subsequently enlarged, neglected and burned down – had, at the beginning of the twentieth century, been extravagantly remodelled. By 1960 Brownsea Castle was again derelict. The castle and the island were acquired by the National Trust who leased them to the John Lewis Partnership.

JLP restored the castle bit by bit and it was reborn as a 'corporate hotel' – another perk for Partners. Yet another, from the mid-1970s, was Winter Hill, a championship golf course at Cookham. Spedan had acquired its 200 acres for this purpose back in 1938, but the war put a stop to it. In the last year of Miller's chairmanship planning permission was given to realise Spedan's project. Winter Hill Golf Club, owned and managed by JLP, is run as a commercial business, Partners paying only a fraction of the fees.

These amenities were earned. The highest peak in a mountain range of peaks and troughs between 1955 and 2000, according to a graph of profitability prepared by Peter Cox, was reached in 1970, two years before Miller's retirement.

JLP's method of ensuring a smooth internal succession has been quaint, possibly devised by Enid Locket before she retired as legal adviser in 1958. In case of their own unexpected death or incapacity, an incoming chairman was required to place in a sealed brown envelope the name of their chosen successor. They could change the name in the envelope at any time but must confirm to the board annually that this nomination was duly recorded, and the sealed brown envelope safely deposited, to be opened when the chairman reached retirement. The name in Miller's brown envelope was that of Peter Lewis, Director of Trading, thereby restoring the Partnership's identity as a family firm, even though it was a nephew not a son of the Founder who took up the mantle. 'Oswald has all the luck,' as Spedan would have said.

The end came at this time for the brothers' old family home, Spedan Tower, the setting for much anger and unhappiness. No other family had made it their home. Post-war, Spedan Tower had been a nurses' hostel and a training centre. In the early 1970s the property was bought by Camden Council. The house was demolished, and the grounds and garden covered over with housing; there is a Spedan Lane and a Spedan Close.

Peter Lewis held the fort, impeccably adhering to Spedan's core values, but without Spedan's flamboyance, for twenty-one years. The Partnership opened a new head office in Bracknell and acquired the Ambleside Hotel in the Lake District as a facility for Partners employed in northern branches, to balance the Odney Club and Brownsea Castle in the south. Partners were given more generous leisure time; those with twenty-five years' service got six months' leave, and from 1984 there were five weeks' annual holiday for everyone with three years' service. For the first time since 1929, the bonuses in 1978 surpassed 20 per cent.

Lewis did not always see eye to eye with the government; in the 1970s there was a policy of wage restraint, which many businesses got round by enhancing executives' pay by various means and with impunity. Lewis, committed to transparency, let his disquiet be known. But increasingly, owing to competitiveness across key industries, wage restraint for many top CEOs fell off the menu and off the wall.

Towards the end of Peter Lewis's regime there was a controversy about Sunday trading, prohibited by law and pressed for by most of the retail sector including the department stores. The government was inclined to comply. Lewis set out the pros and cons of Sunday opening to the Partnership and came down in favour of retaining Sunday closing. Waitrose disagreed and, like many other shops, started opening up on Sundays even before the law was changed. Discussion filled the columns of the *Gazette*. Lewis published his correspondence – trenchant, on his side – with Kenneth Baker, the Home Secretary. These matters – and perhaps because he did not take up outside appointments to the same extent – may or may not have had a bearing on the fact that, unlike his predecessor and his two successors, Peter Lewis did not receive a knighthood.

By 1993, Lewis's last year in office, the hundredth Waitrose supermarket had opened. The following year, across the Atlantic, Jeff Bezos launched a high-tech operation which he called Amazon.com. An event of no apparent significance at the time.

Peter Lewis had the name of Stuart Hampson in his sealed brown envelope. Hampson, previously in the civil service, joined JLP in 1982 and had been on the JLP board as Director of Research and Expansion since. Because of Peter Lewis's unusually long tenure, the changeover necessarily occasioned some new thinking and modernisation, like the generational refurbishment of a profitable ancestral estate. Hampson smartened up the London flagships – Oxford Street and Sloane Square. Electronic point-of-sale systems were introduced in Peter Lewis's time, but his own secretaries were still using 'golf-ball' typewriters and carbon paper, and he expressed surprise when Hampson brought a computer into the chairman's office.

Hampson was to be an effective public advocate for the Partnership – explicating its culture and ethos, and the virtuous circle by which shared values and 'the power of We' paid off in happiness and healthy profits, with no outside investors hungry for their dividend; the 50 per cent of profits not shared between Partners was reinvested in the business.

The early 1990s were a reputational high point. The name 'John Lewis' spelt reliability, good value and a wide choice, just as, *mutatis mutandis*, in Spedan's father's time. The furnishings, fabrics and bed linens were of good quality; modern without being edgy or flashy – conservative contemporary. The 'look', like the established customer base, exactly fitted Spedan's original plan: quiet good taste. If it seemed unexciting to some, there were very many who were entirely comfortable with it. The visual branding had always been strong, simple and, with variations, consistent – dark green geometric motifs or slanting dark green bars on a clear white field. No problem about 'differentiation': a John Lewis carrier bag was and is recognisable from afar.

John Lewis was the darling of consumer publications such as *Which?*, and won awards across nearly all categories in consumer satisfaction polls. Stuart Hampson let in the cameras for a BBC documentary, *Meet the Partners*, in a series about contemporary Britain.

The tone of the film is celebratory, with a hint of irony in a soundtrack featuring 'Rule, Britannia' and numbers from Gilbert and Sullivan. There is the clip of old Spedan in the garden at Longstock outlining his theories of co-ownership and fairer shares; though comment is made that he always spoke and wrote 'fair*er* shares', not 'fair shares', and that the chairman's pay at this time was around £300,000 p.a. His successor, in his last year in the chair, was to take home rather more than £1 million. This escalation, however, had less to do with CEO competitiveness than with a decision to take JLP executives out of the pension scheme which, paid at two-thirds final salary, had become un-viable. The executives, with no pensions, were compensated with higher salaries and cash supplements.

Here, in the documentary, are smiling sales assistants, happy to be Partners, happy in their work and in feeling valued; happy about the wonderful places where they can stay cheaply for holi-days. Smiling women customers in Peter Jones, praising the helpful service: 'It's what English people used to be like', and 'It's so English.' Indeed, there is little apparent diversity among either Partners or customers.

The cameras dip into branch council meetings and into committees – industrial democracy in action. Partnership is likened to being in the army or navy. (The phrase 'Rank and File' is still used.) If you share in the ethos, the culture, the sense of common purpose, and keep the rules, 'they look after you'.

Disgruntlements are expressed and addressed, at length, in accordance with the democratic structure. There is too much pointless 'nannying', too many petty rules, and wages are too low, comments a male Partner swabbing a washroom floor.

Meet the Partners aired on BBC Two in December 1995. The series title was 'Modern Times'. Viewed now, it seems an elegy for a past world. By this stage, Amazon.com had been unleashed, at first selling online just books and music, and exploding over the next twenty years to become the go-to online marketplace for virtually everything that people need, or think they need – to use the aspirational nineteenth-century formula, 'Universal Providers' – with keen prices, a nimble supply chain and an efficient distribution and delivery service sustained by a vast freelance workforce: the 'gig economy'.

Distance shopping was nothing new. Americans had been buying from catalogues put out by big stores for generations. In the UK after World War II, women of the higher economic classes in the shires ordered clothes from top London department stores 'on approval' – familiarly, 'on appro'. 'Mail order' was soon catering for the general population. With internet technology, shopping online became easy, easier, easiest. The John Lewis Partnership began selling online in 2001.

Stuart Hampson's outside appointments included the deputy chairmanship of London First, a body set up to champion planning for the capital after the Thatcher government abolished the Greater London Council, and he received a knighthood in 1998. He was president of the not-for-profit Employee Ownership Association (EOA), founded (under another name) in 1979 by the economist and social reformer Robert Oakeshott. The EOA became a campaigning membership association in 2000, providing information and support to firms in all industries who followed, or wished to follow, that route. JLP, as an original trustee member, still contributes financial backing, and JLP director Stephen May was on the EOA's board until 2017.

Before retiring in 2007 Hampson modified the sealed brown envelope ritual. It was now to be just an emergency measure, only to be opened in the event of a chairman's death or incapacity. The appointment of his successor was revealed in a more conventional manner, and the ground prepared. Sir Stuart's choice fell on Charlie Mayfield.

Mayfield was chip off a different kind of block. From a military family, he went from school to the Royal Military Academy, Sandhurst, and pursued a successful army career, serving as a very young officer in Northern Ireland during the Troubles of the 1980s and 1990s. Leaving the army, he gained an MBA and there followed spells in banking, commerce and management consultancy. He joined JLP in 2000 as head of Business Development, becoming a member of the board a year later, as Development Director.

Continuing success for JLP was now a question of strategy in a transitional retail climate. Mayfield rejigged the management team. Andy Street, turned down by M&S for their graduate trainee scheme, joined JLP in 1985 as a trainee at the Brent Cross branch, worked his way up towards the top as Supply Chain Director, and was appointed general manager of JLP. The Partnership survived the crash of 2007/8; and during Street's time JLP doubled the number of stores, with an increase in sales of more than 50 per cent to over £4 billion. In 2016 Andy Street was selected as the Conservative candidate in the election of the first mayor of the West Midlands and left the Partnership.

Another keen player who also moved along in 2016 – two years after she was named Black British Business Person of the Year – was Margaret Casely-Hayford, a dynamic barrister who had served for a decade as the Partnership's Director of Legal

Services and company secretary. She was a reformer, while bent on enhancing the Founder's vision of Partnership; she spoke of Spedan as 'a genius'. But his notions of industrial democracy and inclusivity, enshrined in the constitution more than seventy years earlier, seemed shopworn and less than radical, and Casely-Hayford worked towards the further empowerment of the 'Rank and File'.

A forward-looking move was Mayfield's appointment in 2009 of Patrick Lewis, Peter Lewis's son – with a law degree from Oxford and already on the board – as Partners' Counsellor, a crucial position addressing issues between Partners and the board, and traditionally held by a seasoned senior Partner. Patrick Lewis was in his early thirties and as committed as Casely-Hayford to enhancing the role of Partners and strengthening their connection with senior managers who, in his view, should think of themselves as 'employed' by the Partners. On a wider front, Casely-Hayford and her legal department, under the chairman, had engaged with the government over corporation law, arguing for JLP's constitutional exceptionalism; what worked for the majority would not work for the Partners. The aim was to leave the Partnership 'future-proof'. If only.

Mayfield embraced the challenge of online shopping and threw money at it. The imperatives were ample warehousing, a nimble supply chain, and hubs for distribution; £150 million was invested in a state-of-the-art automated distribution centre near Milton Keynes, and then three more, to pack and dispatch thousands of parcels a day. 'Never Knowingly Undersold' had long been restricted to like-for-like from other department stores, but in the face of Amazon's pricing strategy it was becoming untenable. Doing the same as always, only better, might not work any more.

Two years into his chairmanship, Mayfield began laying the ground for his most radical innovation: opening up the succession to external as well as internal candidates. An internal appointment, taken by Spedan as axiomatic, was not enshrined in the constitution. But the change must surely transform irrevocably what was still in some wider sense a family business, into which sons followed fathers, and daughters followed mothers, where many Partners spent their whole working lives, and a new chairman was always a devil you knew. Mayfield was tightening up the Partnership's familiar, highly personalised style of governance with measures which did involve changes in the constitution, requiring approval from two-thirds of the council, which was forthcoming.

There followed several years of reflection, briefing, discussion and consultation with Partners at all levels; they could never say they had been rushed into anything. Mayfield appointed a nominations committee consisting of two elected directors (Partners) and two non-executive directors, led by himself. The change in the selection process was announced in 2018. Internal candidates (who included Patrick Lewis) met with the same firm of headhunters as were engaged by the nominations committee to consult on external candidates. The Partnership Council, though not involved, was kept in the loop. In June 2019, at a meeting of the council, the chairman made his recommendation, and the sixth chairman of the John Lewis Partnership was appointed.

The new chairman of JLP attracted a lot of publicity. Dame Sharon White, in her early fifties, of Jamaican heritage, is a Cambridge-educated high-profile economist. She joined the civil service in 1989, working in senior roles at the Treasury, then for the British embassy in Washington and in the policy unit at 10 Downing Street under Tony Blair. She was chief executive of Ofcom, the government's communications regulator, before joining the Partnership, and in the 2020 New Year Honours was created a Dame of the British Empire for public service.

Dame Sharon walked into a whirlwind. The traditional retail model was broken; leave Amazon and its imitators out of it: online sales exceeded in-store sales, and the future of the high street was bleak. On taking up her chairmanship in February 2020, she announced a startling strategy of diversification – JLP would expand into estate agency, finance, house-building and more. JLP was running at a loss. Only Waitrose made a profit. The tail was wagging the dog. White assembled her executive team, only two of whom were already on the board of JLP – they were late Mayfield appointments. Peter Lewis, finance director, departed in autumn 2020; new senior posts went to 'outsiders', who were now actually the insiders.

Then the Covid-19 pandemic struck. Only seven weeks after White's accession, the UK was plunged into its first lockdown, and all 'non-essential' shops were closed. A drastic reconfiguration which may well have happened anyway, over a decade, was under-taken in a single year. Many already unprofitable businesses went under completely. Others, including JLP, bleeding money, would not be reopening all their branches after the successive lockdowns; though JLP would not share the fate of Debenhams, an inter-national chain of 130 department stores with a history even longer than that of John Lewis. When the pandemic hit, JLP had reserves of £1.25 billion. Debenhams, with no or insufficient reserves, went bust. The brand, and its website, and stock, but none of the physical shops, were bought by the online-only fashion retailer Boohoo for £155 million, with the loss of around 2,000 jobs.

There had been 83,000 Partners, running Waitroses and John Lewis. Permanent closures of stores were announced in groups of two or three, and in clusters – eight, mostly in the south, then another eight mostly in the north including Scotland. Staff bonuses were slashed and then scrapped. Even the emblematic John Lewis store on Oxford Street has not wholly escaped. It will become 'dual use', losing 45 per cent of its selling floors, designated for office space. Thousands of jobs have already been lost. Dame Sharon – this is not her own simile – is perhaps like a surgeon cutting bits out of a patient in order to save his life.

The list of permanent closures is not yet complete. Will John Lewis & Partners – as it is now styled – become in the aftermath of Covid-19 a chain of high-end grocery supermarkets supporting a handful of stores and an online household goods business? Dame Sharon, when first appointed, gave herself five years to turn the business round. It is unlikely that she will abandon her initial programme of diversification. What was then a strategy can become, may already be, the plan.

Did Spedan Lewis's experiment fail? Not at all. It was never unique, except in so far as Spedan himself was unique, and he certainly was. Co-ownership, in various and sometimes diluted forms, has long been practised worldwide and still is. It does not become the business norm partly because most owners do not look beyond the standard capitalist model, making money for themselves – like Spedan's father, perpetuating an 'us and them' culture and sporadic industrial strife. That is a discussion for another place. This story has been about just one extraordinary family, and one family member's achievement.

Sir Charlie Mayfield was driven by the winds of a changing retail environment into charting a course leading, Covid or no Covid, to a transformation of the John Lewis Partnership as generations had known it. He did not reject the principles of Partnership. He was president of the Employee Ownership Association until 2020 (to be followed in that office by Patrick Lewis). The EOA had 200 UK members in 2015 and more than 450 in 2021.

The philosopher Michael Oakeshott – a kinsman of Robert Oakeshott EOA – wrote the following about the world of politics, but it is relevant to any complex communal undertaking. Oakeshott is in his maritime imagery channelling the novelist Joseph Conrad, whom he admired: 'Men sail a boundless and borderless sea; there is neither harbour for shelter nor floor for anchor, neither starting place nor appointed destination. The enterprise is to keep afloat on an even keel ...'

Bon voyage.

May 2021

ACKNOWLEDGEMENTS

This book was not read in advance by anyone connected with the company, but I am indebted to the following Partners, past and present, who kindly responded to my questions, including to some I had not thought to ask: Margaret Casely-Hayford, Peter Cox, Judy Faraday (*see also* A Note on Sources), Sir Stuart Hampson, Stephen May, Sir Charlie Mayfield, Peter Miller, Patrick Lewis, Peter Lewis (*see also* A Note on Sources) and Dame Sharon White DBE.

I thank the following for sharing unpublished material and special knowledge, and for information, research assistance, memories, insights, contact and connections: Jane Appleyard-Hobbs, Mark Blackett-Ord, Richard Cohen, Amanda (Lewis) Cornish, Richard Davenport-Hines, Hazel Walford Davies, Nick Dent, Sir Jeremy Dixon and Julia Somerville, Sarah Gerwens,

Hugo Glendinning, Matthew Glendinning, Paul Glendinning, Simon Glendinning, Frances Jowell, Caroline Keely, Joyce and David Keetley, Richard Lambert, Michael Lee, Paul Lewis, Philippa Lewis, Keith Perreur-Lloyd, Thomas Seymour, Richard Thomas and Stephen Young.

I would like to include in this list my husband Kevin O'Sullivan, the great encourager, who did not live to see this book published.

Many thanks too for generous help from the following institutions and organisations: The Athenaeum (Jennie de Protani); College of Arms (David White); Employee Ownership Association (Keely Read); Girton College, Cambridge (Naomi Sturges); King's College, London (Frances Pattman); North London Collegiate School (Sue Stanbury, Angela Kenny); Somerset Archives and Local Studies (Graeme Edwards, Liz Grant); Somerset Heritage Centre (Philip Hocking); Somerville College, Oxford (Elizabeth Cooke, Andrew Parker, Kate O'Donell); Swanage Town Council, for Godlingston Cemetery (Cara Johnston); Wellcome Library (Amelia Walker); Westminster School (Elizabeth Wells); The Women's Library at the London School of Economics (for the unpublished memoir by Enid Locket).

Very many thanks to Stephen Young and Rod Ellis at Platform 1 Design for image preparation; and, from first to last, to my agent Andrew Gordon, and at HarperCollins/William Collins for the support of Arabella Pike and of Katy Archer, Kate Johnson, Jo Thompson and Nicola Webb. And special thanks to champion proofreader Elisabeth Ingles.

A NOTE ON SOURCES

The John Lewis Partnership Heritage Centre at Odney is a business and textile archive, open to Partners and to the public. Accessible only with permission – for which I thank previous chairman Sir Charlie Mayfield – it is a seemingly inexhaustible collection of books, complete runs of the Partnership's *Gazette*, business and legal papers, wills and personal letters and papers mostly deposited by Spedan Lewis – those he chose not to burn – particularly valuable for material by and concerning his wife, Beatrice, and his correspondence with Eleanor McElroy. There is neither a digital nor a printed catalogue available to researchers, which is challenging, and I am grateful beyond measure to the Centre's manager, Judy Faraday, and to her colleagues, for their continual help and guidance, and also for facilitating my stays at the Odney Club during research visits. I have also availed myself of the numerous John Lewis Memory Store web-pages.

The second principal source, without which the narrative of this book would have been hollow, has been nine large cardboard boxes in the possession of Peter Lewis containing bundles of personal, and sometimes explosive, family letters dating from Spedan's and Oswald's childhoods, and also including those from their mother to Oswald, whose bound diaries form part of the accumulation of family material. I owe Peter Lewis an unpayable debt of gratitude for his hospitality on numerous research visits, and for his patience and generosity throughout the writing of this book.

Since this is a book about people rather than balance sheets, I would refer readers who want more business details to Peter Cox's *Spedan's Partnership*, to back issues of the *Gazette* and to trade papers such as *Retail News* and *Retail Gazette*.

SELECTED BIBLIOGRAPHY

Reginald Airey, *Westminster* (George Bell & Sons, 1902)

Anonymous, *The Beauties of England: Or, a Comprehensive View of the Antiquities of This Kingdom; the Seats of the Nobility and Gentry; the Chief Villages ... Intended As a Travelling Pocket Companion* (L. Davis and C. Reymers, 1764)

Jane Appleyard-Hobbs, *Waitrose: Seeking to Attain Perfection* (Acton History Group, 2009)

H.E. Baker, (Max) anonymously, *Retail Trading: The Philosophy and Practice of John Spedan Lewis* (John Lewis & Co. Ltd)

Rudolf Bing, *5000 Nights at the Opera* (Hamish Hamilton, 1972)

Hester W. Chapman, *Long Division* (Secker & Warburg, 1943)

Richard A. Chapman, *Leadership in the British Civil Service* (Croom Helm, 1984)

John Collinson, *History and Antiquities of Somerset* (R. Cruttwell, 1791; Franklin Classics, 2018)

Peter Cox, *Spedan's Partnership: The Story of John Lewis and Waitrose* (Labatie Books, 2010)

Emily Davies, *The Higher Education of Women* (A. Strahan, 1866; Cambridge University Press, 2011)

Fred Davis, *A Shepton Mallet Camera, Vol IV* (Shepton Mallet Amenity Trust, 1996)

David Erdal, *Beyond the Corporation: Humanity Working* (The Bodley Head, 2011)

John E. Farbrother, *Shepton Mallet: Notes on its History, Ancient, Descriptive and Natural* (Albert Byrt, 1859)

John Galsworthy, *Strife* (1909; McAllister Editions, 2016)

Jonathan Glancey, *A Very British Revolution: 150 Years of John Lewis* (Laurence King, 2014)

P.C. Hoffman, *They Also Serve: The Story of the Shop Worker* (Porcupine Press, 1949)

Lady Margherita Howard de Walden, *Pages From My Life* (Sidgwick & Jackson, 1965)

Julian Huxley, *Memories* (Allen & Unwin, 1970)

Simon Jenkins, *England's Thousand Best Churches* (Allen Lane, 1999)

Carol Kennedy, *Business Pioneers: Family, Fortune and Philanthropy* (Random House, 2000)

John Spedan Lewis, *Partnership for All* (Kerr-Cross, 1948)

— *Fairer Shares* (Staples Press, 1954)

— *Inflation's Cause and Cure* (Museum Press, 1958)

Oswald Lewis, *Because I've Not Been There Before* (Duckworth, 1929)

— *I'd Like To Go Again* (Newman Neame, 1954)

Peter Lewis, *John Lewis 1836–1928* (Ripe Digital, 2009)

— *Oswald* (2012)

— *Spedan* (2013)

Frank McElroy, *Death of a Purser* (Author House, 2011)

Hugh Macpherson (ed.), *John Spedan Lewis 1885–1963: Reminiscences by some of his Contemporaries* (John Lewis Partnership, 1985)

Michael Oakeshott, *Rationalism in Politics and Other Essays* (Methuen, 1962)

Rev W. Phelps, *History and Antiquities of Somerset Vol II* (J.B. Nicholls & Son, 1836)

Charles Reilly, *Scaffolding in the Sky: A Semi-Architectural Autobiography* (Routledge, 1938)

Thomas Seymour, *Battle on Holles Street: Howard de Walden vs. Lewis & the 999 Year Lease* (available from Wilton65 GU33 7DD, privately printed in 2019)

Edward Short, *I Knew My Place* (Macdonald, 1983)

Barbara Stephen, *Emily Davies and Girton College* (Constable and Co Limited, 1927)

— *Hypericon* (1976)

— *Girton College 1869–1932* (Cambridge University Press, 1933)

Alan Stone, *Shepton Mallet: A Visible History* (Shepton Mallet Local History Group, 2005)

Lawrence Tanner, *Westminster School* (Country Life, 1934)

Anthony Trollope, *The Three Clerks* (Bentley, 1858)

H.G. Wells, *Kipps* (1905) and *The History of Mr Polly* (1910), in one volume (Wordsworth Classics, 2017)

Emile Zola, *The Ladies' Paradise* (*Au bonheur des femmes*) (Vizetelly, 1883; Oxford World Classics, 2008)

Also census returns, newspapers, videos, innumerable online genealogical, biographical, literary, historical, political, medical and topographical articles, arcane uploads and websites.

MONETARY
CONVERSION TABLE

Purchasing power of £100 in a given year expressed by value in 2020 prices.

2000 – £172.73	1910 – £12,405.83
1980 – £438.53	1900 – £12,569.50
1960 – £5,724.75	1880 – £12,302.13
1940 – £5,724.75	1860 – £12,434.31
1930 – £6,684.39	1840 – £10,487.02
1920 – £4,570.15	

Figures from the Bank of England website.

LIST OF ILLUSTRATIONS

John Lewis as a young man (by kind permission of Peter Lewis)
John Lewis's first wife, Ellie Baker (Peter Lewis)
Artist's view of old Shepton Mallet (Peter Lewis)
Line drawing of shop terrace (Peter Lewis)
Ellie with Spedan and Oswald (Peter Lewis)
Tower Hampstead, the family home (Peter Lewis)
John Lewis's sister, Elizabeth (Peter Lewis)
Nelly Breeks, John Lewis's first love (Peter Lewis)
Peter Jones, Sloane Square (by kind permission of John Lewis
    and Partners)
The silks counter of John Lewis (John Lewis and Partners)
John Lewis shopfront on a street with horse-drawn carriages
    (John Lewis and Partners)
Spedan on entering the company (Peter Lewis)

Oswald on entering the company (Peter Lewis)

The Peter Jones exterior (John Lewis and Partners)

The interior of Peter Jones (John Lewis and Partners)

Eleanor McElroy playing cricket at Grove Farm (Peter Lewis)

Grove Farm exterior (Peter Lewis)

Leckford Abbas exterior (Peter Lewis)

Arthur Rose (Acton History Group)

Wallace Waite (Acton History Group)

The Waitrose exterior (John Lewis and Partners)

Spedan (Peter Lewis)

Beatrice Hunter, Spedan's wife (Peter Lewis)

Spedan and Beatrice with their children (Peter Lewis)

Spedan with his son John (Peter Lewis)

Spedan and Beatrice's home, Longstock House (Peter Lewis)

The garden at Longstock House (Peter Lewis)

Oswald (Peter Lewis)

Frances Cooper, Oswald's wife (Peter Lewis)

Oswald as a young officer (Peter Lewis)

Oswald and Frances with dog (Peter Lewis)

Oswald and Frances's home, Beechwood House (Peter Lewis)

The swimming pool of Beechwood House (Peter Lewis)

The John Lewis store post-bombing (John Lewis and Partners)

Fire officers attempting to hose the building (John Lewis and
   Partners)

John Lewis in later years (Peter Lewis)

Spedan with chess board (Peter Lewis)

Peter Lewis (Peter Lewis)

The Peter Jones building (John Lewis and Partners)

Modern John Lewis building with Barbara Hepworth's *Winged
   Figure* (John Lewis and Partners)

INDEX

Council, 226, 247, 263;
Second World War cut-backs,
232–3; non-contributory
pension scheme, 233, 296;
public service roles of senior
staff, 235; Heritage Centre at
Odney, 236, 307–8; staff
departures after Second World
War, 250–1; 'Second
Constitution,' 259–60; Miller
named Spedan's successor,
261–3, 291; rebuilding of West
House in 1950s, 265; General
Council, 278–9; Spedan
sidelined after retirement, 278,
279; centenary celebrations
(1964), 286, 292; memorials to
Spedan, 286; after Spedan's
death, 291–303; Hepworth's
centenary sculpture, 292;
internal succession method,
293, 298, 299–300; executive
pay, 294, 296; early 1990s as
reputational high point, 295–6;
Hampson as chairman, 295–8;
Hampson introduces
computers, 295; *Meet the
Partners* (BBC documentary,
1995), 296–7; Employee
Ownership Association (EOA),
297–8, 302–3; online sales,
297, 299; Mayfield as
chairman, 298–300, 302;
succession opened to external
candidates, 299–301; Sharon
White as chairman, 300–2;

Partnership Council, 300;
impact of Covid-19 pandemic,
301–2; White's strategy of
diversification, 301, 302; now
styled John Lewis & Partners,
302
John Lewis Partnership Heritage
Centre (Odney), 236, 307–8
John Spedan Lewis Trust, 286
Jones, C.M., 201
Jones, Maurice, 210, 264, 275
Jones, Peter, 83–4, 149
Jones, Terry, 210, 264
Jones Bros (Holloway Road), 27

Kay, Phyllis, 211, 239, 244, 269,
278
Kendal's (Manchester department
store), 26
Kenwood House (Hampstead),
188
King, Ann (JL's aunt), 13, 14,
33–4, 54

Labour Party, 142, 231, 249, 252
Lander, John St Helier, 172
Langhorne House, Shepton
Mallet, 15
leasehold system: and department
store expansion, 30, 38, 41–2,
70–1, 83–4; landlords, 70–3,
77, 93–4, 96–8, 105–6,
114–15; JL's campaign for
reform of, 70, 72–3, 96–8,
105–6, 114–15; de Walden's
'Marylebone Scheme,' 106

Lewis, Spedan (*cont ...*)
  diaries, 5–6, 281–2; retirement
  of (1955), 5, 275; burns father's
  diaries, 6, 16, 29, 55, 281, 285;
  on Jews and Welshmen, 10;
  investigates family pedigree
  (1930s), 12, 212–15; on JL's
  business methods, 38, 39–40;
  birth of (1885), 53; on his
  mother, 53, 178; explanation
  of his name, 54–5; childhood,
  56–7, 59–63, 64–7; as a
  'diverger'/non-conformer, 57,
  67, 273; education of, 57,
  59–63, 64, 65–7, 78–9; height
  of, 58, 108; as Queen's Scholar
  at Westminster, 59–63, 64,
  65–7, 78–9; and religion, 61;
  few close friends of, 64–5;
  'excitable brain' of, 64, 81,
  87–8, 125–6, 204, 205; violent
  temper, 64, 87–8, 169–70,
  178–9, 257–8; management
  style of, 65, 137–9, 239, 245,
  247; natural history as passion
  of, 65, 102, 109, 179–80, 210,
  241–2, 248–9, 286; moves
  straight into family business,
  66–7, 79; as always blaming
  others, 66, 158; cultural
  interests, 78, 209–10, 255; and
  JL's imprisonment, 78; health
  of, 79, 85, 88, 107–9, 112,
  123, 137, 148, 239, 245, 276;
  made director of Peter Jones,
  84; and women, 85, 87, 90, 95,
  116, 145, 161–2, 166–70, 199;
  handwriting of, 86; reorganises
  showrooms, 86; engagement to
  Nettie, 87, 89, 90, 205; at
  Fly-Fishers' Club, 89–90, 102;
  'kidnapping' of mother, 89–90,
  92; Oswald sues, 92–3;
  punctures lung in fall from
  horse, 95–6, 98, 102;
  convalesces, 98–9, 102, 107–9;
  personal finances of, 98–9,
  101–2, 112–13, 115, 131–2,
  137, 160–1, 173, 175, 176,
  180, 196; fluent
  communication skills, 99, 180,
  198–9, 211; and motor cars,
  101, 104, 191, 283–4;
  ultimatum to JL, 104; has
  second operation, 107, 108;
  relationship with Eleanor
  McElroy, 108–12, 113–14, 116,
  125–6, 128, 137, 162, 170,
  171, 172–3, 182; returns to
  work, 113; differing values/
  attitudes to brother, 116; skiing
  in Switzerland, 118; at John
  Lewis and Peter Jones, 125–6;
  truce with JL, 125–6; physical
  appearance of, 126–7, 216,
  254–5, 275; takes dancing
  lessons, 127; ceases to be
  partner at John Lewis (1915),
  131–2; rejection of luxury
  trade, 136–7; leases Coombe
  House, 137; loss of Grove
  Farm, 137, 257, 282, 284; and

"THE MODERN" CRETONNE
1/9½ yd.
31 ins. wide. A Cretonne with attractive modern design. It is very hardwearing & can be used for curtains, cushions and loose covers. In Green/Blue, Wine Blue, Orange/Fawn.

"THE JACOBEAN" PRINTED JUTE
1/6½ yd.
31 ins. wide. An inexpensive fabric for curtains, cushions and loose covers. The design is printed in a combination of Green, Red, Blue, and Brown, on a Natural or Fawn ground.

"THE WARWICK" PRINTED LINEN
2/11½ yd.
31 ins. wide. We believe that this material is unobtainable elsewhere under 3/11. At our price of 2/11½ it is wonderful value. The colours are dark Red, Blue, and Green, on Natural ground.

"THE TULIP" CRETONNE
1/11½ yd.
31 ins. wide. An excellent fabric for curtains, cushions and loose covers. The attractive modern design is printed in Gold, Orange and Green on a fawn ground.

"THE ROYAL" DAMASK
6/11 yd.
48 ins. wide. A fadeless Damask of Artificial Silk that is very suitable for curtains. It is smoothly woven and has a modern design. In five good furnishing colours: Blue, Beige, Brown, Copper and Green.

"THE GRANVILLE" TAFFETA
6/11 yd.
48 ins. wide. A lustrous silk & Rayon Taffeta that wears well in curtains, bedspreads and cushion covers. It is available in twenty-two very good colours including Rose, Gold, Beige, Blue and Green.

JOHN LEWIS
AND COMPANY LIMITED
MONTHLY SPECIAL NOTICES

1932

Any shop can say it sells cheaply and nearly every shop does say so.

We mark our goods in plain figures and leave them to speak for themselves.

APRIL